AF752321

FOCUS ON DISABILITY: TRENDS IN RESEARCH AND APPLICATION, VOLUME II

Focus on Disability: Trends in Research and Application, Volume II

Thilo Kroll
Editor

Nova Biomedical Books
New York

Copyright © 2008 by Nova Science Publishers, Inc.

All rights reserved. No part of this book may be reproduced, stored in a retrieval system or transmitted in any form or by any means: electronic, electrostatic, magnetic, tape, mechanical photocopying, recording or otherwise without the written permission of the Publisher.

For permission to use material from this book please contact us:
Telephone 631-231-7269; Fax 631-231-8175
Web Site: http://www.novapublishers.com

NOTICE TO THE READER

The Publisher has taken reasonable care in the preparation of this book, but makes no expressed or implied warranty of any kind and assumes no responsibility for any errors or omissions. No liability is assumed for incidental or consequential damages in connection with or arising out of information contained in this book. The Publisher shall not be liable for any special, consequential, or exemplary damages resulting, in whole or in part, from the readers' use of, or reliance upon, this material.

Independent verification should be sought for any data, advice or recommendations contained in this book. In addition, no responsibility is assumed by the publisher for any injury and/or damage to persons or property arising from any methods, products, instructions, ideas or otherwise contained in this publication.

This publication is designed to provide accurate and authoritative information with regard to the subject matter covered herein. It is sold with the clear understanding that the Publisher is not engaged in rendering legal or any other professional services. If legal or any other expert assistance is required, the services of a competent person should be sought. FROM A DECLARATION OF PARTICIPANTS JOINTLY ADOPTED BY A COMMITTEE OF THE AMERICAN BAR ASSOCIATION AND A COMMITTEE OF PUBLISHERS.

LIBRARY OF CONGRESS CATALOGING-IN-PUBLICATION DATA

Focus on disability : trends in research and application / Thilo Kroll (editor).
p. ; cm.
"Volume II."
Includes bibliographical references and index.
ISBN-13: 978-1-60021-792-0 (hardcover)
ISBN-10: 1-60021-792-3 (hardcover)
1. Chronically ill--Medical care. 2. Chronically ill--Rehabilitation. 3. People with disabilities--Medical care. 4. People with disabilities--Rehabilitation. I. Kroll, Thilo.
[DNLM: 1. Disability Evaluation. 2. Rehabilitation. 3. Activities of Daily Living. 4. Disabled Persons--rehabilitation. WB 320 F652 2008]
RA644.5.F63 2008
362.4--dc22 2007029779

Published by Nova Science Publishers, Inc. ✦ New York

CONTENTS

PREFACE

This volume of 'Disability and Health' covers a broad range of topics by researchers from several countries, including Canada, Germany, Japan, the United Kingdom and the United States. The selection of papers reflects current research trends and applications at the intersection of disability and health. The book contains disability-related topics stretching across the life span from childhood obesity and the assessment of health and function in older adults. It is a core principle of 'Disability and Health' publications to combine the expertise of researchers from various disciplinary backgrounds including psychology, sociology, public health, health services research, health policy, disability studies, medicine, and rehabilitation research.

Traditionally, public health and population medicine have been concerned with acute infectious diseases, nutrition, and health care provision and studied these issues primarily in terms of inequitable access to services. Public health researchers have paid relative little attention by comparison to long term or chronic disabling conditions (Yach, 2006). There are clear differences in terms of health risk exposure, morbidity and mortality for chronic conditions such as cardiovascular disease and cancer by sex, race, ethnic group and socioeconomic status. And we should add people with disabilities to this list due to their 'thinner' margin of health (DeJong et al., 2002).

WHAT IS A DISABILITY?

The literature is filled with attempts to distinguish 'disability', 'function', 'impairment' and 'participation' (Altman, 2001). Many disability studies researchers and consumer advocates who have adopted a social or relational model rather than an individual model of disability (Priestley, 2003) have viewed disability as a product of social oppression and view the social model as a useful framework through which processes of social exclusion translate impairment into disability. In the social model view physical impairment is not seen through the lens of medical professionals who seek to determine and alleviate the conditions that they believe are responsible for causing the impairment but rather conceptualized as a product of inaccessible environments and social intolerance of human diversity.

More recently, some disability researchers have expressed their discomfort with automatically equating disability with social impression and with the tendency of social model advocates to ignore physical impairment as a reality (Shakespeare, 2006). Even in a legislative and physical world approximating near complete equality for people with disabilities disadvantages may remain. And these disadvantages are not necessarily the product of intentional marginalization of people with disabilities. Post-structural and postmodern researchers (Zola, 1991; Shakespeare, 2006) have argued for a pragmatic, albeit critical stance towards using the social or individual models of disability in researching disability. It is a move away from the attempt to identify and adopt an all encompassing framework for the study of 'disability'. In the words of Corker (1998, p.232) *"Poststructuralist discourse on disability does not "reject" the social model. Rather it suggests that, since disability is now located in a postmodern world, it is appropriate to begin to look at the relationship between the individual and society rather than to focus on the individual or society."*

Most conceptual models and frameworks of disability now portray it as the product of an interaction person- and environmental factors (for a comprehensive discussion see Altman, 2001).

In this book the editor and authors follow a broad pragmatic understanding of disability. 'Disability' is characterized as a phenomenon that is socially constructed in multiple ways (e.g. person-focused, socially determined, culturally determined, environmentally determined) by various actors (e.g. researchers, policymakers, practitioners, the public) for specific purposes (e.g. classification, measurement, program development, evaluation) combining person, social, environmental and sociohistorical/cultural factors. In other words, the understanding and conceptualization of disability is variable depending on who is defining it, when, where and for what purpose.

Equally challenging to grasp is the concept of 'health'. Health is increasingly regarded as being distinctively different from being merely the absence of 'illness'. Health is being viewed as a multidimensional concept that includes psychological or emotional and social in addition to physical well-being. It has been characterized as culture, time and context bound, and is linked to well-being. The World Health Organisation (WHO) has defined it in 1946 as 'the state of complete physical, social and spiritual well-being, not simply the absence of illness'. This definition however ignored economic and cultural influences (Marks et al., 2005, p. 4), and it is questionable whether such an ideal state is ever attainable. In this book, 'health' is understood as *a life-long process during which varying degrees of physical, emotional and social well-being co-exist that are dynamically shaped by psychological, social, environmental, economic and cultural factors.* This is an operational or working definition that allows for an inclusion of broad health topics.

Why Focus on Disability and Health?

Disability and health are not to be considered synonymous concepts. However, there are multiple reasons for why disability and health should be examined together:

1. Chronic or long term conditions are becoming increasingly prevalent in most parts of the world, especially in developed countries. It has been estimated that ten percent of the world's population live with a physical, sensory, intellectual, or mental health impairment that impacts their daily lives (Groce, 2006).
2. With continuous increase in life expectancy and unprecedented medical advances, more people with long term conditions are expected to reach old age but are simultaneously at greater risk for developing health problems.
3. Formerly invariably fatal conditions, such as HIV/AIDS are now manageable but often at the cost of activity limiting impairments.
4. Social and physical barriers make access to needed health care services more challenging for people with disabilities.
5. People with disabilities are frequently excluded from medical and health-related research studies.
6. People with long term conditions are increasingly recognized as experts in their own right and can provide critical information to policymakers and service providers how to best support them in managing the impact of physical or mental impairment or ill health.

The health of people with disabilities is an area of research that has only recently received more attention.

Disability Classification

The most obvious reason to seek agreement on how to classify 'disability' is to have a basis to compare health and social service utilization figures for people with disabilities with those for the general population. Measuring or counting disability may also serve as a basis to determine where people with long term conditions are confronted with barriers to accessing services to which they are entitled and to identify factors that constrain their quest for health, well-being and personal independence. In another volume of 'Disability and Health' we have focused specifically on inclusive research designs and research methods for people with disabilities (See Kroll, Keer, Placek, Cyril & Hendershot, 2006).

The World Health Organisation's (WHO) International Classification of Functioning, Disability and Health (ICF) is an effort to promote comparability of research concerning health-related outcomes at individual and population levels across countries. The ICF characterizes how people live with particular conditions that potentially impact health and well-being. The ICF is not a disability classification system. It rather focuses on health and health-related domains, such as body functions, structures, activities and participation. Apart from person factors the ICF includes environmental characteristics.

In this book, three articles discuss the links between the ICF classification approach and functional characteristics in older adults. Lise Poissant and colleagues are examining how established functional measures can be linked to ICF components. The creation of ICF-coded functional status indicators can provide a way to determine functional status irrespective of the instrument used by researchers or clinicians. The authors discuss to what extent future availability of these codes in administrative databases can be of benefit to population health surveillance, epidemiologic research and health services planning. The second article by Kristine Mulhorn explores how the ICF can be linked to a Japanese health status measure for community-living elderly. The application of ICF coding holds the potential for cross-national comparisons. The third chapter by Jiro Okochi and Tai Takahashi provides a Japanese perspective on how ICF codes may be used as qualifiers for health assessments. The authors used Rasch modeling to compare ICF with other functional measures.

In the fourth paper that focuses on disability classification based on the ICF, Sayay Arthanat and James Lenker discuss the use of the ICF as a framework for assistive technology practice. They examine compatibility of the ICF model with AT assessment elements, and outline future developments of an ICF-based AT assessment.

HEALTH PROMOTION

Health promotion and health and wellness programs are increasingly targeted towards various populations of people with disability. While health promotion has traditionally focused on overcoming individuals' motivational barriers to engaging in healthy behaviors and lifestyles. Health promotion activities for people with disabilities need to take into consideration the need for environmental accommodations and accessibility. People with physical disabilities often have a greater susceptibility to health risk factors that ultimately may lead to poorer health outcomes and preventable secondary conditions (Jones & Bell, 2004). In fact, research has demonstrated that people with disabilities are at least as likely if not more likely to engage in health risk behaviors (Jones & Beatty, 2003; Iezzoni, McCarthy, Davis & Siebens, 2000). At the same time, people with disabilities face an array of barriers to access primary preventive services and are frequently excluded from health promotion programs. Commonly cited barriers include among others the lack of accessible provider offices and screening equipment, lack of awareness of these services, and the providers' inability to look beyond the primary disabling condition towards other preventive care needs. Community-based health education initiatives are beginning to address the issue through targeted campaigns and programs (Kroll, Jones, Kehn & Neri 2006).

There is increasing policy emphasis on programmes that combine education, self management and health promotion. The Expert Patient Programme (EPP) is an example of lay led interventions that have been rolled out across England to address health and well-being of people with various long term conditions. The Expert Patient Programme is a self-management course that teaches individuals how to manage the impact of long term conditions on their lives. It is facilitated by voluntary tutors and topics include 'goal setting', 'healthy eating', 'exercise', 'communication with health professionals', and 'managing depression and isolation' (www.expertpatients.nhs.uk). In their chapter, Turner, Barlow and Heathcote-Elliott review the experience with lay led self management programs for people with long term health conditions in the UK.

Parents of children with disabilities or long term chronic health conditions face multiple challenges and stressors in managing physically and emotionally consuming caregiving tasks while maintaining their own health. Powell and Barlow have developed a training and support program for parents of children with disabilities or chronic illness to mitigate the stress impact. Their chapter describes the development of the program and its subsequent testing.

Complementary and alternative medicine has received considerable media attention. However, this topic is being mostly discussed in combination with general health and fitness concerns or in terms of managing cancer with other means. Little attention has been given to what extent people with disabilities or long term conditions turn to alternative and complementary medicine. Matthew Carlson and Gloria Krahn examine in their chapter the utilization of complementary and alternative medicine services among people with disabilities based on a survey study conducted with over 800 adults in the United States.

HEALTH CARE DELIVERY

It is increasingly recognized that designing and implementing services that address the needs of people with disabilities is best accomplished when all stakeholders participate in the processes involved. As stated for the United Kingdom in a recent paper *"The UK policy of actively encouraging consumers to engage with researchers has its basis in prevailing notions of accountability rather than evidence-based practice. User involvement has become established in service development and audit in order to facilitate a more democratic and open provision of service delivery...The concept has been extended into the area of health research, and is beginning to be accepted by NHS (National Health Service) trusts...*(Boote, Telford & Cooper, 2002, p. 214)*"*

The policy initiatives in the United Kingdom have produced service user involvement in Department of Health and National Health Service (NHS) development programs. INVOLVE is an initiative to engage the public in research. It has been set up to enhance the relevance of research for the general population and people with particular health and social care concerns in particular (www.invo.org.uk).

Similarly, in the United States, service user involvement in research and service development has been mandated by several Federal agencies. The US Department of Education, National Institute on Disability and Rehabilitation Research, for example, emphasises such an involvement in a notice of research priorities *"...Involve individuals with disabilities, their family members, and consumers, as appropriate, in all stages of the research process and related activities..."* [Federal Register: May 6, 2002 (Volume 67, Number 87)] http://www.ed.gov/legislation/FedRegister/proprule/2002-2/050602e.html, accessed June 1, 2006. And the Interagency Committee on Disability Research (ICDR) also supports this approach.

> *"...ICDR should prioritize participatory action research to encourage people with disabilities to become researchers and principal investigators. Likewise, researchers should be encouraged to include people with a broad range of disabilities in their study samples, including those with multiple and/or hidden disabilities..."* (cf. Letter of the American Psychological Association's (APA) Letter to the U.S. Department of

Education Interagency Committee on Disability Research (ICDR), http://www.apa.org/ppo/issues/icdrltr704.html, accessed June 1,2006)

In this book, Ken Hergenrather and Scott Rhodes provide an overview of community-based participatory research and discuss the application of participatory research strategies to the areas of health and disability. They describe innovative research methods, such as photovoice that are conducive to building community relationships and that transcend cultural and linguistic barriers. The chapter includes findings from HIV/AIDS-related research and positions HIV/AIDS as a long term condition. Erin Hayes and Fabricio Balcazar examine the role of peer mentoring in the delivery of health services to people with disabilities from low income backgrounds. Peers, i.e. individuals with shared life experiences (i.e. being disabled), are introduced as crucial links between formalized health delivery contexts and the communities in which individuals live. This type of 'community health worker' can maximize health resources and holds the potential of delivering better health outcomes. Peers also serve as important intermediaries in community-based data collection processes.

Living with Long Term Disabling Conditions

Petra Warschburger discusses factors that increase the risk of long-term impairment including heart disease and diabetes in children with obesity. Obesity is emerging as a major threat to public health and in personal well-being and a costly bi-product of contemporary life styles in industrialized nations that is characterized by lower levels of physical activity and greater consumption of higher calorie fast foods. Children are at a particular risk for long term health consequences and consequently should be considered a primary target group for prevention efforts.

Maria Fotiadou examines the challenges for families to cope with the implications of cancer. Cancer as a group has traditionally been viewed as an acute condition. With increasing survival rates the focus is increasingly directed towards how individuals and their families manage the impact of cancer and its disabling consequences on their lives.

In their chapter Jörg Klewer, Dieter Pöhlau and Joachim Kugler discuss the healthcare service experiences and quality of life of people with myasthenia gravis in Germany. Myasthenia gravis has rarely attracted the attention of health researchers. This study is the largest to date with a sample of people diagnosed with myasthenia gravis.

While this volume of Disability and Health is very broadly conceptualized several key areas within disability have been omitted. It is expected that other fields of study at the intersection of disability and health can be addressed in future volumes.

References

Altman, B. (2001). Disability Definitions, Models, Classification Schemes, and Applications. In G.L. Albrecht, K.D. Seelman & M. Bury (Eds.), *Handbook of Disability Studies* (97-122). Thousand Oaks: Sage.

Boote, J., Telford, R. & Cooper, C. (2002). Consumer involvement in health research: A review and research agenda. *Health Policy, 61*, 213-236.

Corker, M. (1998). Disability Discourse in a Postmodern World. In T. Shakespeare (Ed.), *The Disability Reader: Social Science Perspectives* (221-233). London: Cassell.

DeJong, G, Palsbo, SE., Beatty, P.W., Jones, G.C., Kroll, T. & Neri, M.T. (2002). The Organization and Financing of Health Services for Persons with Disabilities. *Millbank Quarterly, 80*(2), 261-301.

Groce, N.E. (2006). People with Disabilities. In. B.S. Levy & V.W. Sidel (Eds.), *Social Injustice and Public Health* (145-160). New York: Oxford Press.

Iezzoni, L.I., McCarthy, E.P., Davis, R.B. & Siebens, H. (2000). Mobility impairments and use of screening and preventive services. *American Journal of Public Health, 90,* 955–961.

Jones, G.C. & Beatty, P.W. (2003). Disparities in preventive service use among working-age adults with mobility limitations. In B.M. Altman, S.N. Barnartt, G.E. Hendershot & S.A. Larson (Eds), *Using Survey Data to Study Disability: Results from the National Health Interview Survey on Disability. Special Issue: Research in Social Science and Disability, 3*, (109-130). Oxford: Elsevier.

Jones, G.C. & Bell, K.T. (2004). Adverse health behaviors and chronic conditions in working-age women with disabilities. *Family and Community Health, 27*(1), 22-36.

Kroll, T., Jones, G.C., Kehn, M.E. & Neri, M.T. (2006). Barriers and Strategies Affecting the Utilization of Primary Preventive Services for People with Physical Disabilities: A Qualitative Inquiry. *Health & Social Care in the Community, 14*(4), 284 – 293.

Kroll, T., Keer, D., Placek, P. Cyril, J. & Hendershot, G. (Eds.) (2006). *Towards Best Practices for Surveying People with Disabilities.* Hauppage, NY: NovaScience.

Marks, D. F., Murray, M., Evans, B., Willig, C., Woodall, C. & Sykes, C.M. (2005). *Health Psychology. Theory, Research & Practice.* London: Sage, 2nd edition.

Priestley, M. (2003). *Disability. A life course approach.* Cambridge: Polity.

Shakespeare, T. (2006). *Disability rights and wrongs.* Oxon: Routledge.

Yach, D. (2006). Chronic Diseases. In. B.S. Levy & V.W. Sidel (Eds.), Social Injustice and Public Health (253-276). New York: Oxford Press.

Zola, I (1991). Bringing Our Bodies and Ourselves Back In: Reflections on the Past, Present and Future Medical Sociology. *Journal of Health and Social Behaviour, 32*, 1-16.

DISABLITY CLASSIFICATION

In: Focus on Disability: Trends in Research and Application ISBN: 978-1-60021-792-0
Editor: Thilo Kroll, pp. 3-22 © 2008 Nova Science Publishers, Inc.

Chapter I

Linking the Barthel Index, Reintegration to Normal Living Index and OARS-IADL to the ICF to Characterize Community-Dwelling Elders

Lise Poissant[1,*], *Sara Ahmed*[1] *and Nancy E. Mayo*[2,3]
[1]Clinical and Health Informatics, [2]Clinical Epidemiology, [3]School of Physical and Occupational Therapy, McGill University, Montreal (Qc), Canada.

Abstract

Introduction: Adequate health services planning and programming priorities necessitate the availability of detailed information on health status of individuals. Despite the increased recognition towards the need for data on functional status, one of the challenges arises from the non-agreement among clinicians and researchers as to which instrument should be used. The creation of ICF-coded Functional Status Indicators (FSI) will provide in a standardized manner, relevant information on functional status irrespective of the instrument used by researchers or clinicians.

Objective: This paper will demonstrate the feasibility of generating a set of coded functional status indicators derived from three outcome measures; the Barthel Index, the Reintegration to Normal Living Index (RNL) and the OARS-IADL and will identify key FSI that best characterize a population of community-dwelling elders.

Methods: A group of eleven rehabilitation professionals independently assigned codes to each items on the three measures. Items that did not reach full agreement were

* Correspondence concerning this article should be addressed to: Lise Poissant, PhD, Clinical and health Informatics Research Group, McGill University, Morrice House, 1140 Pine Ave. west, Montreal (Qc), Canada H3A 1A3, Tel: (514) 934-1934 ext 32980; Fax: (514) 843-1551; Lise.poissant@mcgill.ca.

reviewed by two expert raters. Data available on 488 community-dwelling elders, average age, 62 years, were analyzed to address the second objective of this paper.

Results: The overall agreement on all items that could be linked was 83.3%. Out of the pool of 28 items, 11 reached 100% agreement at the 3 digit level. The OARS-IADL was the easiest to map to the ICF. Among items that reached full agreement, seven were assigned a four-digit code, providing a more granular level of information.). Two items remained with a *no code* qualifier. These are; being comfortable with yourself when in the company of others' (RNL10) and spending your day in an activity that is important to you' (RNL5). Analyses revealed that older individuals are significantly more likely to experience limitations and restrictions than community-dwellers who are less than 65 years of age, in 12 ICF activities. Being 65 years and older had a significant impact on *being occupied in an activity important to one's self, family relationships* and *doing housework.* Individuals aged 75 years and over were found to experience difficulties in; *recreation and leisure, using transportation, moving around outside the home, family relationships, socializing, self-care, walking short distances, washing whole body, doing housework, preparing meals, looking after one's health and shopping.* Eight activity domains referring mostly to mobility and basic activities of daily living were problematic for women only.

Conclusion: ICF-coded FSI have the capacity to characterize in a standardized and meaningful way an aged population living in the community. These indicators will allow comparisons across populations groups, and monitoring of patient's progress within a continuum of care. Future availability of these codes on administrative databases will facilitate population health surveillance, epidemiologic research and health services planning.

BACKGROUND

Effective and efficient planning of health services delivery has become a priority to meet the needs of an ageing population. In Canada, 12.7% of the population is aged 65 years and over and this proportion is expected to increase to 16.5% in 2016 [1]. With an average life expectancy of 78.3 years of which 12,4% will be lived with some disability, elders are likely to experience some limitations or restrictions of their activities in their late years of life [2,3]. The higher prevalence of chronic conditions among elderly and the costs associated with managing chronic diseases [4-6] emphasizes the need to establish programs that will be adapted to the population's needs. Indeed, the presence of only one chronic condition has shown to have a significant impact on functional status of elderly individuals [7]. This impact spans a wide range of impairments, activity and participation domains. Community-dwelling individuals who live with a chronic disease such as stroke, arthritis or COPD must often cope on a day-to-day basis with impairments such as pain, muscle weakness and cognitive deficits that may limit activity domains such as self-care, mobility, housework, or day time work [8]. For many individuals, these will have lasting consequences that have an impact on physical and mental health status [8,9], influence their health related quality of life (HRQL) [10,11] and increase their risk of mortality [12,13].

The need to capture these health outcomes for population health surveillance, epidemiologic research and health services planning has been well documented [14-18]. Furthermore, detailed information on functional status of community-dwelling elders must be made available for effective communication processes and to facilitate continuity of care [19]. Haggerty et al [20] identifies informational continuity as an essential component to develop care continuums. Informational continuity is defined as the knowledge one must have on a patient (for example, his/her diagnoses, preferences, living environment) to bridge individual care episodes and ensure patient's needs are met. Informational continuity necessitates the information to be comprehensive but most importantly, relevant and meaningful to the different care providers. To date, informational continuity remains difficult to achieve, even more so, on functional status of individuals. Health surveys, research data provide a wealth of information on functional status of community-dwelling individuals. However, the absence of a common language across the different data sources has limited the scope of utilization of this information. Classifications aim at providing a uniform language and framework to describe a universe of constructs. Among the most commonly used classifications for health-related constructs are the International Classification of Diseases, Disorders and Injuries (ICD) [21] and the Classification of Functioning, Disability and Health [22].

The World Health Organization's International Classification of Disease (ICD 9/10) is the coding system used almost universally to code diseases, disorders, and injuries. ICD codes are available on administrative databases following completion of the hospital discharge abstract and are therefore extensively used for health services planning. However, there are recognized limitations to the ICD as it does not provide information on the severity of a health condition nor on functional status. In some chronic diseases this information is crucial for adequate planning of services and valid interpretation of administrative information. Over the years, the ICD has proven to be highly useful and met several purposes; however, when used solely, its specific medical content can be seen as a limitation to summarize patient's information [17].

The World Health Organization's International Classification of Functioning and Disability (ICF) is a universal system developed over the past two decades to classify the consequences of diseases. This classification is complementary to the ICD and optimizes data quality by adding standardized, conceptually organized information on functioning and disability. The ICF is a relatively small classification, comprising around 4,000 codes that are subdivided into two main parts; Functioning and Disability and Contextual Factors. Body Functions and Structures, Activities and Participation are the main components of Functioning and Disability and the core of ICF in its actual version. The ICF meets most characteristics identified by Rose and colleagues as key elements of good code sets [23]. Indeed, the ICF is hierarchical, allows for different levels of granularity, has unique concepts and has the capacity to evolve.

There is no doubt that the ICF is a useful classification to conceptualize the health problems of chronic populations [24] and to code functional status information for future integration on administrative databases [25]. But, the integration of the ICF into clinical practice remains a challenge. One option is to impose the adoption of a new measure comprising ICF-coded clinical indicators. This measure would need to be generic and valid among different disease groupings, capture a large range of disease severity and obviously carry meaningful information to clinicians. This is highly unrealistic as the required set of items in this measure would be much too large to be manageable. This would likely result in poor acceptance of the new measure and enhance the likelihood of having incomplete information. One viable option is to use existing clinical information obtained from outcome measures that are routinely used by multidisciplinary teams and link those to the ICF to create ICF-coded functional status indicators (FSI). This avenue is of interest and efforts have been made to link the Western Ontario and McMaster Universities ostheoarthritis measure [26] and health-related quality of life measures including the SF-36 and EQ-5D [27], the SF-12 [28] and the Osteoporosis Assessment Questionnaire [29]. Several outcome measures remain to be linked to the ICF to encompass all possible domains of functioning, disability and health.

This paper will demonstrate the feasibility of generating a set of ICF-coded constructs derived from three outcome measures; the Barthel Index (BI), the Reintegration to Normal Living Index (RNL) and the OARS-IADL and will identify key ICF-coded FSI that best characterize a population of community-dwelling elders.

METHODS

The Study Population

The data we used for this study were obtained from the Montreal Stroke Cohort Study that was established to examine the long-term impact of stroke [30]. A control group comprised of community dwelling individuals without stroke was assembled for comparison. Community-dwelling individuals were identified through randomly generated computerized telephone listings. The control group (n=488) were matched to individuals with stroke on age and gender. All participants were interviewed over the telephone on the Barthel Index, the OARS-IADL and the Reintegration to Normal Living Index (RNL). Basic demographics and presence/absence of 19 specific chronic conditions were also collected through self-report.

Description of the Measures

The Barthel Index (BI) is a well-known, widely used 10-item measure of functional independence in personal care and mobility [31]. It was originally developed for persons with neuromuscular or musculoskeletal disorder [31,32]. The information is most often obtained from the client themselves or health care professionals. Domains covered by the BI are; feeding, personal hygiene, dressing, bathing, bladder control, bowel control, getting to the toilet, transfer from bed to chair, walking 50 meters and going up and down stairs. If the person is unable to walk, an item assessing the person's capacity to use a wheelchair is scored. Each item has 3 to 4 response levels scored 0, 5, 10 or 15. Total scores range from 0 to 100, with a score of 100 indicating complete independence. Interpretation of scores suggest that scores under 20 reflect total dependence, 21 to 60 severe dependence, 61 to 90 moderate dependence and 91 to 99 slight dependence [19,32].

The OARS-IADL (Older Americans Resources and Services Scale-Instrumental Activities of Daily Living)[33] [34] is a short, easy to administer, seven-item questionnaire used to provide a profile of functioning of elderly individuals living at home. Each item is scored on a three-point scale: 0=unable, 1= with help and 2=without help. Items cover domains of shopping, meal preparation, telephone use, housework, medication, finances and transportation use. Items' scores are summed up. OARS-IADL scores range between 0 and 14, the latter indicating independent functioning in these activities. A ceiling effect has been reported among community-dwelling elders [35].

The Reintegration to Normal Living Index (RNL)[36] was developed to assess global functional status of individuals living in the community. The RNL comprises 11 declarative statements that the person is asked to rate as: 1= yes, it describes my situation 2= it partially describes my situation or 3=no, it does not describe my situation. The RNL covers the following domains; indoor, community and distance mobility; self-care, work, recreational, social activities, family roles, personal relationships, level of comfort with others and coping skills. A total score is obtained by summing up all items. Scores range from 0 to 22, with higher scores reflecting greater difficulty to go back to one's normal pattern of activities.

Linkage to the ICF

Eleven rehabilitation professionals (7 physiotherapists, 3 occupational therapists and one kinesiologist) independently assigned ICF codes to the 28 items encompassed by the BI, OARS-IADL and RNL. All raters were familiar with the ICF and its underlying concepts. All of them had previously used these outcome measures (RNL, BI, OARS-IADL), either during research or clinical activities. Six of them were involved in a previous rating exercise, while others were considered novice raters. All were provided a standardized set of instructions including a coding example. For each item, raters were asked to identify the 4-digit ICF code that best captured the construct conveyed by the item. The aim for 4-digit codes was to achieve the highest granularity the ICF can offer. However, if they could not identify a 4-digit code, a 3-digit code was accepted. They were instructed to give, if possible, only one code per item and describe any difficulties associated with the selection of that code. If, for example, more than one code could be associated to an item, raters were instructed to list the other potential code(s). For each item, raters had to identify their final decision. The following options were thus available; i) item is associated to a 4 or 3-digit code, ii) item cannot be matched (*no match*) to a specific code due to multiple constructs within the item or iii) item cannot be associated to any ICF-code (*no code*).

Our instructions followed the ten rules established by Cieza et al [27] except for rule number three that specifies that all constructs encompassed by a single item should be linked to the ICF. One of the examples they provide links 'How much does pain interfere with your personal care' to *pain* (b280), *self-care unspecified* (d599) and *mobility, unspecified* (d499). In a previous project from one of the authors (N.M.) [28], a similar item originating from the SF-12 [37] was linked to the ICF. In that project, our raters associated the code (b280) to; 'How much does pain interferes with your work or usual activities' indicating that they felt the construct of this item to be more directly associated to pain than work. Their interpretation is consistent with the SF-36 scale developers who use this question to estimate a score on the Pain subscale of the SF-36. Keeping in mind that the goal of this project is to generate coded, standardized functional status indicators (FSI), it was necessary to impose our linkage rule to ensure the selection of one unique code per item assessed on outcome measures. ICF-coded FSI will have the capacity to be integrated in administrative databases only if they have a standard format (one 4-digit code per FSI) and can be interpretable by clinicians, researchers and decision-makers. Combining codes enhances the precision of the information. However, the information remains relevant only if the codes are kept combined, an attribute not yet possible with administrative databases.

ICF codes are alphanumeric and raters were requested to clearly label the ICF component connected to each code using the appropriate letter that precedes each ICF code. The letter 'b' preceding an ICF code is unique to an impairment of a body function or structure. The letter 'd' describes an activity limitation or a participation restriction with no distinction between these two ICF components. Finally, codes that are preceded by an 'e' are attached to an environmental factor. Raters were also instructed to assign one severity qualifier decimal to each response option of the set of items. The qualifiers used were those defined by the ICF; 0: no difficulty or impairment, 1: mild difficulty or impairment, 2: moderate difficulty or impairment, 3: severe difficulty or impairment and 4: complete or total difficulty or impairment. For the purpose of this exercise, raters were not offered choices "8" (not specified) or "9" (not applicable) as possible severity qualifiers.

In past studies, the linkage of outcome measures to the ICF, has been commonly performed by two raters [26,29]. In this study, a larger number of raters was involved. Items for which one unique code (either at the 3- or 4-digit level) was assigned, reached 100% agreement across raters and were thus, automatically assigned that code. All others were reviewed independently by two-expert raters who assigned the ICF code that best reflected the meaning of the item. If agreement could not be reached among the two expert-raters, a third person was asked to provide an opinion. The percent agreement was calculated at the 3-digit level. In order to ensure uniformity of code format, items that were assigned a 3-digit code through raters or experts agreement, were added a fourth digit; the value "9" (unspecified). This decision is consistent with the conceptual organization of codes in the ICF and does not influence the interpretability of the construct carried by the ICF-code. Indeed, when looking at the description of the ICF codes d920 *Recreation and leisure* and d9209 *Recreation and leisure, unspecified*, both remain generic constructs with a very similar level of granularity.

Statistical Analyses

Descriptive statistics were used to describe the level of impairment, activity limitation and participation restriction of community-dwelling individuals aged 65 years and over. Means for the total score of the Barthel Index, OARS-IADL and the RNL index were calculated and comparisons were made across age groups. The expected association between age and functional status was assessed using logistic regressions controlling for gender and co-morbid conditions (one or more). The three-level ordinal scales of each outcome measures were collapsed into dichotomous scales with 0= no impairment/limitation/restriction, and 1= presence of an impairment/limitation/restriction. Age was categorized as follows; younger than 65, 65-74, 75 and older. Odds ratios and 95% confidence intervals were computed for each item. The experiment-wise p-value of 0.05 was accepted as statistical significance.

Table 1. Raters selection of codes and Expert-consensus selected ICF descriptor for items on the Reintegration to Normal Living Index

Item from RNL Index	% Agreement 3-digit Level	Raters-Selected ICF-item	ICF code	Number of raters	Expert-Consensus Selected ICF-item
Able to move around your living quarters (RNL1)	100%	Moving around within home Moving around in different location	*d4600* *d460*	10 1	Moving around within home
Able to move around community (RNL2)	100%	Moving around outside the home Moving around in different location	*d4602* *d460*	10 1	Moving around outside the home
Be able to take trips out of town (RNL3)	55%	Using transportation Recreation and leisure Moving around outside the home Moving around using transportation, other unspecified	*d470* *d920* *d4602* *d489*	6 3 2 1	Using transportation
Be comfortable with how your self-care needs are met (RNL4)	55%	Caring for body parts Self-care, unspecified Washing whole body Carrying out daily routine Ensuring one's physical comfort	*d520* *d599* *d5101* *d230* *d5700*	2 6 1 1 1	Self-care, unspecified
Spend most of your days occupied in an activity that is important to you (RNL5)	36%	Recreation and leisure Recreation and leisure, unspecified Informal associations Carrying out daily routine, unspecified Major life areas, other specified No Code	*d920* *d9209* *d9100* *d2309* *d898* -	3 1 1 1 1 3	No code
Able to participate in recreational activities you want (RNL6)	100%	Recreation and leisure Recreation and leisure, unspecified	*d920* *d9209*	4 5	Recreation and leisure
Participate in social activities with family friends (RNL7)	64%	Socializing Informal relationships with friends Community life, unspecified Family relationships	*d9205* *d7500* *d9109* *d760*	7 1 2 1	Socializing
Assume a role in family (RNL8)	82%	Family relationships Family relationships, unspecified Interacting according to social rules Domestic life, unspecified	*d760* *d7609* *d7203* *d699*	5 4 1 1	Family relationships

Table 1. Continued

Item from RNL Index	% Agreement 3-digit Level	Raters-Selected ICF-item	ICF code	Number of raters	Expert-Consensus Selected ICF-item
Be comfortable with your personal relationships (RNL9)	36%	Basic interpersonal interactions	*d710*	3	Basic Interpersonal relationships
		Appreciation in relationships	*d7101*	1	
		Family relationships	*d760*	1	
		Interpersonal interactions and relationships, unspecified	*d799*	1	
		General interpersonal interactions, others specified and unspecified	*d729*	1	
		Particular interpersonal relationships, other specified and unspecified	d779	2	
		Informal relationships with friends	*d7500*	1	
		Confidence	*b1266*	1	
Be comfortable with self when in company of others (RNL10)	36%	Basic interpersonal interactions	*d710*	3	No code
		Interpersonal interactions and relationships, unspecified	*d799*	1	
		Informal relationships with friends	*d7500*	1	
		Informal social relationships	*d750*	1	
		Confidence	*b1266*	1	
		Range of emotion	*b1522*	1	
		No Code	-	3	
Can deal with life events when they happen (RNL11)	64%	Handling stress and other psychological demands	*d240*	5	Handling stress and other psychological demands
		Handling responsibilities (1)	*d2400*	1	
		Handling stress and other psychological demands, unspecified *d2409* (1)	*d2409*	1	
		Managing daily routine *d2301* (1)	*d2301*	1	
		Appropriateness of emotions *b1520* (1)	*b1520*	1	
		Regulation of emotions *b1521* (1)	*b1521*	1	
		No Code (1)	-	1	

Results

Linkage Process

The 28 items that were linked to the ICF are presented in Tables 1 to 3. To facilitate reading, items are listed by outcome measures and sequenced in the same order as they would be on the original measure. Eleven items reached full agreement at the three-digit level. Three originated from the RNL Index, four from the BI and four from the OARS-IADL. Items from the OARS-IADL measure were the easiest to map to the ICF with more than half of the items reaching 100% agreement and the three others obtaining 55%, 82% and 91% agreement. Among items that reached full agreement (11/28), seven were mapped to the ICF at a more granular level and were given a four-digit code – four digit codes that ends with a '9' are excluded from this as they are not seen as being more granular than the 3-digit code of the activity they refer to. These items are: able to move around your living quarters (RNL1) - *d4600 (moving around within home)*; able to move around the community (RNL2) - *d4602(move around outside the home)*; bathe or shower (BI3); *d5101 (washing whole body);* walk 50 yards (BI9) – *d4500 (walking short distances)*; go up and down stairs (BI10) – *d4551 (climbing); u*se the telephone (OARS-IADL1 - *d3600 (use telecommunication devices;* and, go shopping (OARS-IADL3) – *d6200 (shopping).*

Table 2. Raters selection of codes and Expert-consensus selected ICF descriptor for items on the Barthel Index

Items from Barthel Index	% Agreement 3-digit Level	Raters-Selected ICF-item	ICF Code	Number of raters	Expert-Consensus Selected ICF-item
Feed oneself (BI1)	91%	Eating Drinking *d560* (1)	*d550* *d560*	10 1	Eating
Do own personal hygiene (BI2)	55%	Caring for body parts Caring for body parts, unspecified Washing oneself Washing body parts Maintaining one's health	*d520* d5209 *d510* *d5100* *d5702*	5 2 2 1 1	Caring for body parts
Bathe or shower (BI3)	100%	Washing oneself Washing whole body	*d510* *d5101*	5 6	Washing whole body
Dress one's self (BI4)	100%	Dressing Putting on clothes Dressing, unspecified	*d540* *d5400* *d5409*	6 3 2	Dressing
Get to the toilet on your own (BI5)	73%	Toileting Toileting, unspecified Transferring oneself while sitting Moving around within the home	*d530* *d5309* *d4200* *d4600*	5 3 2 1	Toileting
Bowel incontinence (BI6)	55%	Faecal continence Defecation functions Regulating defecation	*b5253* *b525* *d5301*	5 1 5	Faecal continence
Bladder incontinence (BI7)	45%	Regulating urination Urinary continence Urination functions Urinary excretory functions, unspecified	*d5300* *b6202* *B620* *B6109*	5 4 1 1	Urinary continence
Transfer from bed to chair (BI8)	73%	Transferring oneself Transferring oneself, unspecified Transferring oneself while lying Transferring oneself while sitting Changing basic body position Sitting Missed	*d420* *d4209* *d4201* *d4200* *d410* *d4103* -	2 1 1 4 1 1 1	Transferring oneself
Walk 50 yards (BI9)	100%	Walking short distances Walking long distances Walking d450	*d4500* *d4501* *d450*	8 2 1	Walking short distances
Go up and down stairs (BI10)	100%	Climbing Moving around	*d4551* *d455*	10 1	Climbing

Table 3. Raters selection of codes and Expert-consensus selected ICF descriptor for items on the OARS-IADL

Items from OARS-IADL	% Agreement 3-digit Level	Raters-Selected ICF-item	ICF Code	Number of raters	Expert-Consensus Selected ICF-item
Use the telephone (OARS1-IADL1)	100%	Using telecommunication devices Using communication devices and techniques, others specified Using communication devices and techniques	*d3600* *d3608* *d360*	8 1 2	Using telecommunication devices
Get to places out of walking distances (OARS-IADL2)	82%	Using transportation Using public motorized transportation Using transportation, unspecified Moving around using transportation, other specified and unspecified	*d470* *d4702* *d4709* *d489*	6 1 2 2	Using transportation
Go shopping (OARS-IADL3)	100%	Shopping Acquisition of goods and services	*d6200* *d620*	9 2	Shopping
Prepare own meals (OARS-IADL4)	100%	Preparing meals Preparing simple meals Preparing meals, unspecified	*d630* *d6300* *d6309*	5 2 4	Preparing meals
Do own housework (OARS-IADL5)	100%	Doing housework Doing housework, unspecified	*d640* *d6409*	7 4	Doing housework
Take own medicine (OARS-IADL6)	91%	Maintaining one's health Looking after one's health, unspecified Looking after one's health, others specified Looking after one's health Undertaking a simple task	*d5702* *d5709* *d5708* *d570* *d2100*	5 1 2 2 1	Looking after one's health
Handle own money (OARS-IADL7)	55%	Personal economic resources Basic economic transactions Basic economic transactions, unspecified Financial assets	*d8700* *d860* *d8609* *e1650*	4 5 1 1	Basic economic transactions d860

Among all items that did not reach full agreement across the eleven raters, only one could clearly be identified as a coding error. Feed oneself (BI1) was mapped by 10 raters as *d550 (eating)* but one rater linked it to *d560 (drinking)* which specifically excludes in its definition the activity of eating [22]. All other items obtained agreement levels ranging from 36% to 91%. On some items, the selection of codes by raters varied substantially, with some items being attributed codes associated to different ICF components ('b' vs 'd' vs 'e' codes). For example, bowel incontinence and bladder incontinence were associated to body functions by 55% of raters while the others associated these two incontinence items of the BI as 'd' codes, interpreting them as limitations of an activity rather than impairments of a body function. Following experts' review, these two items were respectively assigned the codes b5253 (*fecal incontinence*) and b6252 (*urinary incontinence*).

Two items were assigned the same ICF codes. Able to take trips out of town (RNL3) and able to get to places out of walking distances (OARS-IADL2) were linked to the same ICF code, *d4709 (using transportation)*. The percent agreement reached on each of these two items was fairly good (55% and 82% respectively).

From the pool of 28 items, only two items originating from the RNL scale could not be mapped to the ICF and were assigned a *no code*. The item 'being comfortable with yourself when in the company of others' (RNL10) could not be mapped to the ICF. This item was seen by some raters as being associated to one's emotions (body function domain) and by others as relating more to relationships with friends or society in general. Likewise, the item 'spending your day in an activity that is important to you' (RNL5) also reached 36% of agreement and was assigned a *no code* by three raters. It remained without a code upon review by the expert raters.

Table 4. Population characteristics and mean scores on Barthel Index, OARS-IADL and RNL for community-dwelling individuals under or above 65 years of age

	Individuals < 64 years old n=265	**Individuals 65 to 74 years old** n=148	**Individuals > 75 years old** n=73
Age			
mean (sd)	52.9 (8.6)	68.7 (2.8)	79.9 (4.4)
Gender			
Female **(%)**	69%	64%	71%
Co-morbid conditions			
None (%)	28%	14%	-
One or more (%)	72%	86%	100%
Barthel Index			
Mean (sd)	99.5 (3.6)	99.3 (2.7)	98.4 (6.9)
RNL Index			
Mean (sd)	0.47(1.5)	0.98 (2.6)	1.7 (3.0)
OARS-IADL			
Mean (sd)	13.9(0.3)	13.8 (1.0)	13.5 (1.4)

Population Characteristics using total Scores on BI, OARS-IADL and RNL Index

The study population (n=488) was mainly composed of women (66%) with the higher proportion of women remaining constant across age groups. The mean age of individuals across groups was 62.2 years (sd:12.2). Individuals who were less than 65 years of age (n=221) were aged 52.9 years (sd:8.6) in comparison to the oldest group of community-dwelling elders (n=73) who were 79.9 years old (sd: 4.4). Table 4 indicates the mean scores on the three outcome measures for individuals across all three age groups. On all three measures, being aged 75 years and more was significantly associated to more limitations and restrictions in the areas captured by the BI, OARS-IADL and RNL index, when compared to individuals aged less than 65 years of age. Reaching the age of 65 years was associated with a significant increase in the RNL total score reflecting the impact of age on an individual's capacity to return to a normal life pattern.

Table 5. Comparisons across age groups on presence of impairments/activity limitations and participation restrictions on ICF-coded domains of RNL, BI and OARS-IADL using odds ratio (OR) and 95% confidence interval (95% CI)

Expert-consensus ICF item	Presence of impairments/limitations/restrictions				Odds[1] of having an impairment/limitation/restriction compared to individuals < 65 years of age			
ICF items from RNL Index	< 65 years n (%)	65- 74 years n (%)	>74 years n (%)	< 65 years ref	65 – 74 years OR 95%CI		>74 years OR 95% CI	
Recreation and leisure (d920)	11 (4.1%)	13 (8.8%)	14 (19.2%)		2.4	1.0 – 5.5	5.8	2.5 – 13.8
Using transportation (d470)	9 (3.4%)	11 (7.4%)	14 (19.2%)		2.5	1.0 – 6.2	7.7	3.1 – 19.1
Being occupied in an activity that is important to oneself (no code)	11 (4.1%)	18 (12.2%)	13 (17.8%)		3.2	1.5 – 7.1	5.1	2.1 – 12.3
Moving around outside the home (d4602)	2 (<1%)	4 (2.7%)	5 (6.9%)		3.6	0.6 – 20.2	8.8	1.6 – 47.8
Family relationships (d760)		13 (8.8%)	7 (9.6%)		3.4	1.3 – 8.8	3.4	1.1 – 10.2
Self-care (d599)	2 (<1%)	2 (1.4%)	4 (5.5%)		1.6	0.2 – 11.6	6.5	1.1 – 37.6
Socializing (d9205)	19 (7.1%)	14 (9.5%)	14 (19.2%)		1.4	0.7 – 3.0	3.4	1.6 – 7.4
Moving around within home (d4600)	1 (<1%)	2 (1.4%)	2 (2.7%)		3.5	0.3 – 40.6	6.0	0.5 – 73.0
Basic Interpersonal relationships (d710)	4 (1.5%)	3 (2.0%)	1 (1.4%)		1.4	0.3 – 6.6	0.9	0.1 – 8.4
Be comfortable with self when in company of others (no code)	7 (2.6%)	3 (2.0%)	4 (5.5%)		0.8	0.2 – 3.2	2.3	0.6 – 8.2
Handling stress and other psychological demands (d240)	9 (3.4%)	5 (3.4%)	6 (8.2%)		1.1	0.3 – 3.3	2.5	0.8 – 7.7

Table 5. Continued

ICF items from BI								
Walking short distances (d4500)	3 (1.1%)	3 (2.0%)	4 (5.5%)		2.4	0.5 – 12.0	6.9	1.4 – 33.5
Washing whole body (d5101)	1 (<1%)	1 (<1%)	4 (5.5%)		1.7	0.1 – 28.0	12.1	1.3 – 116.7
Urinary continence (b6202)	5 (2.0%)	5 (3.4%)	5 (6.9%)		1.8	0.5 – 6.2	3.7	1.0 – 13.7
Climbing (d4551)	3 (1.1%)	4 (2.7%)	2 (2.7%)		2.7	0.6 – 12.7	2.7	0.4 – 17.1
Eating (d550)	2 (<1%)	3 (2.0%)	1 (<1%)		2.9	0.5 – 17.9	2.0	0.2 – 23.3
Transferring oneself (d420)	4 (1.5%)	2 (1.4%)	1 (<1%)		1.0	0.2 – 5.9	1.0	0.1 – 9.3
Faecal continence (b5253)	4 (1.5%)	2 (1.4%)	3 (4.1%)		0.8	0.1 – 4.5	2.5	0.5 – 11.8
Caring for body parts (d520)	1 (<1%)	0	1 (<1%)		-	-	1.7	0.1 – 28.5
Dressing (d540)	2 (<1%)	0	1 (<1%)		-	-	1.3	0.1 – 16.1
Toileting (d530)	1 (<1%)	0	1 (<1%)	1.0	-	-	1.7	0.1 – 28.5
ICF items from OARS-IADL								
Doing housework (d640)	4 (1.5%)	8 (5.4%)	15 (20.6%)	1.0	3.7	1.1 – 12.7	17.1	5.4 – 54.4
Preparing meals (d630)	1 (<1%)	4 (2.7%)	4 (5.5%)	1.0	7.2	0.8 – 65.6	16.6	1.8 – 155.4
Using transportation (d470)	1 (<1%)	4 (2.7%)	4 (5.5%)	1.0	7.2	0.8 – 65.7	13.9	1.5 – 130.7
Looking after one's health d570	1 (<1%)	2 (1.4%)	4 (5.5%)	1.0	3.3	0.3 – 37.7	14.3	1.5 – 134.7
Shopping (d6200)	2 (<1%)	4 (2.7%)	4 (5.5%)	1.0	3.8	0.7 – 21.0	8.3	1.4 – 47.5
Using telecommunication devices (d3600)	0	1 (<1%)	2 (2.7%)	1.0	-	-	-	-
Basic economic transactions (d860)	0	4 (2.7%)	3 (4.1%)	1.0	-	-	-	-

[1] Adjusted for age, gender and presence or not of a chronic condition.

Population Characteristics using ICF-Coded Items on BI, OARS-IADL and RNL Index

Table 5 shows the number of individuals within each age group who presented with some degree of impairment, limitation or restriction on each of the 28 expert-consensus ICF items. Contrasts are made between age groups with all odds ratio being adjusted for gender and co-morbid conditions. Confidence intervals are presented and those that exclude 1 indicate statistical significance. Analyses revealed that older individuals (75 y.o and more) are significantly more likely to experience limitations and restrictions than community-dwellers who are less than 65 years of age, in 12 ICF activities. These are; *recreation and leisure, using transportation, moving around outside the home, family relationships, socializing, self-care, walking short distances, washing whole body, doing housework, preparing meals, looking after one's health and shopping.* The impact of being 75 years and older was very strong on *recreation and leisure* (OR 5.8; 95% CI: 2.5 – 13.8) and *using transportation* (OR 7.7; 95% CI 3.1 – 19.1). Being 65 years and older had a significant impact on *being occupied in an activity important to one's self, family relationships* and *doing housework.*

Figure 1. Impairments, activity limitations and participation restrictions across gender among individuals aged 65 years and more (n=221).

Figure 1 illustrates differences between men and women who are aged 65 years and older (>64 years, n=221). Eight activity domains referring mostly to mobility and basic activities of daily living were problematic for women only. This specificity was not seen for men. Our results show that men and women are similarly affected in their capacity to participate in their r*ecreational and leisure* activities and in s*ocializing* activities. However, engaging in activities that are important to one's self (RNL5) is a challenge faced more frequently by men (18.7%) than by women (11.6%). Similarly, more men experience u*rinary incontinence* problems (6.7% vs 3.4% for women), and limitations in m*eals preparation* (5.3% vs 2.7% for women). Conversely, women reported greater difficulty handling f*amily relationships* (11.0% vs 5.3%) and were more limited than men in their capacity to h*andle stress* (6.2% vs 2.7%) and m*ove around outside the home* (4.8% vs 2.7%). None of these differences between men and women reached statistical significance.

DISCUSSION

The use of ICF-coded functional status indicators was shown to be useful to characterize community-dwelling elder although there were few problems in this population. Total summary scores on the RNL, Barthel Index, and OARS-IADL measure were misleading and provided an increased sense of 'healthiness' of community-dwellers. Indeed, our results as presented in Table 4, do not highlight any major difficulties in the areas covered by the three measures. However, when looking at the various body functions, activities and roles captured by the RNL, BI and OARS-IADL, almost half of those are problematic among elderly individuals. We identified twelve ICF-coded FSI, all of them from the activity and participation component of the ICF. Older individuals (>75 years) were found to have more difficulty moving around outside the home, using transportation, shopping, preparing meals, doing housework, bathing themselves (washing whole body) and managing their medication (looking after one's health). Difficulties in activities such as walking, shopping, bathing, doing housework and preparing meals contribute to the burden associated with ageing [38]. These activities are essential to community living and are important to an individuals' health-related quality of life. On the other hand, they can be compensated for if a difficulty arises. While the spouse or caregiver will most often take over these roles or provide physical assistance when necessary, community services also have the responsibility to adapt their resources to meet those needs. The wide range of goods and services that can now be delivered and provided at home is one example of community services that adapted to the needs of the elderly population. Identifying those needs early in the disability process will optimize service delivery and program planning. The venue of clinical information systems is expected to facilitate this and provide the infrastructure necessary to create FSI in a timely manner.

Our results also showed that individuals aged 75 years and over experience greater difficulty in their capacity to participate in the recreational and leisure activities of their choice. Access to certain recreational activities is dependent upon the capacity of an individual to be mobile in his/her community or to use transportation. Consequently, it was of no surprise to see the strong association between age and difficulties in recreational and leisure activities among those 75 years and older in light of their mobility limitations. Engaging in an activity that is important to one's self (RNL5) was challenging for all individuals over the age of 65 years. Four raters mapped that item (RNL5) and RNL6 to the same ICF code (d920 recreation and leisure). These raters indicated through their code selection that these two items captured the same construct. Interestingly, our results showed that older men did not interpret these two items the same way. Approximately 19% of men reported some restriction in their ability to engage in an activity that was important to them compared to 13% who expressed limitations in their capacity to engage in recreational activities. One possible reason for this discrepancy is that men, even after retirement, still consider work as the most important activity. This was not an issue with women who may have a wider range of activities (work, housework or family relationships) that they consider important and continue to perform at older ages.

Among our study population, almost 25% of items were problematic for women but not men. This may be a consequence of the longer life expectancy of women who then become more at risk of experiencing limitations. It may also be that women are more inclined then men to report activity limitations [3]. Nevertheless, consideration must be given to these gender specific restrictions.

Undoubtedly, the added-value of ICF-coded FSI will be achieved only if outcome measures routinely used in clinical practice or research are computerized and an integrated algorithm automatically translates each item score into ICF-codes. Semi-automated coding is currently available to translate clinical information and ICD codes into a SNOMED code [39]. The feasibility of translating clinical information into ICF codes is dependent upon the availability of a large pool of ICF-coded items originating from outcome measures. It is also dependent upon the convergence of the different sources that could generate a same ICF-coded FSI. The potential problems associated with providing one unique code to two different items originating from two outcome measures is well illustrated with the ICF descriptor 'using transportation'. Both 'being able to take trips out of town' and 'going to places out of walking distances' were interpreted by raters as linking to the same ICF code (agreement of 55% and 82% respectively). However, the proportion of individuals reporting any difficulty using transportation is quite different depending upon the item used to flag this problem. The convergence of these two sources is not optimal and would create a major challenge that would need to be addressed if FSI are to be automated using electronic health records. Statistical methods such as Rasch or Item-response theory may prove useful to identify the most appropriate data source to be used to generate ICF-coded FSI.

There are limitations to this project. First, the study population of community-dwelling elders was, overall, rather healthy. The low prevalence of impairments/limitations and restrictions limited our statistical power to detect significant differences across age groups and gender. Second, our method to control for the presence of co-morbid conditions did not take into account the type of chronic condition. The presence of certain chronic conditions, like arthritis, may have more impact on a person's functioning than age itself. Co-morbidities were self-reported by community-dwelling individuals at the time of interview. In the context of this paper, it was not possible to verify the accuracy of the information, and decided to take a more conservative approach.

The relatively large number of raters involved in the linkage process and our decision to measure agreement at the 3rd level, reduced our capacity to reach full agreement on some items. The long list of codes on certain items inflated the impression of poor agreement and hid the fact that many of them had high agreement at the second level. On the 26 items that were assigned a code, the overall agreement at the 3-digit level was 78.7% and compares advantageously with the overall agreement of 74.9% documented by Cieza and colleagues in their study assessing the validity of ICF linkage rules [27]. Having a large group of raters perform the linkage of items to the ICF has some benefits. First, having eleven raters agree on one unique ICF code strengthens the validity of this code and increases its reliability. Second, by exposing clinicians to the ICF in the context of a linkage process may reinforce the usefulness of the ICF in clinical practice and enhance clinician's acceptance of a standard vocabulary framework.

We recognize that associating one unique code on items such as, "how comfortable are you with how your self-care needs are met" restricts its interpretation to one concept, in this case, *self-care* without capturing any other underlying concept (here, comfort). The decision to prioritize the main concept was supported by the idea of having the ICF-coded FSI integrated into administrative databases. In our opinion, having one code, although not detailed, is better than no code at all. On the other hand, the code must reflect as accurately as possible the difficulty the person is experiencing. Cognitive debriefing would need to be performed to examine the clarity and degree of ambiguity of each item. This technique is frequently used for newly developed scales, and our results indicate that it may become a necessary step to be done early in future linkage processes of outcome measures to the ICF. Future research is required to assess differences in clinicians, patients and researchers' interpretation of items to be linked to the ICF.

The development of a linkage protocol with detailed rules and steps is currently under development (Mayo et al, unpublished work). This study aligned itself quite closely with the proposed recommendations by Mayo and colleagues. They propose 70% agreement as the minimal percent agreement for a given code to be endorsed as the "best" code. According to this rule, 17 items (61%) from our pool received the 'best' code after independent rating by individual raters. Their protocol recommends the use of a Delphi approach to allow raters to modify their codes or select another code in light of other raters' choices. This second step will not only enhance the validity of selected codes but will also allow linkage errors to be captured by raters and be removed from the final percent agreement. The Delphi approach will need to be undertaken to validate the set of selected codes on the BI, RNL and OARS-IADL

CONCLUSION

ICF-coded functional status indicators were useful to characterize community-dwelling elders and provided a level of detail otherwise not available using total scores on the Barthel Index, Reintegration to Normal Living Index and the OARS-IADL. The ICF has the capacity to create coded FSI that are meaningful to clinicians, researchers and decision-makers. ICF-coded FSI will allow comparisons across populations groups, and monitoring of patient's progress within a continuum of care, regardless of the outcome measures used. Further work is required to expand the pool of ICF-coded items, and test their capacity to characterize other population groups. The emergence of clinical information systems will make possible the integration of ICF coded functional status indicators on administrative databases.

Acknowledgments

We would like to thank the raters on this project; Jane Boucher, Diana Chin, Nancy Cox, Diana Dawes, Lois Finch, Johanne Higgins, Carolina Moriello, Sandra Prizio and Nancy Salbach. L. Poissant is financially supported by a New Emerging Team grant from the Canadian Institute of Health Research (CIHR).

References

[1] www.statcan.ca. Statistics Canada. 2004.

[2] Brach JS, FitzGerald S, Newman AB, Kelsey S, Kuller L, VanSwearingen JM et al. Physical activity and functional status in community-dwelling older women: a 14-year prospective study. *Arch Intern Med* 2003; 163(21):2565-2571.

[3] Murtagh KN, Hubert HB. Gender differences in physical disability among an elderly cohort. *Am J Public Health* 2004; 94(8):1406-1411.

[4] Hoffman C, Rice D, Sung HY. Persons with chronic conditions. Their prevalence and costs. *JAMA* 1996; 276(18):1473-1479.

[5] Murray CJ, Lopez AD. Global mortality, disability, and the contribution of risk factors: Global Burden of Disease Study. *Lancet* 1997; 349(9063):1436-1442.

[6] Murray CJ, Lopez AD. Regional patterns of disability-free life expectancy and disability-adjusted life expectancy: global Burden of Disease Study. *Lancet* 1997; 349(9062):1347-1352.

[7] Stuck AE, Walthert JM, Nikolaus T, Bula CJ, Hohmann C, Beck JC. Risk factors for functional status decline in community-living elderly people: a systematic literature review. *Soc Sci Med* 1999; 48(4):445-469.

[8] Eisner MD, Yelin EH, Trupin L, Blanc PD. The influence of chronic respiratory conditions on health status and work disability. *Am J Public Health* 2002; 92(9):1506-1513.

[9] Clarke P, Marshall V, Black SE, Colantonio A. Well-being after stroke in Canadian seniors: findings from the Canadian Study of Health and Aging. *Stroke* 2002; 33(4):1016-1021.

[10] Rubenstein L. *Quality of Life for Patients Diagnosis and Screening, or to Evaluate Treatment. Quality of Life and Pharmacoeconomics in Clinical Trials*. Lippincott-Raven, 1996.

[11] Whiteneck GG. The 44th annual John Stanley Coulter Lecture. Measuring what matters: key rehabilitation outcomes. *Arch Phys Med Rehabil* 1994; 75(10):1073-1076.

[12] Carey EC, Walter LC, Lindquist K, Covinsky KE. Development and validation of a functional morbidity index to predict mortality in community-dwelling elders. *J Gen Intern Med* 2004; 19(10):1027-1033.

[13] Parker MG, Thorslund M, Nordstrom ML. Predictors of mortality for the oldest old. A 4-year follow-up of community-based elderly in Sweden. *Arch Gerontol Geriatr* 1992; 14(3):227-237.

[14] Liang MH, Shadick N. Feasibility and utility of adding disease-specific outcome measures to administrative databases to improve disease management. *Ann Intern Med* 1997; 127(8 Pt 2):739-742.

[15] Selby JV. Linking automated databases for research in managed care settings. *Ann Intern Med* 1997; 127(8 Pt 2):719-724.

[16] Hornbrook MC, Goodman MJ. Chronic disease, functional health status, and demographics: a multi-dimensional approach to risk adjustment. *Health Serv Res* 1996; 31(3):283-307.

[17] Iezzoni LI. Assessing quality using administrative data. *Ann Intern Med* 1997; 127(8 Pt 2):666-674.

[18] Roger France FH. WHO views on perspectives in health informatics. *Int J Med Inf* 2000; 58-59:11-19.

[19] Shah S, Vanclay F, Cooper B. Predicting discharge status at commencement of stroke rehabilitation. *Stroke* 1989; 20(6):766-769.

[20] Haggerty JL, Reid RJ, Freeman GK, Starfield BH, Adair CE, McKendry R. Continuity of care: a multidisciplinary review. *BMJ* 2003; 327(7425):1219-1221.

[21] WHO. International Classification of Diseases, Disorders and Injuries. 10th revision ed. Geneva: 1994.

[22] WHO. International Classification of Functioning, Disability and Health. Second revision ed. Geneva: 2001.

[23] Rose JS, Fisch BJ, Hogan WR, Levy B, Marshal P, Thomas DR et al. Common medical terminology comes of age, Part One: Standard language improves healthcare quality. *J Healthc Inf Manag* 2001; 15(3):307-318.

[24] Fransen J, Uebelhart D, Stucki G, Langenegger T, Seitz M, Michel BA. The ICIDH-2 as a framework for the assessment of functioning and disability in rheumatoid arthritis. *Ann Rheum Dis* 2002; 61(3):225-231.

[25] Iezzoni LI, Greenberg MS. Capturing and classifying functional status information in administrative databases. *Health Care Financ Rev* 2003; 24(3):61-76.

[26] Weigl M, Cieza A, Harder M, Geyh S, Amann E, Kostanjsek N et al. Linking osteoarthritis-specific health-status measures to the International Classification of Functioning, Disability, and Health (ICF). *Osteoarthritis Cartilage* 2003; 11(7):519-523.

[27] Cieza A, Brockow T, Ewert T, Amman E, Kollerits B, Chatterji S et al. Linking health-status measurements to the international classification of functioning, disability and health. *J Rehabil Med* 2002; 34(5):205-210.

[28] Mayo NE, Poissant L, Ahmed S, Finch L, Higgins J, Salbach NM et al. Incorporating the International Classification of Functioning, Disability, and Health (ICF) into an

electronic health record to create indicators of function: proof of concept using the SF-12. *J Am Med Inform Assoc* 2004; 11(6):514-522.

[29] Borchers M, Cieza A, Sigl T, Kollerits B, Kostanjsek N, Stucki G. Content comparison of osteoporosis-targeted health status measures in relation to the International Classification of Functioning, Disability and Health (ICF). *Clin Rheumatol* 2004.

[30] Mayo NE, Wood-Dauphinee S, Cote R, Durcan L, Carlton J. Activity, participation, and quality of life 6 months poststroke. *Arch Phys Med Rehabil* 2002; 83(8):1035-1042.

[31] Mahoney FI, Barthel DW. Functional evaluation: The Barthel Index. *Md State Med J* 1965; 14:61-65.

[32] Finch E, Brooks D, Stratford P, Mayo N. *Physical Rehabilitation Outcome Measures.* Second Edition ed. Hamilton, Ontario: BC Decker, 2002.

[33] Center for the Study of Aging and Human Development. Multidimensional Functional Assessment: the OARS methodology: a manual. 1975. Durham (NC).

[34] Fillenbaum GG, Smyer MA. The development, validity, and reliability of the OARS multidimensional functional assessment questionnaire. *J Gerontol* 1981; 36(4):428-434.

[35] Doble SE, Fisher AG. The dimensionality and validity of the Older Americans Resources and Services (OARS) Activities of Daily Living (ADL) Scale. *J Outcome Meas* 1998; 2(1):4-24.

[36] Wood-Dauphinee SL, Opzoomer MA, Williams JI, Marchand B, Spitzer WO. Assessment of global function: The Reintegration to Normal Living Index. *Arch Phys Med Rehabil* 1988; 69(8):583-590.

[37] Ware JE, Jr., Kosinski M, Keller SD. *How to Score the SF-12 Physical and Mental Health Summary Scales*. 2nd ed. Boston, MA: 1995.

[38] Gill TM, Kurland B. The burden and patterns of disability in activities of daily living among community-living older persons. *J Gerontol A Biol Sci Med Sci* 2003; 58(1):70-75.

[39] Buemi A. BMACR. Transcodage SNOMED – CIM-10: proposition pour une meilleure indexation des dossiers médicaux. *Actes des 9ièmes Journées Francophones d'Informatique Médicale* 2003; 16(2002):371-378.

In: Focus on Disability: Trends in Research and Application ISBN: 978-1-60021-792-0
Editor: Thilo Kroll, pp. 23-30 © 2008 Nova Science Publishers, Inc.

Chapter II

Cross-walking ICF to the TMIG-IC—Tokyo Metropolitan Institute of Gerontology's Index of Competence: An Application of ICF to Community-Living Elderly

Kristine A. Mulhorn

University of Michigan-Flint, Department of Health Sciences and Administration, Flint, MI 48502, USA.

Background

The International Classification of Functioning, Disability and Health presents a significant opportunity to develop a common language for cross-national comparisons of disability measures for elderly populations. Thus far, the ICF has been applied to aging populations in institutional settings. The present study considers ICF for those populations living in the community. This project follows the methodology introduced the ICF to current measurement systems, such as those in national health and disability surveys (Swanson, Carrothers, Mulhorn, 2003) in health records (Ustun, Chatterji, Kostansjek, & Bickenbach, 2003), in various health status instruments (Cieza, Brockow, Ewert, Amman, Chatterji, & Stucki, (2002)), and in other assessment tools used in the care of the elderly (Takahashi, Okochi, Takamuku, Matsuda, 2004); Teare, Berg, Ikegami, Resnick, Kairy, 2004; Poissant, Mayo & Ahmed, 2004). In all these cases the goal meets some of the recommendations of the WHO to make ICF reach its potential as "a common language" for practitioners and researchers (WHO, 2002). The first step was to follow the methodology presented by Cieza, et al., (2002) to cross-walk ICF to both the TMIG-IC (Koyano, et al., (1991) and the additional items added to TMIG-IC for the frail elderly. This may be the first attempt at linking a Japan-based health status measurement tool (TMIG-IC) to the ICF following the recommended methods and rules proposed and followed by Cieza, et al., 2002).

Table 1a. Cross-walking Results for Investigator 1

TMIG-IC Item (1-13)	Component	Chapter 1st Level	2nd Level	3rd Level	4th Level	Additional Information
1. Can you use public transportation (bus or train) by yourself?	d	4	70	0		
2. Are you able to shop for daily necessities?	d	6	20	0		
3. Are you able to prepare meals by yourself?	d d	6 6	30 30	0 1		simple meals complex meals
4. Are you able to pay bills?	d	8	60			
5. Can you handle your own banking?	d	8	65			
6. Are you able to fill out forms for your pension?	d	8	70			
7. Do you read newspapers?	d	1	66			
8. Do you read books or magazines?	d	1	66			
9. Are you interested in news stories or programs dealing with health?	d d	5 5	70 70	 9		
10. Do you visit the homes of friends?	d d	9 9	20 20	 5		
11. Are you sometimes called on for advice?	d	7	78			
12. Are you able to visit sick friends?	d d	9 9	20 20	 8		
13. Do you sometimes initiate conversations with young people?	d	7	79			

METHODS

Based on the evidence of activities involving the ICF and the aging population presented at the 10th Annual NACC Conference in 2004, there is a growing literature and several groups actively engaged in addressing the use of ICF for assessment tools for institutionalized elderly (Stucki, et al., 2001; Takahashi, et al., 2004; Teare, et al., 2004). Work that integrates Cieza, et al. outline a clear methodology for cross-walking measurement systems to the ICF and this was followed by three investigators who independently coded the items on the TMIG-Index of Competence used for assessing the functional status for elderly living in the community. Each item in the index was coded appropriately at the 1st, 2nd and 3rd levels following the recommended format. The results for each are included in Tables 1.a.,

1.b, and 1.c. This cross-walking exercise points to the Then, a brief summary of these results was compiled to address the differences.

Table 1b. Cross-walking Results for Investigator 2

TMIG-IC Item (1-13)	Component	Chapter 1st Level	2nd Level	3rd Level	4th Level	Additional Information
1. Can you use public transportation (bus or train) by yourself?	d	4	70	2		
2. Are you able to shop for daily necessities?	d	6	20	0		
3. Are you able to prepare meals by yourself?	d	6	30	9		
4. Are you able to pay bills?	d	8	60			paying bills
5. Can you handle your own banking?	d	8	60			handling own banking
6. Are you able to fill out forms for your pension?	d	1	70			forms for pension
7. Do you read newspapers?	d	1	66			newspaper
8. Do you read books or magazines?	d	1	66			books or magazines
9. Are you interested in news stories or programs dealing with health?	nd					
10. Do you visit the homes of friends?	d	9	20	5		
11. Are you sometimes called on for advice?	nd					
12. Are you able to visit sick friends?	d	9	20	5		
13. Do you sometimes initiate conversations with young people?	d	3	50	0		with young people

The methodology was patterned after the systematic strategy for linking the ICF to other tools introduced by Cieza et al., 2002. After becoming familiar with ICF and its components in both Part 1(Functioning and Disability)—Body Functions (b) and Structure (s) and Activities and Participation (d) and in Part 2 (Contextual Factors) with the components Environmental Factors (e) and Personal Factors. The next step was to link each item in TMIG-IC (and later the items for the frail elderly) to the most precise category in the ICF, using the linking rules set forth by Cieza, et al. The coding described by Cieza, et al., such as *nd* for not definable and *nc* for not covered. We then document what is not explicitly covered by ICF. The linking was completed across three researchers independently. After the linking is complete, a combined table was created with the necessary columns—component, Chapter 1st level, 2nd level, 3rd level, 4th level and additional information.

Table 1c. Cross-walking Results for Investigator 3

TMIG-IC Item (1-13)	Component	Chapter 1st Level	2nd Level	3rd Level	4th Level	Additional Information
1. Can you use public transportation (bus or train) by yourself?	d	4	70	2		
2. Are you able to shop for daily necessities?	d	6	20	0		
3. Are you able to prepare meals by yourself?	d	6	30	0		
4. Are you able to pay bills?	d	2	20	8		
5. Can you handle your own banking?	d	2	20	8		
6. Are you able to fill out forms for your pension?	d	2	20	8		
7. Do you read newspapers?	d	1	66	0		
8. Do you read books or magazines?	d	1	66	0		
9. Are you interested in news stories or programs dealing with health?	d	5	70	8		
10. Do you visit the homes of friends?	d	7	50	0		
11. Are you sometimes called on for advice?	c	3	99			
12. Are you able to visit sick friends?	d	9	20	5		
13. Do you sometimes initiate conversations with young people?	d	7	60	0		

First, following the model set by Rune Simeonson (Simeonsson, 2003) in his effort to develop an ICF for Children and gather an international working group to address the integration of ICF into to areas of research on the aging population: 1) assessment tools measuring the health and functioning of elderly living in the community and 2) reimbursement and tools used for caregiving for elderly living in long-term care settings. Such tools include SNOMED CT and MDS, both known to require attention as they relate to ICF (Harris, et al., (2003). While SNOMED CT is a terminology of medical terms and ICF is a classification system, in order for both to coexist, it is agreed that there needs to be more work in this area. This stage of the project can be seen as an outgrowth of the work began by Stucki and others in Germany linking the ICF to other measurement instruments from rehabilitation medicine and general health status tools, such as SF-36. This work has been referred to as one of the "core sets" projects.

Second, I propose that TMIG staff and I follow the methodology presented by Cieza, et al., (2002) to cross-walk ICF to both the TMIG-IC (Koyano, et al., (1991) and the additional items added to TMIG-IC for the frail elderly. This can happen fairly quickly and I will outline the recommended steps. This may be the first attempt at linking a Japan-based health status measurement tool (TMIG-IC) to the ICF following the recommended methods and rules proposed and followed by Cieza, et al., 2002). I have summarized the steps that need to be taken to complete this methodology.

STEPS:

i) Become familiar with ICF and its components in both Part 1(Functioning and Disability)—Body Functions (b) and Structure (s) and Activities and Participation (d) and in Part 2 (Contextual Factors) with the components Environmental Factors (e) and Personal Factors.

Part 1: Functioning and Disability
Components: b, s, d
Part 2: Contextual Factors
Components: e, personal factors

ii) Link each item in TMIG-IC (and later the items for the frail elderly) to the most precise category in the ICF, using the linking rules set forth by Cieza, et al. on page 206 of their article.
iii) Use the coding described by Cieza, et al., such as *nd* for not definable and *nc* for not covered. Then document what is not explicitly covered by ICF.
iv) The linking should be done by at least three researchers, independently. Three researchers—the author and two representatives from TMIG—completed the task.
v) After the linking is complete, a combined table can be created with the necessary columns—component, Chapter 1st level, 2nd level, 3rd level, 4th level and additional information. This will provide the basis for the remainder of the work proposed here but will also allow for an innovative step towards bringing ICF to current measures of functional status.

RESULTS

The first stage of the project was to develop an international working group made up of researchers and clinicians familiar with ICF who are actively addressing health and disability of elderly populations living in the community. This project began with the meeting of researchers at TMIG in Tokyo in 2004, following the NACC meeting. The results presented here are based on that stage of the project. Future work will reflect the other members from France and Canada.

The results demonstrate a close approximation of the TMIG-IC items with categories and specific codes in the ICF. The complete breakdown of the cross-linking by all three investigators is displayed in Tables 1a, 1b, and 1c. The item most problematic because it is not defined clearly by ICF and may also be an item unique to Japan or not regularly included by other instruments is item No. 13, “initiating conversations with young people”. This is a key indicator of being needed and included for the elderly in Japan and consistently suggests health, but is not specifically identified in the ICF. The result for each of the investigators for this item was d779, “interpersonal interactions and relationships, other specified”.

There were a few other items that would require a new code or would meet the require a code with the “other specified” clarification. These include items 9 through 13 from the TMIG-Index of Competence. Please see Table 2 for items 9 through 13 where the description of the TMIG-IC items are listed with the recommendations and possible cross-links. These areas confirm what Cieza et al. have found—that “it is not at all simple and straightforward to link specific items to the ICF” (Cieza et al., 2002).

Table 2. Cross-walking to TMIG-1C Challenges

TMIG-1C Item	Possible Cross-links	Recommendations
9. Are you interested in news stories or programs dealing with health?	d 5709 d 5708	d 5709 Seeking health information from books, newspapers, other news sources…
10. Do you visit the homes of friends?	d 9205 d 7500	
11. Are you sometimes called on for advice?	d 778 e 399 nd	Others seek advice from you
12. Are you able to visit sick friends?	d 9208 d 9205	d 9208 Visiting sick friends or relatives
13. Do you sometimes initiate conversations with young people?	d 779 d 760 d 3500	d 779 Initiating conversations with young people

The remainder of the codes linking ICF to the TMIG-IC tool were identical across the investigators with agreement across all three levels. These items are good candidates for comparisons across countries. The cross-linking demonstrates the versatility of many items in the TMIG-IC and the potential for TMIG-IC to be used for cross-national comparisons of measures of functioning for community-living elderly.

Conclusion

There are two sets of conclusions—one set based on the status of ICF for aging populations and the other based on the cross-walking results of the first stage of this long-term project on community living elderly.

ICF for Aging Populations

Consider classification and other tools used in various long-term care settings (such as Minimum Data Set in Canada and the US) in addition to SNOMED CT. This may be done with these instruments in mind. This is at the technical level. Make decisions about items that may belong in ICD (like dementia and associated functioning areas such as aphasia, apraxia, and dysphagia). Aphasia is not currently in ICF, but apraxia and dysphagia are. Since ICF is a classification system and not intended to include all diagnoses or symptoms, the significance of this absence is yet unclear. Such issues, however, could be addressed more systematically by those adapting ICF to other instruments. At an administrative level (i.e., for reimbursement, standards of care and caregiving), consider use of ICF in various long-term care settings. These include the home, nursing care facilities (nursing homes), home health care services. Continuing the work of DISTAT and consistent with the goal of ICF as a "common language", there should be a goal of comparing demographic trends and consequences of functional characteristics over time and across countries. Consider demographic questions like whether there is an expanding or decreasing morbidity as populations age. Consider comparability across countries given there is a range of long-term care settings even when rates of population subgroups (e.g., 65-74, 75-84, and 85+) are similar. Consider the implications of the results for training and education, especially those seeking careers in long-term care facilities. Consider the integration of ICF to various reimbursement / payment / program eligibility systems so that persons 65 and older AND persons under 65 can be compared in terms of function and disability.

Cross-walking the TMIG-IC to the ICF

Cross-walking the TMIG-IC to the ICF presents an example of an examination of the potential of an assessment tool for international comparisons. The results indicate some areas of disagreement across only three investigators who independently conducted the cross-walking, but it also demonstrated that several TMIG-IC items could lend themselves to international comparisons. Items such as using transportation by oneself, shopping, preparing meals, paying bills, banking, reading newspapers, and reading resulted in high levels of consensus. These were consistent with other tools measuring IADLs and participation in community activities. Other items, such as the ability to visit sick friends and initiating conversations with young people are not directly identified in the ICF, and were areas where there was a lack of consensus. The exercise follows the work of Poissant, et al. (2004) who suggest we develop a bank of ICF-coded items based on cross-walking to the items the most common outcome measures used in clinical practice across various settings. The TMIG-IC has been in use since the early 1990s and has already been useful in research in Asia, but now has the potential to reach others. More discussion across investigators who regularly use TMIG-IC and other assessment tools for community-living elderly will provide additional steps for the recommended use of TMIG-IC in other work.

REFERENCES

Cieza A, Brockow T, Ewert T, Amman E, Kollerits B, Chatterji S, Üstün TB,Stucki G. (2002). Linking health-status measurements to the international classification of functioning, disability and health. *Journal of Rehabilitation Medicine*, Sep;34(5):205-10.

Hendershot, G.(2003). Disability International Standard Tablations (DISTab or DISTAB): Methodological Issues in International Comparisons: The International Classification of Functioning, Disability and Health (ICF). *Forum on International Collaborative Research in Rehabilitation*, July.

Koyono, W., Shibata, H., Nakazato, K., Haga, H., Suyama, Y. (1991). Measurement of competence: reliability and validity of the TMIG Index of Competence. *Archives of Gerontology and Geriatrics, 13*: 103-116.

Mulhorn, K.A. (2004). Considerations of ICF for the Aging Population. *Presentation at the 10th North American Collaborating Center Conference on ICF* (June).

Poissant, L., Mayo, N., Ahmed, S. (2004). Linking the ICF to the Barthel Index, the OARS-IADL and the RNL Index to characterize community-dwelling elders, *Presentation at the 10th North American Collaborating Center Conference on ICF* (June).

Simeonsson, R.J. and Leonardi, M. (2003). "A V ersion of the IC for Children and Youth: Status Report." *Presented at the ICF Meeting in Cologne, Germany.*

Stucki, G. Cieza, A., Ewert, T, Kostanjsek, N., Chatterji, S., , Üstün T.B. (2002). Application of the International Classification of Functioning, Disability and Health (ICF) in clinical practice. *Disability and Rehabilitation, 24*(5): 281-282.

Swanson, G., Carrothers, L., Mulhorn, KA. (2003). Comparing Disability Survey Questions in Five Countries: a study using ICF to guide Comparisons, *Disability and Rehabilitation, 25*(11/12): 665-675.

Takahashi, T., Okochi, J., Takamuku, K., Matsuda, S. (2002). TAI (Typology of the Aged with Illustrations) based Assessment System, *Proceedings*, POS/E.

Teare, G.F., Berg, K, Ikegami, N., Resnick, L. Kairy, D. (2004). Cross-walking the RAI-Home Care Assessment to the ICF. *Presentation at the 10th North American Collaborating Center Conference on ICF* (June).

Üstün T.B., Chatterji, S., Kostansjek, N., Bickenbach, J. (2003). WHO's ICF and Functional Status Information in Health Records. *Health Care Financing Review, Spring, 24*(3): 77-88.

WHO (2002) Towards a Common Language for Functioning, Disability and Health: ICF. Geneva, Switzerland.

In: Focus on Disability: Trends in Research and Application ISBN: 978-1-60021-792-0
Editor: Thilo Kroll, pp. 31-38 © 2008 Nova Science Publishers, Inc.

Chapter III

EVALUATING THE ICF AS A FRAMEWORK FOR CLINICAL ASSESSMENT OF PERSONS FOR ASSISTIVE TECHNOLOGY DEVICE RECOMMENDATION

Sajay Arthanat and James A. Lenker
Department of Rehabilitation Science, School of Public Health and Health Professions, University at Buffalo, New York, USA.

ABSTRACT

Assistive technology (AT) supports function and independence in life roles for persons with disabilities. AT assessment, intervention planning, and outcomes measurement are complicated by the heterogeneity of user populations, AT devices, contextual environments, and participation needs of device users. This paper (chapter/section?) will discuss the potential for the International Classification for Health, Disability and Functioning (ICF) (World Health Organization, 2001) to be used as a clinical assessment tool that supports AT device recommendation. The paper will highlight the relevance of the ICF to AT practice, illustrate compatibility of the ICF model with AT assessment elements, and discuss the need for development of an ICF-based AT assessment.

WHY DO WE NEED ICF-BASED ASSESSMENTS?

The use of the ICF as a framework for functional assessment and intervention planning has been proposed in the literature (Ustun, Chattergi, Bickenbach, Kostanjsek & Schneider, 2003). Operationally, this requires an understanding of the interactions among the ICF concepts of *Body Structure and Functions* and *Environmental* and *Personal Factors*, all of which impact on an individual's *Activity and Participation*. The ICF (as a classification model) describes overall health and functioning by pointing out "what the individual can do" as opposed to "what the individual wants to do." ICF-based assessments could help clinicians understand an individual's collective needs and prioritize goals for intervention. As an example, the Rehabilitation Problem Solving Form (RPF-Form) is an ICF-based assessment tool that identifies problems from patient and clinician perspectives, relates problems to modifiable factors, and provides a basis for intervention planning that addresses patient goals (Steiner et al., 2002). Condition-specific ICF instruments based on core sets of musculoskeletal, neurological, internal medicine, and pain conditions are also being developed in a collaborative effort by the University of Munich and the WHO (Stucki, Ewert, & Cieza, 2003).

Is the ICF Compatible with AT Practice?

The ICF is a holistic, bio-psychosocial framework (Stucki et al., 2003). Its components (*Body Structure and Function*, *Activity and Participation*, and *Environmental* and *Personal Factors)* address the elements inherent in AT assessment and intervention. Furthermore, the ICF speaks a language that is common to multiple disciplines (Arthanat, Nochajski, & Stone, 2004), and ICF terminology is appealing to researchers and practitioners in the multidisciplinary field of AT (Lenker & Jutai, 2002).

How Can the ICF Framework be Mapped to Elements of AT Assessment?

It is impractical to use the ICF in its entirety for assessments. Creation of condition- or intervention-specific ICF assessment tools has been proposed to improve the ICF's usability in clinical practice (Stucki et al., 2003). By virtue of its broad and descriptive framework, the ICF model can be mapped to the diversity of AT assessment elements involving the users, devices, and contexts.

A myriad of motor, sensory, perceptual, cognitive, and psychosocial functions or abilities of the AT user are relevant to two objectives of assessment and intervention: (a) that an AT be used to enable participation in activities that involve the compromised functions; and (b) that the user be able to interact effectively with the AT device. The domains within the ICF component *Body Structures and Functions* encompass all abilities of the AT user.

A prospective AT user has up to five contexts requiring AT needs identification and intervention planning: (a) Activities of Daily Living (ADL), (b) Instrumental Activities of Daily Living (IADL), (c) education, (d) vocation, and (e) recreation, which are relevant to home, school, workplace, and community settings. These five contexts can be classified within the ICF component of *Activity and Participation.*

AT devices primarily include mobility and seating, computer access, self-care, communication, and sensory devices. These are listed under the ICF component of *Environmental Factors* within the domain of *'Products and technology.'*

Table 1. AT Evaluation Areas and their Corresponding ICF Components & Domains

<table>
<tr><th colspan="2">Assistive Technology Assessment Elements</th><th colspan="2">ICF Conceptual Framework</th></tr>
<tr><td colspan="2" rowspan="3">User Abilities</td><td colspan="2">Part I: Functioning & Disability</td></tr>
<tr><td colspan="2">Component: Body Structures & Functions</td></tr>
<tr><td>Chapters: Body Functions</td><td>Chapters: Body Structure</td></tr>
<tr><td colspan="2">Motor</td><td>Neuromusculoskeletal and Movement-Related Functions,
Voice & Speech Functions</td><td>• Structures of the nervous system
• Structures related to movement
• Structures involved in voice and speech</td></tr>
<tr><td colspan="2">Sensory</td><td>Sensory Functions and Pain</td><td>• Structures of the nervous system
• The eye, ear, and related structures
• Skin and related structures</td></tr>
<tr><td colspan="2">Perception</td><td>Mental Functions</td><td>• Structures of the nervous system
• Structures related to movement
• The eye, ear, and related structures
• Skin and related structures</td></tr>
<tr><td colspan="2">Cognition</td><td>Mental Functions</td><td>• Structures of the Nervous system</td></tr>
<tr><td colspan="2">AT Application</td><td colspan="2">Component: Activity & Participation</td></tr>
<tr><td rowspan="5">Life Roles</td><td>Activities of Daily Living (ADL)</td><td colspan="2">• Self-care
• General tasks and demands
• Mobility
• Communication</td></tr>
<tr><td>Instrumental Activities of Daily Living (IADL)</td><td colspan="2">• Domestic life</td></tr>
<tr><td>Education</td><td colspan="2">• Major life areas
• Learning and applying knowledge
• General tasks and demands
• Communication
• Interpersonal interactions and relationships</td></tr>
<tr><td>Vocation</td><td colspan="2">• Major life areas
• Learning and applying knowledge
• General tasks and demands
• Communication
• Interpersonal interactions and relationships</td></tr>
<tr><td>Recreation</td><td colspan="2">• Community, social, and civic life
• Interpersonal interactions and relationships</td></tr>
</table>

Table 1. (Continued)

AT Devices		Part II: Contextual Factors
		Component: Environmental Factors
		Chapter: Products & Technology
Assistive Technology Assessment Elements		**ICF Conceptual Framework**
Mobility		Products and technology for personal indoor and outdoor mobility and transportation
Self-Care		Products and technology for personal use and daily living
Sensory	Vision	Products and technology for communication
	Hearing	Products and technology for communication
Communication		Products and technology for communication
Computer Access		Products and technology for education Products and technology for employment
Seating		NOT CLASSIFIED
Environmental Influences		Facilitators or Barriers
Physical Environment		Products and technology (Design of Environments) Natural environment and human-made changes
Social Environment		Support and relationships Services, systems, and policies
Attitudinal Environment		Attitudes
Psychosocial Attributes		*Component: Personal Factors*
Perceived Benefit		
Motivation		
Self-Esteem		
Perceived Competence		
Personal Resources		
Experience		
Education		
Socioeconomic Status		
Demographic Status		

Environmental factors affect the efficiency of AT usage during task performance. They include physical, social, and cultural contexts (Cook & Hussey, 2002), which in essence match the five *Environmental Factors* of the ICF framework. An AT assessment must identify environmental attributes that enable or hinder activity performance, which are classified by the ICF as '*Facilitators'* and *'Barriers.'*

Personal resources can have profound impact on the potential user of AT. Pertinent factors including socioeconomic status, age, education, employment, and experience with technology can be classified within the ICF component *Personal Factors*. Also, the user's psychosocial attributes such as, competence, self-esteem, and perception of the device's benefits are critical to acceptance and usage of the technology. The skills acquired by prior experiences with technologies can also be defined as a variable within *Personal Factors.*

Table 1 illustrates the mapping of the AT assessment areas to the components and chapters of the ICF. Figure 1 depicts the influences of ICF components on *Activity and*

Participation, illustrating the potential for an ICF-based assessment to identify the needs and goals most vital to an individual's life roles.

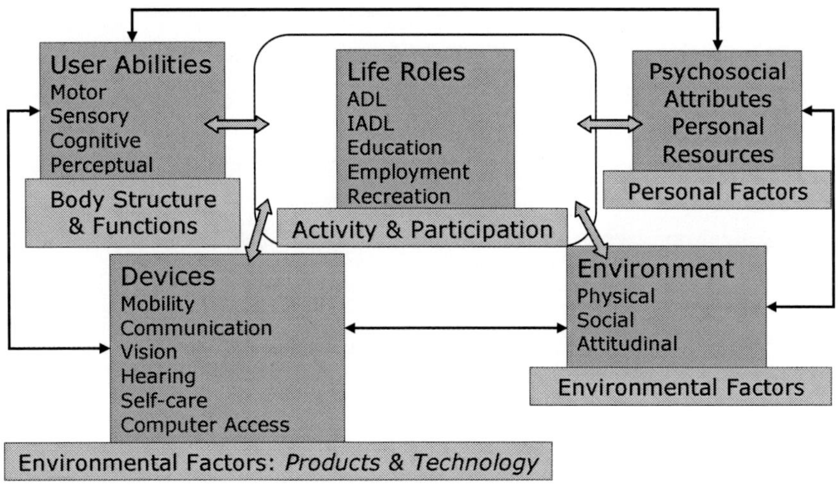

Figure 1. ICF-Based AT Assessment Needs Identification and Goal Setting.

AT Intervention Planning and Outcomes Measurement: What is the Role of the ICF?

AT assessments seek to identify efficient strategies for achieving *Activity and Participation* goals. Toward this end, AT devices are evaluated in conjunction with five so-called "parallel interventions": (a) enhancement of user abilities, (b) change in user technique, (c) modification of task, (d) alteration of environment, and (e) use of personal assistance (Smith, 2002). One or more of the parallel interventions may be complementary to the use of AT devices, or they may be an alternative to AT devices. Goal identification and prioritization are not explicitly addressed in the ICF Checklist, though they seem to fit within *Personal Factors*. Among the six parallel intervention options, enhancement of user abilities corresponds to *Body Structure* and *Function*; change in technique and task relate to *Activity and Participation;* and the remaining strategies, such as environmental modification, use of personal assistance, and use of AT devices, are part of *Environmental Factors*.

Two additional assessment components merit attention. First, it is important for practitioners to document the quantifiable characteristics composing AT assessment and invention, i.e., the 'treatment strength' (Keith, 1997). For example, an assessment can be characterized in terms of duration (hours), number of sessions, professional disciplines of practitioners conducting the assessment, qualifications of practitioners, or the trial period of the AT device allowed during the assessment. The intervention itself can be described in terms of the AT device and parallel interventions that support *Activity and Participation* goals. Implementation of the AT intervention can be characterized in terms of type of AT device, use of parallel interventions that support device use, number of hours spent on device configuration, number of hours spent on user training, and qualifications of practitioners providing the device configuration and training services. Essentially, these elements are among the independent variables that can affect the individual's performance outcomes. All these elements can be characterized within the ICF component domain *Environmental Factors*.

Second, it is important for practitioners to capture baseline performance data at the time of assessment so that longitudinal outcomes research can be more readily conducted. The AT field has not yet reached consensus regarding a core set of outcome domains, although it has been suggested (Lenker et al., 2003) that the core domains should include four factors: device usage; device usability including effectiveness, efficiency, and user satisfaction (International Standards Organization, 1993); quality of life impact; and social role performance impact. With respect to the ICF, many device usage and usability factors, as well as social role performance, are measurable variables within *Activity and Participation* and *Personal Factors*. Quality of life is a personal gestalt that reflects all ICF components; thus, it is not classifiable within a specific component.

Are Current Approaches in AT Assessment Relevant to the ICF?

The ICF components are implicit in some well-established AT assessment instruments. The Canadian Occupational Performance Measure (COPM) uses a semi-structured interview format to elicit a consumer's five highest-priority problem areas relating to self-care, productivity, and leisure (Law et al., 2004). For each problem area, consumers rate their current performance and satisfaction. For practitioners, the COPM can highlight the level of AT performance necessary to fulfill the identified participation needs of the client. The COPM appears to have two limitations with regard to AT intervention: (a) it does not systematically assess users' abilities, psychosocial status, and environmental factors; and (b) its open-ended format does not include questions specific to selection of AT devices.

The Individually Prioritized Problem Assessment (IPPA) developed by Wessels et al. (2002) is a structured assessment and goal-setting process that asks clients to rate the importance and difficulty associated with up to seven problem areas. The IPPA checklist includes queries in nine activity areas: self-care, mobility, transportation, housework, safety, leisure, communication, role activities, and social interaction. All are relatable to the ICF component of *Activity and Participation*. The IPPA can measure effectiveness of AT in terms of reduced difficulty of activity performance in the areas of priority. Similar to the COPM, the IPPA does not systematically assess user abilities or personal and environmental factors, and it does not include AT-specific questions.

The Matching Person Technology (MPT) is perhaps the most comprehensive assessment framework in AT provision. It consists of a battery of instruments designed to match individuals with AT devices based on the person's current needs, skills and abilities, environmental factors, and functions and features of the technology (Scherer & Craddock, 2002). The assessment process encourages consumer–clinician collaboration, ultimately seeking to characterize a client's predisposition to use various forms of technology. ICF components are embedded within the content of the MPT instruments, which seek to identify 'consumer needs and preferences' (i.e., *Activity and Participation* and *Personal Factors)* 'and milieu' (i.e., *Environmental Factors)*.

WHAT ARE THE POTENTIAL LIMITATIONS OF ICF-BASED AT ASSESSMENT?

The ICF classifies AT devices according to functional domains; it does not include detailed functions and features for the diversity of technologies. Also, no single assessment tool can be expected to serve as a prescriptive guide for AT recommendation. AT practitioners must rely on their knowledge, experience, and clinical reasoning to identify technology options. Device selection is also at times dictated by the availability of third-party reimbursements. In addition, the distinction between *"Capacity"* and *"Performance"* in the ICF is only theoretical at the moment, as this requires operationally defining the *current* and *standard* environments in terms of all the involved environmental variables. Moreover, the conversion of specific ICF qualifiers and codes to quantify the efficacy of interventions is vital. The ICF needs to further classify AT by including seating interventions involving postural support and pressure relief systems, which is a significant AT practice domain.

DISCUSSION: WHAT CAN BE CONCLUDED?

Assistive technology practitioners do not typically use standardized assessments. Nonetheless, practitioners must synthesize information that considers the gamut of ICF component areas in order to develop AT recommendations that maximize achievement of *Activity and Participation* goals. Future development must occur in five areas:

1. Detailed exploration of all ICF components is not practical in AT clinical settings; therefore the AT field needs to identify a streamlined set of ICF components that are most crucial to the needs of specific AT applications, such as wheeled mobility and seating, computer access software, and devices that augment communication, hearing, or vision.
2. Consensus is needed on a standard set of indicators that reflect AT treatment strength.
3. Consensus is needed on a standard set of AT outcome measurement domains.
4. Once identified, core AT outcome indicators must be incorporated into the ICF-based AT assessment. This would support longitudinal outcomes measurement, setting the stage for evaluating efficacy of AT services within and between countries.
5. Ultimately, researchers will need to demonstrate improvements in outcomes resulting from use of an ICF-based AT assessment.

References

Arthanat, S., Nochajski, S.M., & Stone, J. (2004). The International Classification of Functioning, Disability and Health and its application to cognitive disorders. *Disability and Rehabilitation, 26*(4): 235-245.

Cook, A.M., & Hussey, S.M. (2002). *Assistive technologies principles and practice* (2nd ed.). St.Louis: Mosby.

International Standards Organization. (1993). ISO CD 9241-11.2. In *Ergonomic Requirements for Office Work with Visual Display Terminals (VDTs): Guidance on Usability Specification and Measures*. Geneva: International Standards Organization.

Keith, R.A. (1997). Treatment strength in rehabilitation. *Archives of Physical Medicine and Rehabilitation, 78*, 1298-1304.

Law, M., Baptiste, S., Carswell, A., McColl, M., Polatojko, H., & Pollock, N. (2004). *The Canadian Occupational Performance Measure: Description*. Retrieved May 10 2004 from: http://www.caot.ca/copm/description.html.

Lenker, J.A., & Jutai, J.W. (2002). *Assistive technology research and practice: What role for ICF?* Paper presented at the 8th North American Collaborating Center (NACC) Conference on ICF, Toronto, ON.

Lenker, J.A., Scherer, M.J., Fuhrer, M.J., Jutai, J.W., & DeRuyter, F. (2003). Psychometric and administrative properties of measures used in assistive technology device outcomes research. *Assistive Technology, 17,* 7-22.

Scherer, M.J., & Craddock, G. (2002). Matching Person & Technology (MPT) assessment process. *Technology and Disability, 14*(3), 125-131.

Smith, R.O. (2002). Assistive technology outcome assessment prototypes: Measuring "INGO" variables of "outcomes". In R. Simpson (Ed.), *RESNA 25th Annual Conference Proceedings* (pp. 239-241). Minneapolis, MN: RESNA Press.

Steiner, W.A., Ryser, L., Huber, E., Uebelhart, D., Aeschlimann, & Stucki, G. (2002). Use of the ICF model as a clinical problem-solving tool in physical therapy and rehabilitation medicine. *Physical Therapy, 82*(11), 1098-1107.

Stucki, G., Cieza, A., Ewert, T., Kostanjsek, N., Chatterji S., & Ustun, T.B. (2002). Clinical commentary. Application of the International Classification of Functioning, Disability and Health (ICF) in clinical practice. *Disability and Rehabilitation. 24*(5):281-282.

Ustun, T.B., Chatterji, S., Bickenbach, J., Kostanjsek, N., & Schneider, M. (2003). The International Classification of Functioning, Disability and Health: A new tool for understanding disability and health. *Disability and Rehabilitation, 25*(11), 565-571.

Wessels, R., Persson, J., Lorentsen, O., Andrich, R., Ferrario, M., Oortwijn, W., Vanbeekum, T., Brodin, H., & de Witte, L. (2002). IPPA: Individually Prioritized Problem Assessment. *Technology and Disability, 14*(3), 141-145.

World Health Organization. *International Classification of Functioning, Disability and Health (ICF),* Geneva: WHO 2001.

In: Focus on Disability: Trends in Research and Application ISBN: 978-1-60021-792-0
Editor: Thilo Kroll, pp. 39-56 © 2008 Nova Science Publishers, Inc.

Chapter IV

APPLICATION OF ICF CODES IN GERIATRIC ASSESSMENT: USE OF ICF QUALIFIERS TO QUANTIFY HEALTH INFORMATION

***Jiro Okochi*[1] *and Tai Takahashi*[2]**
[1]University of Occupational and Environmental Health, Department of Preventive Medicine and Community Health, 1-1 Iseigaoka, Yahatanishi-ku, Kitakyushu-city, Japan;
[2]International University of Health and Welfare, Japan.

ABSTRACT

Objective: The application of the International Classification of Functioning, Disability and Health (ICF) to geriatric health assessment is a new challenge. In this study, the authors measured the ICF with the existing scales of the Typology of the Aged with Illustrations (TAI), with the intention of estimating the TAI scale level [score/?] from the ICF qualifier level using Rasch measurement techniques.

Methods: 788 Japanese older adults aged 65 and older were recruited to measure 85 codes of body function (BF) and 152 codes of activity and participation (AP), using the ICF qualifiers. All participants were assessed by two investigators independently. The ICF items relevant to TAI mobility and mental status scales were selected for cross-validation with the TAI scales. The measurement results were divided into development and validating samples by random selection. The ICF items were further selected until sufficient fitness to the Rasch model was achieved. Then the score of the TAI scales and each ICF item were studied using equating method in the validating samples.

Result: Average ages of men (25%) and women were 79(SD9) and 84(SD8), respectively, in the eligible sample. The average weighted kappa was 0.43 for BF and 0.56 for AP domain. The ordering of the item difficulty is demonstrated using Rasch analysis using the development sample, for mobility-related items in AP domain and mental function–related items in the BF domain. After selecting the ICF items that fit to the Rasch models, the order of the item difficulty of ICF items was identical to the TAI scales of mobility and mental status. Although the estimated scores between ICF mobility-related items and TAI mobility scale were similar in Mobility, deviation was found in Mental function–related items.

Discussion: The average weighted kappa of the measurement using the ICF qualifiers was relatively low. The quantification using ICF items did not consistently [ok?] estimate the score of the extant scale, especially in the analysis of mental function–related items in BF domain.

Conclusions: Constructing quantitative links between extant measures and the ICF items might enable us to describe health status with the common taxonomy of the ICF. However, careful examination of the item response pattern for each ICF item and extant measures is required to use the ICF as a common scale to describe human health status.

Keywords: International Classification of Functioning, Disability and Health; Disability Evaluation; Aged, 65 and over; Reproducibility of Results; Item Response Theory

INTRODUCTION

The challenges of implementing the International Classification of Functioning (ICF) [1] in fields such as medicine, rehabilitation, and long-term or social care include the operationalization and quantification of the ICF categories [2]. Unlike the International Classification of Diseases (ICD), which uses medical records as the source of information, the ICF requires health status measurement. Because an abundance of scales [rating instruments?] already exist that measure daily living activity and functions and that have been more specifically constructed for the intended populations, one solution to ICF implementation is to construct linkages between the extant measures and ICF categories [3,4]. This allows ICF users to tailor the number of ICF categories to handle in their clinical field. Such linkages must be substantiated by quantification, that is, by establishing relationships between the extant measures and related ICF items.

The goal of this study is to establish quantitative links between the Typology of the Aged with Illustrations (TAI) rating instrument and the ICF. If the ICF items and extant scales are measuring the same latent trait, then we can translate results from assessments using the extant scales to the ICF. In other words, we intended to study whether the TAI scales can be a substitute for the ICF, and vice versa. For this purpose, we applied Rasch measurement techniques [5]. In this context, the authors intended to describe the possibility of applying the ICF to describe human health status. In addition, this paper indicates some problems that might be encountered when the ICF codes and qualifiers are applied in a specific field, and presents test–retest reproducibility results.

Typology of the Aged with Illustrations

The authors used two scales -- mobility and mental status -- from the Typology of the Aged with Illustrations (TAI) rating instrument, whose reliability and validity has been previously established [6].

In Japan, the geriatric assessment became an obligation for care service providers as a means to improving the quality of care with the implementation of the long-term care insurance (LTCI) law in 2000 [7]. According to Ministry of Health, Labour and Welfare (MHLW) figures, the average time required for a geriatric assessment just prior to the implementation of LTCI was 1.8 h per person. With the prospect of an increasing workload under the LTCI, the TAI was developed as simple instrument for effective and efficient care management [6,8].

TAI measures functional and activity status with regard to mobility (and transfer), mental (cognitive) status, toileting and eating through observation and interview of the older adult. Each scale is scored on a 6-point scale (see Appendix Figures 1 and 2). TAI scores are identified with a specific level of care, giving care managers an immediate understanding of the type of care the older adult requires [8]. For example, an older adult with a TAI mobility scale score of 3 requires indirect assistance but not direct help from others. Thus, TAI results can be easily coupled to protocols of care.

The instrument has several further advantageous characteristics. The illustrations attached to the scales have improved test-retest reproducibility [6]. The simplicity of the scales [or instrument?] allows us to repeat assessments for large-scale epidemiological studies, as well as to describe status changes of older people in institutions (Okochi, unpublished data).

In addition, the TAI can predict the resource utilization of patients in long-term care institutions. A study of 1260 older adults in long-term care institutions showed an overall explanatory variance of 0.63 using only four TAI scales and one additional simple scale for medical resource use [8]. This figure was as good as that achieved by the case-mix classification system used in the Japanese LTCI (0.62, according to MHLW figures), which employed 79 variables. It also showed high concurrent validity with the Functional Independence Measure (FIM) [6,9].

Rasch Measurement Techniques

This study used the Rasch measurement techniques for analysis. The Rasch model [5] asserts that the easier the item, the more likely it will be answered correctly, and the more able the person, the more likely that he or she will correctly answer an item compared with a less able person [10]. The Rasch method produces a scale-free measures and sample-independent item ‘difficulties’ [11]. Mathematically, this means that the differences between pairs of measures and pairs of item ‘difficulties’ are expected to be relatively sample-independent [12]. When the unidimensionality criterion is met, that is, the single construct or single latent trait is measured, then the subscales that compose the Rasch measurement are additive. Additivity refers to the properties of the measurement units, which are the same size over the entire continuum [13]. These units are called logits and are a linear function of the probability of obtaining a certain score or rating for a person of a given ability [13].

The Rasch model assumes that the probability that a person will be grouped into a particular item category is a logistic function of the difference between the person’s ability (θ) and the difficulty of the task represented in the item (b). The probability of a success (or failure) of a task in a binary question in a scale (such as success or failure in transferring from a bed) can be expressed as

$$Pi(\theta) = \frac{e^{(\theta - b_i)}}{1 + e^{(\theta - b_i)}}$$

where Pi (θ) is the probability that respondents with ability (θ) will answer item i correctly (or be able to do the task specified by that item i). If a person's ability equates to the task difficulty, the probability of success in the item task is 0.5. From this formula, the expected pattern of responses to an item set is determined given that estimated (θ) and b, on person n and items i:

$$\ln\left(\frac{P_{ni}}{1 - P_{ni}}\right) = \theta_n - b_i$$

As expected, the response to the same item by a different person (or to a different item by the same person) can be expressed with simple logit. Therefore, if we know the item difficulty and the respondent behavior, we can estimate the person locations on the scale.

The extension of this model to polytomous, i.e. has items with more than two possible scores, a 'threshold' parameter (τ) can be estimated. The threshold represents the 0.5 probability point between any two adjacent score categories within an item, and k represents the k_{th} threshold within an item.

$$\ln\left(\frac{P_{nik}}{1 - P_{nik}}\right) = \theta_n - b_i - \tau_k$$

When the observed response pattern coincides with or does not deviate too much from the expected response pattern, then the items constitute a true Rasch scale. This deviation is analyzed based on χ square value of fitness of good statistics. The RUMM program used in this study substitutes the parameter estimates back into the model and examines the difference between the expected values predicted from the model and the observed values using two tests of fit: item–trait interaction and item–person interaction [12,14]. The fit statistics approximate a distribution with a mean expected near zero and a standard deviation near one. Negative values indicate a response pattern that fits the model too closely and positive values indicate a poor fit to the model. However, the fit statistic depends on the sample size, and with a large sample size, the result of the fit tends to be poor [15].

Using the Rasch measurement technique, we can estimate [each person's score for each item in the scale. the person location for each score at the scale. Then we can estimate the score of different scales if the scales fit the Rasch model.

METHOD

Participants

788 Japanese older adults aged 65 and over from 34 institutional and 25 home-based services under jurisdiction of the long-term care insurance (LTCI) law were recruited to evaluate the ICF items in the Body Function (BF) and Activity and Participation (AP) domains. The selection criteria for the participants were functional stability during the one-week test–retest interval and written informed consent from the participant or a family member as proxy.

Selection of ICF Items

The authors selected every three-digit item in the BF and AP domains. In addition, four-digit items relevant to the care of older adults were added by consensual recommendations of a panel of physiotherapists, occupational therapists, speech therapists, nurses, social workers and care-managers. As a result, the study instrument comprised 85 BF items (of these 6 items were four-digit) and 152 AP items (of these 71 items were four-digit) [16]. The ICF items related to mobility and mental functions were further selected for the purpose of this study.

Measurement

Between May and October 2003, two evaluators measured each subject independently using 237 ICF codes to study the reproducibility of each code. The body function and performance qualifiers were used for the BF and AP domains, respectively [16]. Qualifiers were graded as defined by the WHO [1]: Level 0 indicates "no problem" (0-4% limitation or restriction); Level 1 "mild problem" (5-24% limitation or restriction); Level 2 "moderate problem" (25-49% limitation or restriction); Level 3 "severe problem" (50-95% limitation or restriction) and Level 4 "complete problem" (96-100% limitation or restriction). Levels 8 and 9 denote the conditions "not specified" and "not applicable" and were analyzed as missing values in this study.

In this study, all the ICF qualifier levels were reversed, so that older adults with higher ability received the higher score. Thus, the score of 4 indicated the qualifier level of 0, the score 3 indicated the qualifier level 1, the score 2 equalled the qualifier level 2, the score of 1 equaled the qualifier level 3, and the score of 0 equaled the qualifier level 4.

In addition, all investigators concurrently measured the participants using the four scales within the Typology of the Aged with Illustrations (TAI). The TAI Mobility and Mental Function scales are shown in Appendix Figures 1 and 2. Evaluators also documented the chronic medical conditions, health behaviors and living status of each subject; however, these data were not used in this particular study.

The authors attached the illustrations to the assessment protocol with the intention of increasing test–retest reproducibility and facilitating understanding of each ICF item, since the illustrations were known to increase reliability [6,17,18]. The illustrations used for the study are available on the authors' website [19,20]. In addition, the authors provided a comprehensive guide to the ICF codes and the qualifiers, based on the text by WHO [1], and a guide to the TAI in advance of the commencement of the evaluation.

Analysis

The test–retest reproducibility statistics of the ICF items used in this study and of the TAI scales were estimated by weighted kappa statistics.

For the Rasch analysis, a randomly selected half of the samples was used as a development sample, and the other half as a validating sample. To test the relative item difficulty and to test the score of TAI scales and ICF codes, the authors first selected relevant ICF items for TAI scales of mobility and mental status. Then the authors further selected the ICF items that showed better fit to the model (development model), using the individual item fit statistics estimated from the RUMM program.

In this process, the authors tried to retain as many ICF items as possible that had the same or similar content to the threshold used in the TAI scale [3] shown to the left in Appendix Figures 1 and 2. Finally, an equating test between the selected ICF items and the TAI scales was performed on the validating sample using the estimated person location of score 3 (qualifier level 1) for each ICF item from the development model. Score 3 is selected because the TAI scales often used the presence or absence of the problem in its threshold (see Appendix Figures 1 and 2).

Because of the large sample size, the item fit statistics were generally poor. Therefore, the authors further evaluated the development model and validation model using five randomly selected subsamples (n=300).

The authors used the RUMM 2020 [14] for the analysis using the Rasch measurement techniques, STATA (version 8.17) for the weighted kappa analysis and SPSS (12.0J) for the rest of the analysis.

Results

Of 1578 measurements performed on 788 participants, 1546 measurements were eligible for the study. Of these, 742 older adults were measured twice by two independent evaluators and provided the data for the test-retest reproducibility. A total of 289 experienced care professionals served as independent evaluators. The evaluators were nurses (24%), therapists (26%), care managers (22%) and social workers and caregivers (28%). Average ages of men (25%) and women were 79 (SD9) and 84 (SD8) respectively. Average weighted kappa statistics were 0.43 and 0.56 for BF and AP domains respectively. The result of the test-retest reproducibility and validity study of the ICF codes will be reported elsewhere in detail [16].

The result of 1546 measurements were then divided randomly into development samples (n=773) and validating samples(n=773).

Mobility and Transfer

In the analysis of mobility- and transfer-related items, the only three-digit ICF item used was 'Moving around using equipment' (d465). Items under 'Moving around using transportation' (d47-) were also excluded, as were 'Running' (d4552), 'Jumping' (d4553) and 'Swimming' (d4554), since these were irrelevant to geriatric care. Table 1 shows response frequencies and reproducibility results. The average kappa of the items studied was 0.60. Most of the items had fair reproducibility. 'Transferring oneself while sitting' (d4200) and 'Walking short distance' (d4501) showed good reproducibility and 'Maintaining a lying position' (d4150) showed poor reproducibility.

Table 1. Distribution of the raw score (reverse of the qualifier level) and weighted kappa (n=742)

Code	Description	4	3	2	1	0	ns/na	Weighted kappa	95%C.I.
d4100	Lying down	415	359	245	177	284	4	0.59	(0.55-0.63)
d4101	Squatting	114	207	253	282	622	6	0.55	(0.51-0.59)
d4102	Kneeling	113	213	243	283	619	13	0.59	(0.55-0.63)
d4103	Sitting	139	234	234	275	593	9	0.55	(0.51-0.59)
d4104	Standing	198	274	282	267	457	6	0.57	(0.53-0.61)
d4105	Bending	239	297	285	266	390	7	0.58	(0.54-0.62)
d4106	Shifting the body's centre of gravity	294	323	275	223	363	6	0.60	(0.56-0.64)
d4150	Maintaining a lying position	553	312	273	156	161	29	0.41	(0.37-0.45)
d4151	Maintaining a squatting position	64	175	210	308	716	11	0.56	(0.52-0.6)
d4152	Maintaining a kneeling position	106	187	219	291	659	22	0.57	(0.53-0.61)
d4153	Maintaining a sitting position	544	353	217	144	217	9	0.54	(0.5-0.58)
d4154	Maintaining a standing position	232	267	238	205	532	10	0.62	(0.58-0.66)
d4200	Transferring oneself while sitting	544	311	191	147	285	6	0.73	(0.69-0.77)
d4201	Transferring oneself while lying	438	282	229	197	319	19	0.66	(0.62-0.7)
d4500	Walking short distances	278	253	207	180	557	9	0.71	(0.67-0.75)
d4501	Walking long distances	38	106	189	239	878	34	0.60	(0.56-0.64)
d4502	Walking on different surfaces	33	121	207	259	837	27	0.61	(0.57-0.65)
d4503	Walking around obstacles	51	125	207	265	802	34	0.58	(0.54-0.62)
d4551	Climbing	117	183	203	267	684	30	0.59	(0.55-0.63)
d4600	Moving around within the home	414	262	201	157	429	21	0.69	(0.65-0.73)
d4601	Moving around within buildings other than home	286	269	193	191	513	32	0.65	(0.61-0.69)
d4602	Moving around outside the home and other buildings	103	156	209	259	715	42	0.65	(0.61-0.69)
d465	Moving around using equipment	76	107	110	140	273	778	0.60	(0.54-0.66)

ns/na; not specified and not applicable.

Figure 1 shows the threshold ordering of relevant ICF items selected for the analysis of mobility and transfer in the development samples, using Rasch measurement technique without consideration of the fit statistics. ‘Walking on different surface’ (d4502) was the most difficult item, and ‘Maintaining sitting position’ (d4153) was the easiest item among the ICF items used.

Some of these ICF items were further deleted until the χ square probability of item–trait interaction reaches the level of P>0.05. Table 1 shows the fit of the ICF mobility-related items after selection (item fit mean -0.24, SD1.50). In this model, the reliability index was 0.96. In item–trait interaction, total item χ square was 64.6 (degree of freedom 54, probability 0.15). However, two ICF items related to TAI, ‘Maintaining a sitting position’ (d4153) and ‘Moving around using equipment’ (d465), were also deleted because of poor item- fit statistics.

By using the five randomly selected subsamples with the size of 300, the fit statistics of the items showed improvement. For example, the total χ square probability of the item–trait interaction ranged between 0.39 and 0.80. Average item fit residuals were 0.89, -1.33, -0.34, -0.77, -1.00 and 0.74 for d4154, d4200, d4201, d4500, d4551 and d4606, respectively.

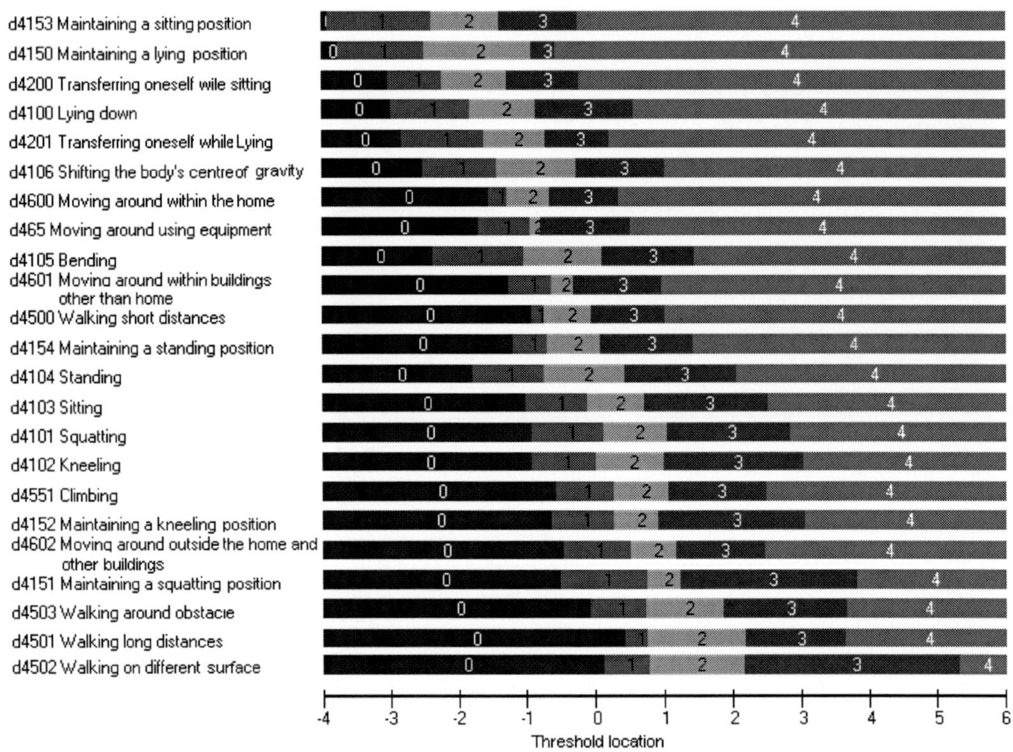

Figure 1. Threshold ordering of ICF item related to mobility and transfer on development samples(n=773) (Figure 1 legend: ICF performance qualifier scores are reversed to indicate the person with higher point has higher ability).

TAI scales use ‘Climb stairs’ (similar to the ICF item of d4551), ‘Walk alone on a flat floor’ (similar to d4500), ‘Moving around using equipment’ (similar to d465), ‘Transfer while sitting’ (similar to d4200), ‘Sit up and maintain seated position’ (similar to d4151) and ‘Rolling over on the bed’ (no closely related item among the ICF categories) to determine the levels of mobility and transfer performance in older adults (Appendix Figure 1). Because d465 and d4153 were deleted during the Rasch purification process, d4551, d4500 and d4200 were used to compare the score for each ICF item and the TAI mobility score by the equating method of the Rasch Model (Figure 2). Item–trait interaction fit statistics (total χ square probability) of the model composed of d4551, d 4500, d4200 and the TAI mobility scale were 0.19, 0.70, 0.72, 0.09 and 0.69 for five random subsamples (n=300), respectively. In these subsamples, all item–fit residual χ square probability was also at an acceptable level of P>0.05.

Table 2. Fit of ICF mobility item to Rasch Model

Code	Item name	Location	SE	Fit Residual	χ_2	Probability
d4154	Maintaining a standing position	0.24	0.056	1.09	9.2	0.42
d4200	Transferring oneself while sitting	-2.00	0.063	-2.48	13.4	0.14
d4201	Transferring oneself while lying	-1.30	0.060	0.49	10.1	0.35
d4500	Walking short distances	0.15	0.055	-1.33	11.4	0.25
d4551	Climbing	1.38	0.059	-0.58	12.7	0.18
d4602	Moving around outside the home	1.54	0.061	1.39	7.8	0.55

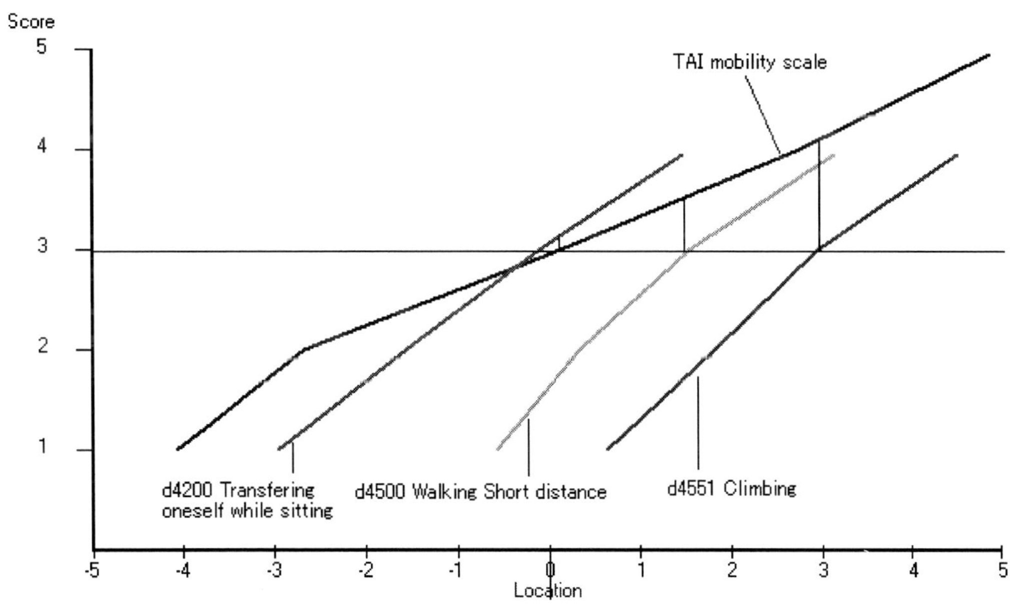

Figure 2. Equating test between three ICF items and TAI mobility scale on validating samples. (Legend for Figure 2: The horizontal line was drawn to show the score level 3 of ICF items (qualifier level 1)).

The participants with a score of 3 for the ICF item 'Climbing' (d4551) had mild restrictions when climbing stairs, and at the same person location, the estimated TAI score was 4.10. TAI level 4 indicates a person who has difficulty climbing stairs, but can walk on a flat floor. Therefore this result suggested that the TAI score of 4 was identical to the score 3 for ICF item d4551 (using performance qualifier, level 1). Similarly, with a score of 3 for the ICF item 'Walking a short distance' (d4500), the estimated TAI score was 3.54. This level indicates the older adult who cannot climb stairs but can walk on a flat floor. For the score of 3 on the ICF item of 'Transferring oneself while sitting' (d4200), the estimated TAI score was 2.92 (expected TAI mobility level 3).

These results suggest the constructive validity of the TAI mobility scale, and that the quantification of the mobility activity using ICF qualifiers produced similar results to the extant TAI ratings system.

Cognitive and Mental Function

The ICF items initially selected for the cognitive and mental functions are shown in Table 3 with the response frequency and test–retest reproducibility result. The average weighted kappa of these items was 0.60.

Table 3. Distribution of the raw score (reverse of the qualifier level) and weighted kappa (n=742)

code	Description	4	3	2	1	0	Ns/ na	Weighted kappa	95%C.I.
b114	Orientation functions	577	306	234	219	124	24	0.68	(0.62-0.74)
b117	Intellectual functions	456	284	247	258	207	32	0.67	(0.61-0.73)
b122	Global psychosocial functions	453	280	259	242	211	39	0.66	(0.60-0.72)
b126	Temperament and personality functions	499	287	280	236	140	42	0.61	(0.55-0.67)
b130	Energy and drive functions	681	312	248	147	64	32	0.51	(0.45-0.57)
b134	Sleep functions	694	410	229	103	36	12	0.42	(0.36-0.48)
b140	Attention functions	483	304	248	238	180	31	0.66	(0.60-0.72)
b144	Memory functions	379	288	309	298	179	31	0.64	(0.58-0.70)
b147	Psychomotor functions	410	350	304	243	129	48	0.54	(0.48-0.60)
b152	Emotional functions	545	320	332	202	61	24	0.53	(0.47-0.59)
b156	Perceptual functions	713	285	238	146	71	31	0.63	(0.57-0.69)
b160	Thought functions	541	240	250	249	156	48	0.63	(0.57-0.69)
b164	Higher-level cognitive functions	419	259	243	259	240	64	0.61	(0.55-0.67)
b167	Mental functions of language	636	297	273	170	87	21	0.63	(0.57-0.69)
b1670	Reception of language	442	308	269	257	182	26	0.62	(0.56-0.68)
b1671	Expression of language	418	264	286	248	242	26	0.56	(0.50-0.62)
b1672	Integrative language functions	379	259	286	265	267	28	0.59	(0.53-0.65)
b172	Calculation functions	332	280	239	271	331	31	0.62	(0.56-0.68)
b176	Mental function of sequencing complex movements	336	254	267	265	326	36	0.64	(0.58-0.70)
b180	Experience of self and time functions	583	267	192	211	192	39	0.57	(0.51-0.63)

ns/na; not specified and not applicable.

Figure 3 shows the threshold ordering of the items related to mental and cognitive functions. The 'Calculation' function (b172) was found to be most difficult, and the 'Consciousness' function (b110) the easiest. Of interest, the location order of the three-digit item of 'Mental functions of language' (b167) and its related four-digit items in the lower hierarchy, namely b1670, b1671 and b1672, were noticeably different.

Table 4 shows the item-fit statistics (item fit mean -0.993, SD 1.819) of the development model. Total χ square probability of item–trait interaction was 0.23 and separation index as reliability index was 0.96.

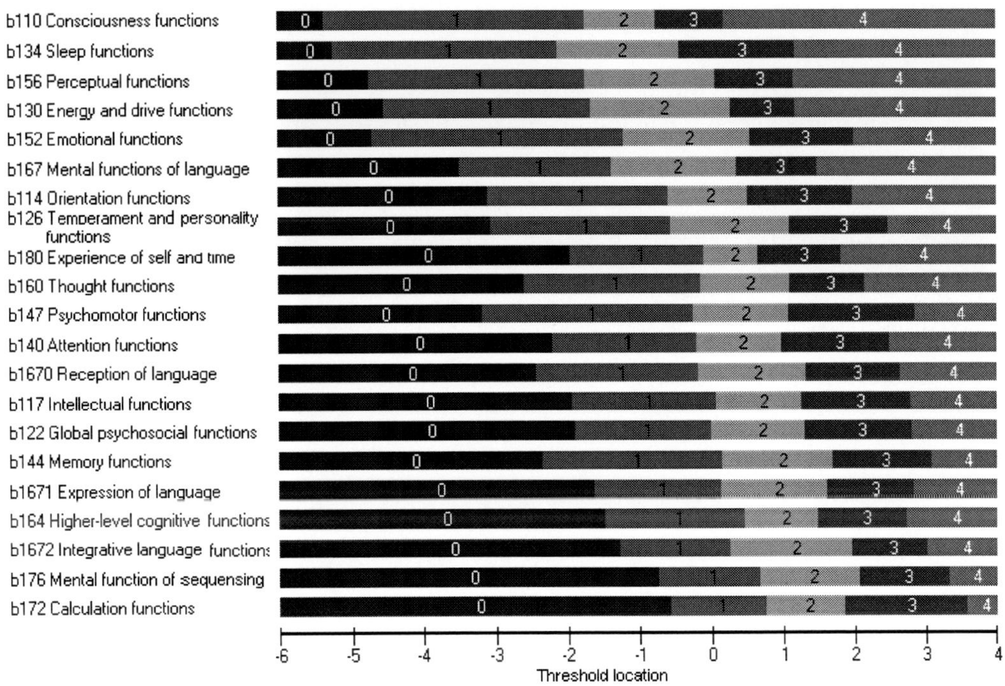

Figure 3. Threshold ordering of ICF item related to mental function on development samples(n=773) (Legend for figure 3: ICF function qualifier scores are reversed to indicate the person with higher point has higher ability).

Table 4. Fit of ICF mental function item to Rasch Model

Code	Item name	Location	SE	Residual	χ_2	Probability
b114	Orientation functions	-0.24	0.069	-1.30	9.4	0.31
b126	Temperament and personality functions	0.22	0.069	1.70	4.8	0.78
b140	Attention functions	0.52	0.067	-0.99	6.2	0.63
b144	Memory functions	1.08	0.069	-1.90	10.5	0.23
b156	Perceptual functions	-1.57	0.074	2.03	15.5	0.05

Total χ square probabilities of item–person interaction of the five subsamples were 0.49, 0.60, 0.21, 0.78 and 0.13. Use of five smaller subsamples (n=300) also showed improved individual item-fit to the model. Average individual item-fit statistics of the five random subsamples for b114, b126, b140, b144 and b156 were -0.91, 1.02, -0.43, -1.16 and 1.40.

The relationship between the four relevant ICF items similar to TAI mental status scale threshold (b144, b114, b126 and b156) and TAI mental status scale were compared by using the equating test of the Rasch Model (Figure 4). Although the 'Consciousness' functions (b110) might be similar to the 0-1 threshold of the TAI mental status scale, the item-fit statistics were poor. Therefore, 'Perceptual function' (b156) was used as an alternative. The ICF item 'Temperament and personality function' (b126) might not be similar to the 'Problem behavior' parameter used in TAI mental status scale. However, there is no ICF item which corresponds to the presence of problem behavior, since ICF is a classification of health condition, not type of disability. The equation between the ICF items and TAI mental status scales is shown in Figure 4. Item–trait interaction fit statistics (total χ square probability) of the model composed of b114, b126, b144, b156 and TAI mental status scale were 0.25, 0.55, 0.16, 0.14 and 0.18 for five random subsamples (n=300), respectively. In these subsamples, the individual item-fit residual χ square probability was also at an acceptable level of $P>0.05$ in all the ICF items used. In three random samples, however, the item-fit statistics of the TAI mental scale were poor ($P<0.05$).

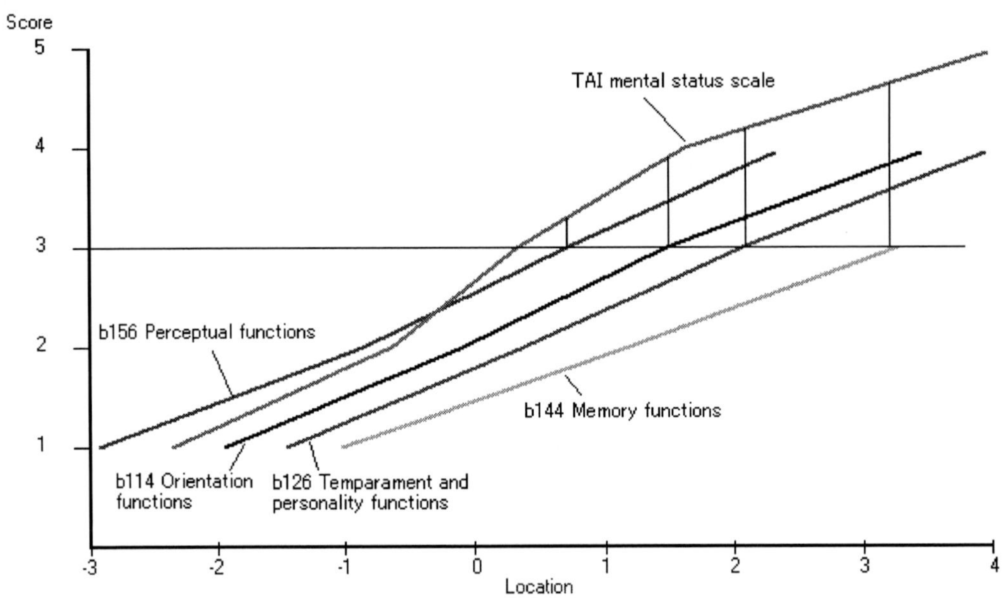

Figure 4. Equating test between three ICF items and TAI mental status scale on validating samples (Legend for Figure 4: The horizontal line was drawn to show the score level 3 of ICF items (qualifier level 1)).

At score 3 for the ICF item of 'Memory function' (b144), the older adult was expected to have mild memory function problems, and at the same person location, the estimated mental status scale score of the TAI was 4.70. TAI mental status level 5 indicates a person who does not have problems in terms of either memory or orientation. The estimate of the ICF

'Memory function' (b144) (using performance qualifier, level 1) was higher than expected from the TAI mental status scale (at TAI level 4). At score 3 for 'Temperament and personality functions' (b126), the expected TAI score was 4.19. At the score of 3 for the ICF item of 'Orientation function' (b114), the estimated TAI score was 3.89. Similarly, at the level of 'Perceptual function' (b156), the expected TAI mental status scale level was 3.30. Therefore, in all equating tests, ICF items showed higher scores compared to the TAI mental status scores. The discrepancy between the ICF score and the estimated TAI score tended to be greater at the lower levels of the TAI mental status scale. However, the order of these three ICF items was identical to the threshold used in the TAI mental status scale.

DISCUSSION

In this study, the authors measured the disability and function of older adults who were covered through LTCI insurance services in Japan, by adopting ICF qualifiers to quantify activity and functional status. To date, little is known on how ICF qualifiers can be applied to the measurement of functional and activity status. Our study, we believe, will contribute information on how ICF codes and qualifiers can be meaningfully used in this field of study.

The ICF is an exhaustive classification and very complex for daily use [21]. To facilitate its use, WHO developed the ICF checklist [22]. However, the generic character of the ICF checklist may be a drawback in specific care settings, such as in geriatric care [21]. The applicability of the ICF checklist for the geriatric care setting is discussed elsewhere [16].

Development of the ICF core sets [23] for use in 12 chronic health conditions is another possibility, especially because these were developed by consensus by international scientific committees. The development of an ICF core set specific to long-term care geriatric care may facilitate the use of ICF codes in this field.

In this study, the authors took a different approach, by first measuring as many ICF items as possible, then evaluating these ICF codes using Rasch measurement techniques to establish a quantitative link between the ICF and the TAI. By applying Rasch measurement techniques, a pure set of items that measure a single latent trait was constructed to compare the results between scales.

The authors found relatively low kappa scores, which indicated low test–retest reproducibility, both in the item related to mobility (AP domain) and mental functions (BF domain). The ICF theoretically can be applied across cultures and age groups because it is based on a universal model. However, in reality, each ICF codes might have different implication for different care settings [16,24], and thus the evaluation using the ICF qualifier could have caused the errors or biases. It is not likely that the low reliability of the ICF items is attributable to investigator bias (i.e. in the sense of limited experience of evaluators in assessing functional status in older adults), since the test-retest reproducibility of the concurrently measured TAI scales was high: "Mobility"0.80 (95% C.I. 0.75-0.84); "Mental"0.75 (0.70-0.80); "Toileting" 0.76 (0.71-0.82); "Eating" 0.78 (0.73-0.83) [16]. On the other hand.no additional training was offered to the data collectors, which may have contributed to the low reproducibility. However, in practice, reliable scales should not require special training. Moreover, a comprehensive training would be costly and may not be fully available to all health workers.

Using Rasch measurement techniques, the authors showed the relative order of item difficulty in the ICF codes (Figure 1 and 3). Although these orders were not fitted to the Rasch model, these might be useful for setting goal for rehabilitation and care-management. For example, for an older person who can relatively easy manage the transfer between chairs from a sitting position, the next rehabilitation goal would be involve a more difficult item, such as transferring from a lying position. The relative order of the difficulty might also differ across cultural and care settings, and also with the presence of different comorbid conditions [25].

It is also worth noticing that the three digit items and their lower hierarchy fourth digits item response pattern were considerably different, for example, when the location between the Mental functions of language (b167) and, its related four digit items in lower hierarchy namely b1670, b1671 and b1672 were compared. Therefore, the upper hierarchy (third digit) ICF items were not the thumbnail sketch of the more detailed lower hierarchy (fourth digit) item quantitatively. The different response characteristics between third and fourth digits items in detail remained to be studied.

On constructing Rasch models, the authors deleted many items in the process with intention to compare the location of each item with that on the TAI scales. A different configuration of item groups may have produced different results. The large sample size, also affected to the poor fit statistics in the Rasch model [15,26]. When we limited the sample size to 300, the item fit statistics improved. Consequently, the use of an adequate sample size might help construct different item sets that better fit the Rasch model.This would require that items at the lower end of the TAI scales could be tested using a different ICF item set.

By equating the TAI scale and the ICF item in the validating sample, the estimated score produced from the location statistics were as expected for mobility related items, but different for mental function related items, i.e. the score of the TAI mental status scale was higher than expected from the ICF items score. This could be attributed to the poor fit of the TAI mental status scales to the Rasch model, and the difficulty in evaluating cognitive function compared to mobility.

The discrepancy between the score of TAI scales and the score of the ICF items was larger at the lower end of TAI mental status scales. This might be explained by the absence of the ICF items closely related in the lower end of TAI in the Rasch model constructed in this study. The conceptualisation of the ICF as a taxonomy of 'normal' functioning made it difficult to meaningfully assess older people with severe functional impairment. In addition, evaluating mental function in terms of assigning a percentage to the problem as defined by the ICF qualifier, may have been problematic [22].

There are a few study limitations to discuss. First, the sample was recruited from the Japanese LTCI settings, and therefore, findings may not be generalizable to populations in different care settings. However, in the absence of the knowledge how to apply the ICF qualifiers, these results illuminate some problem on their use. It is also of important to note that the ICF items may have different properties in other care-settings, and among different cultural and ethnic groups [10,27,28].

It may be possible to improve the test-retest reproducibility by constructing more specific qualifiers, for each ICF codes and for each care setting. However, by applying specific qualifiers for each ICF codes, the advantage of the ICF as a universal tool may be lost. In addition, it would likely be a costly and difficult approach.

The other possible approach is to embed the ICF items within scales such as the TAI scales. TAI scales have a Guttman scale [29] structure. For example, the thresholds used in TAI mobility scale are, 1 for "climbing stairs", 2 for "walking alone on a flat floor", 3 for "moving around using the equipment and transfer while sitting", 4 for "sitting up and maintaining a seated position", and 5 for "rolling over on the bed". These thresholds are arranged in a vertical manner as shown in Appendix Figure 1. And the success or failure to overcome each of these threshold can be coded with 0 (not passed) or 1 (passed). For example, a TAI level that equals '5' is 1, 1, 1, 1, 1 for passing all five items selected , and level 4 is 0, 1, 1, 1, 1: level 3 was 0, 0, 1, 1, 1: level 2; 0,0,0,1,1, level 1;0,0,0,0,1: level 0; 0,0,0,0,0 respectively.

This indicates the possibility that a single TAI like scale can provide a measure across several functions or activities as shown in figures 2 and 4. In addition, the users have knowledge of the ceiling or floor of each item, by using thresholds and illustrations attached to the text. These properties of the TAI scales may be make it possible to embed several ICF codes in a simple scale. The hierarchical structure or scale items can cause some problems. For example, some of the participants can not roll over on the bed, but they are able to walk (e.g., an individual with severe kypho-scoliosis). Incorrect classification on the scale can be prevented by assessing participants using the highest achievable performance or function.

Our next step is to construct TAI-like scales embedding the ICF codes, in order to easily classify and document the health status of a person.

Conclusion

This study examined quantitative links between the ICF items and extant scales of the TAI. Quantification of health status using ICF qualifiers was successful in mobility-related ICF items in the AP domain. However, in mental status–related items, the ICF score showed deviations from the extant scale scores. Therefore, establishing quantitative linkages between extant measures and the ICF codes require a careful examination of the item response patterns for ICF items and extant scales.

Acknowledgement

We would like to appreciate the support of Professor Takashi Hashimoto, Kyushu Rehabilitation College, Dr. Yasuko Arase, Fukuoka City Government, and all of the healthcare professionals who cooperated with this study. The authors also thank Professor Alan Tennant, of the Psychometric Laboratory for Health Sciences at the University of Leeds, UK, for his comments on an earlier version of this paper. This research is funded by Health Labor Science Research Grant;1-15-Seisaku-018.

REFERENCES

[1] World Health Organization. International classification of functioning, disability and health: ICF. Geneva: World Health Organization, 2001.

[2] Stucki G. Applying the ICF in medicine. *J Rehabil Med* 2004(44 Suppl): 5-6.

[3] Cieza A, Brockow T, Ewert T, et al. Linking health-status measurements to the international classification of functioning, disability and health. *J Rehabil Med* 2002; 34(5): 205-10.

[4] Granlund M, Eriksson L, Ylven R. Utility of International Classification of Functioning, Disability and Health's participation dimension in assigning ICF codes to items from extant rating instruments. *J Rehabil Med* 2004; 36(3): 130-7.

[5] Rasch G. *Probablistic Models for some Intelligence and Attainment Tests (expanded edition)*. Chicago: The University of Chicago Press (original work published in 1960), 1980.

[6] Okochi J, Takahashi T, Takamuku K, Matsuda S, Takagi Y. Reliability of a geriatric assessment instrument with illustrations. *Geriatrics and Gerontology International* 2005; (in press).

[7] Matsuda S. The health and social system for the aged in Japan. *Aging Clin Exp Res* 2002; 14(4): 265-70.

[8] Takahashi T, Okochi J, Takamuku K, Matsuda S. The introduction of typology of the aged with illustrations. *Casemix Quarterly* 2001; 3(1): 3-14.

[9] Granger CV, Hamilton BB, Linacre JM, Heinemann AW, Wright BD. Performance profiles of the functional independence measure. *Am J Phys Med Rehabil* 1993; 72(2): 84-9.

[10] Kucukdeveci AA, Sahin H, Ataman S, Griffiths B, Tennant A. Issues in cross-cultural validity: example from the adaptation, reliability, and validity testing of a Turkish version of the Stanford Health Assessment Questionnaire. *Arthritis Rheum* 2004; 51(1): 14-9.

[11] Andrich D. *Rasch models for measurement*. Newberry Park: Sage Publications, 1988. (Lewis-Beck M, ed. Sage University paper series on qualitative measurement in the social science).

[12] Waugh RF. Creating a scale to measure motivation to achieve academically: linking attitudes and behaviours using Rasch measurement. *Br J Educ Psychol* 2002; 72(Pt 1): 65-86.

[13] Conrad KJ, Wright BD, McKnight P, McFall M, Fontana A, Rosenheck R. Comparing traditional and Rasch analyses of the Mississippi PTSD Scale: revealing limitations of reverse-scored items. *J Appl Meas* 2004; 5(1): 15-30.

[14] Andrich D, Lyne A, Sheridan B, Luo G: Rumm. *A Windows-based item analysis program employing Rasch unidimensional measurement models*. Perth: Murdoch University, 1998.

[15] Smith RM, Schumacker RE, Bush MJ. Using item mean squares to evaluate fit to the Rasch model. *J Outcome Meas* 1998; 2(1): 66-78.

[16] Takahashi T, Okochi J. *Reliability and validity of the ICF and ICF Checklist*; (under submission).

[17] Nelson EC, Landgraf JM, Hays RD, Wasson JH, Kirk JW. The functional status of patients. How can it be measured in physicians' offices? *Med Care* 1990; 28(12): 1111-26.

[18] Warren SL, Dadson N. Assessment of anxiety in young children. *Curr Opin Pediatr* 2001; 13(6): 580-5.

[19] Takahashi T. ICF illustration library. 2003 in; http://www.tokyo.image-lab.or.jp/icf/ill/english/.

[20] Sutch S. ICF illustration library. *Bulletin of the World Health Organization* 2004; 82(7): 550-551.

[21] Ustun B, Chatterji S, Kostanjsek N. Comments from who for the journal of rehabilitation medicine special supplement on ICF core sets. *J Rehabil Med* 2004(44 Suppl): 7-8.

[22] World Health Organization. The ICF checklist: Development and Application. In: *Organization*. WH, ed. Geneva: World Health Organization, 2002.

[23] Cieza A, Ewert T, Ustun TB, Chatterji S, Kostanjsek N, Stucki G. Development of ICF Core Sets for patients with chronic conditions. *J Rehabil Med* 2004(44 Suppl): 9-11.

[24] Simeonsson RJ, Leonardi M, Lollar D, Bjorck-Akesson E, Hollenweger J, Martinuzzi A. Applying the International Classification of Functioning, Disability and Health (ICF) to measure childhood disability. *Disabil Rehabil* 2003; 25(11-12): 602-10.

[25] Coster WJ, Haley SM, Andres PL, Ludlow LH, Bond TL, Ni PS. Refining the conceptual basis for rehabilitation outcome measurement: personal care and instrumental activities domain. *Med Care* 2004; 42(1 Suppl): I62-72.

[26] Stone M, Yumoto F. The effect of sample size for estimating Rasch/IRT parameters with dichotomous items. *J Appl Meas* 2004; 5(1): 48-61.

[27] Tennant A, Penta M, Tesio L, et al. Assessing and adjusting for cross-cultural validity of impairment and activity limitation scales through differential item functioning within the framework of the Rasch model: the PRO-ESOR project. *Med Care* 2004; 42(1 Suppl): I37-48.

[28] Tsuji T, Sonoda S, Domen K, Saitoh E, Liu M, Chino N. ADL structure for stroke patients in Japan based on the functional independence measure. *Am J Phys Med Rehabil* 1995; 74(6): 432-8.

[29] Guttman LL. The basis for scalogram analysis. In: Stouffer SA, Guttman LL, Suchman EA, et al., eds. *Measurement and Prediction*. Princeton, New Jersey: Princeton University Press, 1950.

APPENDIX

Appendix Figure 1 Mobility

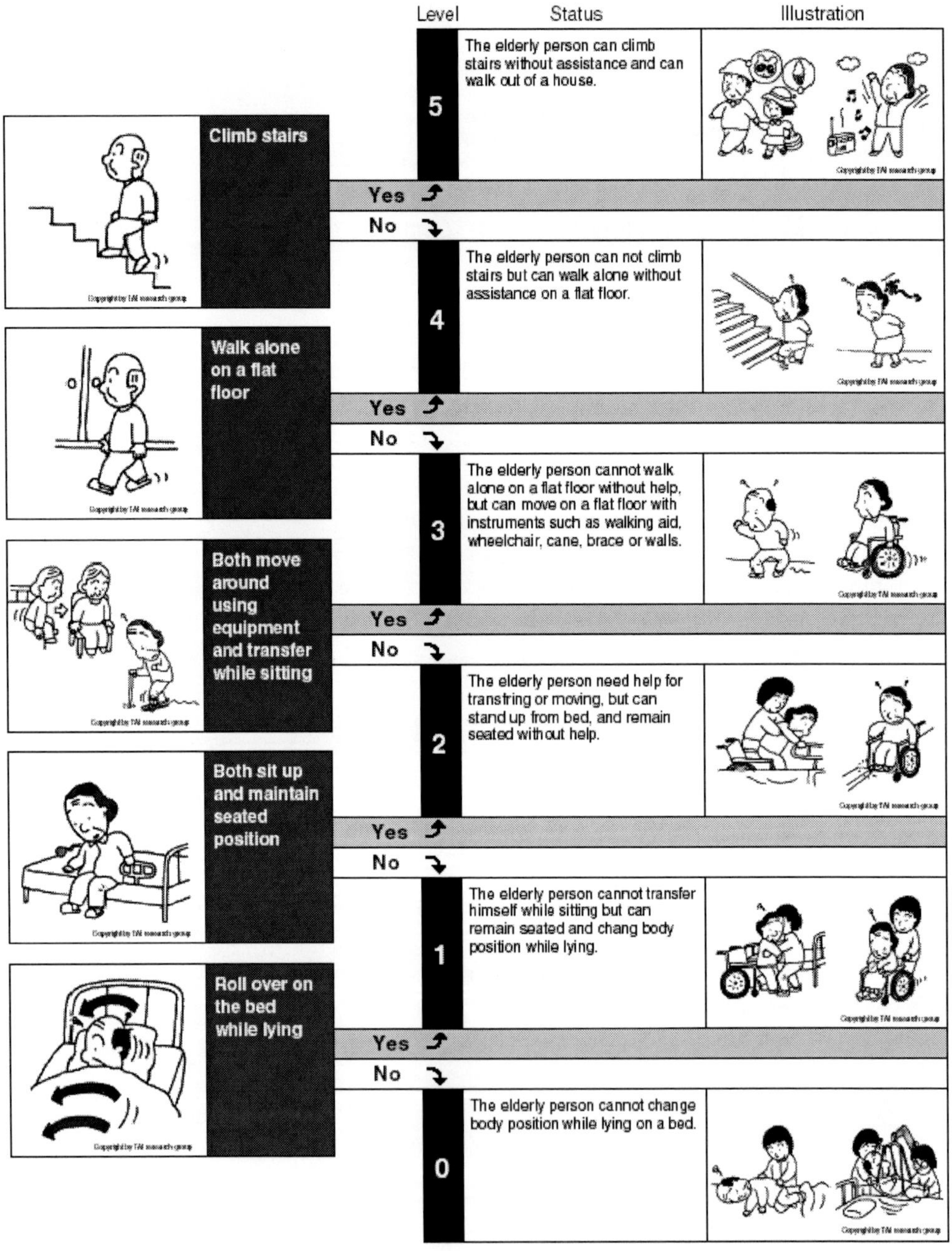

Figure 1.

Health Care Service Delivery

In: Focus on Disability: Trends in Research and Application ISBN: 978-1-60021-792-0
Editor: Thilo Kroll, pp. 59-87 © 2008 Nova Science Publishers, Inc.

Chapter V

Community-Based Participatory Research: Applications for Research in Health and Disability

Kenneth C. Hergenrather[1] and Scott D. Rhodes[2]
[1]Center for Rehabilitation Counseling Research and Education, Department of Counseling, Human and Organizational Studies, The George Washington University, Washington, DC, USA;
[2]Section on Social Sciences and Health Policy, Department of Public Health Sciences, Wake, Forest University School of Medicine, Winston-Salem, NC, USA.

Introduction to Community-Based Participatory Research

Many of the complex health and disability issues that persist into the 21st century, including HIV/AIDS, have proven to be ill-suited for traditional "outside expert" approaches to research and the often disappointing community interventions they have yielded (CDC, 1997; Green 2001; Israel, Schultz, Parker, & Becker, 1998). Instead, research aimed at understanding and eliminating health and disability disparities and promoting community and broader social change has begun to focus attention on alternative orientations to inquiry that emphasize community partnership as integral parts of the research enterprise (Arnstein, 1969; Metzler et al., 2003).

A community-based participatory research (CBPR) approach recognizes that an outsider can work best in partnership, with lay community members and community representatives who are experts on their community environment. CBPR involves a partnership in which all parties (e.g., lay community members, community-based organization members, health department representatives, rehabilitation service providers, and researchers) participate and share control over all phases of the research process to address community concerns. Through partnership, community needs can be addressed, reducing health and disability disparities (Agency for Healthcare Research and Quality, 2002; Rhodes & Benfield, 2005).

CBPR ensures that data are authentic to community experience; creates bridges between communities and researchers; incorporates knowledge and action based upon the lived experiences of community members; and ensures the collaborative development of culturally-appropriate research. Collaborative partnerships enhance the quality, validity, and interpretation of the collected data, and ensure appropriate dissemination of study findings (Institute of Medicine, 2003; Minkler & Wallerstein, 2003). In this chapter we describe the foundations of CBPR and its application in the research process. We then introduce three research methods utilized in a CBPR approach. Finally, we offer two case examples of the application of CBPR through focus group and photovoice methodologies.

Community-Based Participatory Research History and Rationale

In the 1940s and 1950s, social psychologist Kurt Lewin challenged traditional social science research methods. He rejected the positivist belief that the objective world studied by researchers was separate from an inter-subjective world understood by participants living in that world. The positivist paradigm, he contended, was insufficient to understand and address complex human problems. Lewin developed a model of "action research" that promoted the involvement of those affected by the problem in the research process by supporting their participation in the selection of the research methodologies, fact finding and data collection, action or intervention planning, and reflection upon action (Lewin 1946, 1947, 1951; Peters & Robinson, 1984). Action research developed as a means of social change, in which the experimental approaches used by social scientists merged with community-level social action to address identified problems by bringing together various community resources and stakeholders. Action research methodologies have been applied in social, work, and academic settings to solve problems at the group and system levels (Chisholm & Elden, 1993).

Throughout the 1960s, communities worldwide expressed active resistance to societal marginalization based upon such factors as economic status, culture, gender, disability, and stigma. Communities who were traditionally sought for scientific research began demanding changes in their research relationships by restricting entry, calling for partnerships in research design, and requesting reciprocity for resources. Concurrently, Brazilian educator Paulo Friere utilized liberationist ideology for the empowerment of disadvantaged populations to participate in society and promote social change. Freire developed action-based research methodologies, grounded in critical education theory, which emphasized co-learning and critical reflection. He described the development of awareness that occurs when people engage in self-inquiry as "conscientization," an implicit empowering process through which participants, as a group, recognize societal inequity and the mechanisms through which the inequities are perpetuated and explore opportunities to change the inequities (Freire, 1982, 1987; Fals-Borda, 1991). In Latin America, Fals-Borda applied and refined "participatory action research" methods to make critical contributions to mutual inquiry for social change. From the developing world, the recognition of inequitable relationships between researchers and participants emerged. The principles of mutual inquiry for social change were developed through the action research process in Africa, Asia, and Latin America, collectively known as the Southern Tradition. The Southern Tradition was based upon structural crises of societal underdevelopment, critiques of existing theory by social scientists, and the development of new research practice for the purpose of working with communities marginalized by dominant societal globalization (Brown & Tandon, 1983).

By the early 1970s, with the further development of public health services and the field of psychiatry, community representation in research became more widely acknowledged as a means to address social issues. Research professionals initiated participation from both community organizations serving under-represented populations and disadvantaged members of society. Through identifying the causes and solutions to social problems, communities began to develop action plans, becoming empowered for community change. Participant knowledge and personal experience continued to be recognized as a resource to address social issues (Rappaport, 1977, 1990; Schensul & Schensul, 1978; Schensul, Weeks, & Singer, 1999; Zax & Specter, 1974).

In the 1980s, research methodologies promoting university-community partnership emerged and addressed the impact of such social issues as HIV prevention, teen pregnancy, substance abuse, and disability. Fals-Borda applied the phrase "participatory action research" (PAR) to identify the importance of community members being proactive in the research process through collaboration. PAR became a participatory and cooperative research process, engaging community members and researchers in a joint process in which contributions are equitable. For researchers and community members, PAR provided a co-learning process, a method for systems development and capacity building, and empowered community members to enhance community strengths and increase their problem solving abilities. PAR places the emphasis upon the strength of the community members, whose lives are impacted by the issue(s) addressed, and their capacity for problem-solving (Fals-Borda, 1997; George, Green, & Daniel, 1996; Israel, Shurman, & Hugentobler, 1992; Wallerstein, 1999).

In the 1990s, there was an increased commitment from government, health researchers, social science researchers, and professional organizations to develop research collaborations with communities. Empirical evidence supported the significance of a complex set of factors impacting individual health status, extending the factors addressed in the 1960s, which included the physical environmental, poverty, air pollution, racism, and inadequate housing. The research interventions to address the factors associated with health now required a more comprehensive participatory approach (Israel et al., 1998). Community-based participatory research emerged as an approach utilizing a research partnership and equitably involving community members, organizational representatives, academic researchers, and non-academic researchers to share responsibility and ownership of the research for the purpose of enhancing the health and well-being of the community (Israel, Schulz, Parker, & Becker, 2001).

Community-Based Participatory Research Defined

Community-based participatory research (CBPR) is intended to increase the value of the research and knowledge for community members and researchers. A community is characterized by a sense of identification and emotional connection to others, shared norms and values, common interests, and a commitment to meeting needs, which may or may not include geographic location (Israel, Checkoway, Schulz, & Zimmerman, 1994; Steuart, 1993). To truly understand community health and disability issues, community members participate in the research process to validate, guide, and study the intervention design; ensure the appropriateness of measures; and support the interpretation and dissemination of study findings. Community members contribute their expertise and time to gain knowledge of the research issue(s), address impact upon the social and cultural aspects of the community, and integrate newly achieved knowledge into an action plan to improve the health and well-being of the general community and individual members (Green et al., 1995; Hatch, Moss, Saran, Presley-Cantrell, & Mallory, 1993). CBPR relies on community participation to ensure that the developed research question(s) empower the researcher and community members to accumulate knowledge with which to create action plans. It aligns with the critical theory and constructivist theory paradigm, empowering researchers and community member interests to develop the study. The CBPR process is based upon the integration of nine principles, representing ideal goals (Cornwall & Jewkes, 1995; Cornwall, 1996; Green et al., 2003):

1. CBPR recognizes the community as a unity of identity
2. CBPR builds upon the strengths and resources within a community
3. CBPR facilitates collaborative and equitable partnerships throughout the research process
4. CBPR promotes co-learning and capacity building among all partners
5. CBPR integrates and achieves a balance between research and action for the mutual benefit of all partners
6. CBPR emphasizes local relevance of public health problems and ecological perspectives that recognize and attend to the multiple determinants of health and disease
7. CBPR involves systems development through cyclical and iterative process
8. CBPR disseminates findings and knowledge gained to all partners and involves all partners in the dissemination process
9. CBPR involves a long-term process and commitment

CBPR Application to the Research Process

CBPR is a process to increase the value of research and knowledge for the researcher and community members, which ultimately improves community well-being. The research process typically includes: (1) identification of the research question, (2) assessment of community strengths, assets, and challenges, (3) definition of priorities, (4) development of research and data collection methodologies, (5) data collection and analysis, (6) interpretation of study findings, (7) dissemination of study findings, (8) and application of study findings to develop action plans to enhance individual and community well-being (Rhodes & Benfield, 2005).

Identification of the Research Question

CBPR commences with the identification of an issue, by the researcher and community, perceived to assist disenfranchised persons, which is often predicated upon the health disparities associated with socioeconomic status and maginalization (Cooper, Kennelly, Durazo-Arvizu, Oh, Kaplan, & Lynch, 2001; US Department of Health and Human Services, 2001). The issues may be identified through the perceived need of the researcher, reviews of literature, outcomes of researcher meetings with communities facing dilemmas, or expressed community need. Once the researcher initiates in CBPR, a high level of commitment to the community issue is required. However, gaining entry into communities may present challenges. Due to the history of social distance and distrust between the research organizations and the community organizations, researchers should plan to have numerous meetings with various community members to establish and maintain trust, a building block of successful collaboration. The researcher must perceive the CBPR process as a co-learning, in which the contributions of researcher and community are equitable, community member knowledge is legitimate, and both parties are catalysts for community change. Although the researcher can initiate the research process, the community must contribute to defining the research question; enabling the researcher's role to be a process-facilitating role to strengthen community members' awareness of the issue and identify their expertise, skills, and resources to address it (Fals-Borda, 1991; Kidd & Krall, 2005; Rahman, 1991; Reason, 1994; Stoecker & Strubner, 1999).

Assessment of Community Strengths, Assets, and Challenges

Upon entree into the community, the researcher must understand the community and build rapport to become an accepted partner. It is important that the researcher share relevant experience, both personal and professional, with the community to initiate the ongoing process of trust development. This helps align the researcher as a community ally and not an outsider. A history of researcher success is important when collaborating; the community may rely on the reputation of the researcher and affiliated organization in the decision to commit to developing the partnership. If the reputation of the affiliated organization is negative the researcher will have more to overcome.

Community organizations have the capacity to engage "hidden" and "difficult-to-reach" populations who have been unavailable to researchers. Through community partnership, the researcher will be able to engage with populations usually not accessible in traditional research environments. Many community organizations, having a history as research sites, require the identification of the research benefits to both the study population and the community organization. If research study outcomes do not provide immediate benefit, representatives from the organization may view the study as lacking utility and choose to disengage from participation in the partnership. When a study is perceived as beneficial by community approval, community members participate in the research process to guide the study design, ensure the appropriateness of measures, and support the interpretation and dissemination of study findings.

The research collaboration should facilitate a community assessment, which requires significant levels of community support to assess the support of the research question, facilitation and implementation of the research study, and recruitment and retention of study participants. Crucial to the community assessment is the ability of the researcher to "meet the community where it is." An effective strategy meeting the community is to become a part of it through *walking tours* and *windshield tours*. The collaboration partners gain much awareness of community through simple observation and taking notes while walking, biking, or driving slowly through it during different times of the day and days of the week. Community members may serve as informal guides and provide important perspectives on community life. Identifying local community events, reviewing flyer postings, and going to local meeting places (e.g., places of worship, restaurants, convenience stores, bars) may provide insight into the current issues faced by the community. Other assessment methods include interviews with community leaders and community members; Delphi technique; mapping community resources; and mapping community risks (McKnight & Kretmann, 1992; Sim & Wright, 2000; Wekerle & Whitzman, 1995). From such notes and observations, the collaboration partners will identify community themes. The process creates a shared commitment by the researcher and community members to CBPR, acknowledging the wealth of assets community members bring to the process to create knowledge to develop action plans for change (Schensul, Weeks, & Singer, 1999; Sharpe, Greany, Lee, & Royce, 2000).

Definition of Priorities

Through the community assessment, many issues may emerge. The key is to facilitate a discussion in which emerging issues are identified and evaluated as concerns the community members feel deeply enough to pursue. This presents openness to learning, equity in sharing ideas, and a respect for community member knowledge. The roles and responsibilities of community members must be clearly defined and continuously negotiated. When community members are culturally different (e.g., ethnicity, sexual orientation, disability), there may be disagreement with one another. It is important to skillfully facilitate conflict resolution techniques and active discussions when disagreement occurs. The neglect of inter-group conflict may lead to a loss of commitment and resignation of group members. To facilitate the dialogue defining priorities, the researcher engages member discussion to identify specific issues to become the basis for the study and an action plan for social change. Staples (1997) suggests the facilitation of the pros and cons of an issue address the following:

1. Is the community issue consistent with the community agenda?
2. Does the issue unite or divide the community?
3. Will the issue enhance the capacity of the community?
4. In addressing the issue, will leaders and community members further develop consciousness, independence, and skills?
5. Will the community be recognized for success in addressing the issue?
6. Will new partnerships or alliances develop from addressing the issue?
7. Will a concrete action plan be developed and subsequent CBPR studies emerge?

8. Will the issues lead to change for the good of the community?
9. Are enough members vested in the issue to commit to working on it?

Development of Research and Data Collection Methodologies

CBPR methodology is built around the research issue accepted by community members, through which the researcher and community members develop research goals, appropriate methodology, data collection techniques, data analysis, and develop strategies to increase social consciousness and empower change in the lives of study participants and community. Klein, Williams, and Witbrodt (1999) recommend the conceptualization of the research involve both parties and include (1) a mutual understanding of the study, including theoretical foundations and applications of data; (2) study integrity; and (3) investment in, and use of, results. The research process must be amenable to balance of power between the researcher and community members. The sharing of ideas evolves into mutual respect for the legitimacy of member knowledge.

CBPR is aligned with a constructivist research paradigm, supporting the concept that multiple realities exist to be studied and understood (Lincoln, & Guba, 2000). The methods of constructivist research require researchers and community members to be interactively linked, so that the consensus construction of reality is literally created as the study proceeds. Each reality is an intangible construction; rooted in one's personal experiences, based upon how they remember and make sense of the experiences. Because individual constructions of reality are always alterable, the reality is assumed to be more or less "informed," rather than more or less "true." Through CBPR, researchers and community members encounter and consider different perspectives, which may cause them to alter their views. Lincoln and Guba (2000) identify this as *consensus construction of reality*, mutually informed by variations in preceding constructions (including those of the researchers). Such reality can move both community members and researchers toward communicating about action, intervention, and change (Habermas, 1984).

Data Collection and Analysis

After the research methodology is agreed upon, the researcher solicits the support and commitment of community members, including those instrumental to the success of the project. Community members highly supportive of the issue are more likely to be interested in gathering data to address it. Through data collection, researchers learn about the lived experiences of members, their perceived problems and strengths, ways they understand their community, how they receive change, and how change impacts their lives. It is their expertise of their world that drives the CBPR process (Green et al., 1995).

Data collection may follow a qualitative or quantitative approach, by which theory is generated and/or affirmed through gathering data. Analysis and interpretation of any dataset, qualitative or quantitative, using a CBPR approach can be challenging. It is important for the researcher to provide community members the opportunity to participate in the data analysis and not assume members do not want to be involved. Although some community members may lack the time or resources necessary, many community members may choose to participate in the data analysis process. Getting a commitment from one, two, or three community members may be the key to the data analysis. As co-learners, the researchers and community members learn from each other. In developing the research methodology, the group may consider developing a research guide to introduce methodology, outline group processes, discussion protocol, and provide guidelines to elicit participant-identified groups for which to present study findings (Streng, Rhodes, Ayala, Eng, Arceo, & Phipps, 2004).

During quantitative data analysis, researchers should communicate and solicit feedback with community members to keep them current on the statistical approaches, decisions, and rationales. During qualitative analyses, community members review and provide perceptions on possible themes through independent detailed reading and rereading of transcripts. Qualitative data may also be analyzed through program software (e.g., Nvivo, ATLAS.ti, Ethnograph, NUD*IST). The researcher and partners will come together to resolve data discrepancies, and interpret data to identify themes. Themes based in qualitative data are often directional and testable in subsequent research. Examples of themes from qualitative analysis include: (1) *Employment assimilates PLWHA into work environments that are not HIV/AIDS sensitive;* and (2) *Employment increases one's social skills.* Quotations are usually extracted from the transcripts to illustrate themes. Upon completion of the data analysis process, it should be reviewed to ensure it adhered to the CBPR process and generated knowledge meaningful for partners.

Interpretation of Study Findings

The presentation of preliminary study findings to community members further enhances collaboration. This can be conducted through scheduling community meetings in the study timeline, during which findings may be presented in a format (e.g., handouts, booklets, powerpoint). The study findings should be co-presented by the researcher and community members. It is important that the information is presented in a format to meet the needs of community members with disabilities (e.g., visually impaired, hearing impaired, learning disability). Regardless of ability to attend community meetings, all members must be provided the opportunity to comment on the study findings. This can be facilitated through telephone or e-mail. Following a presentation of study findings, the presenters should engage community members in active dialogue to discuss the process, discuss reactions to the findings, suggest alternate interpretations, determine utilization of study findings to further address community needs, and create plans of action. It is important to acknowledge community members' reactions to the study findings and opinions regarding the use of findings. Community meetings are an important part of the collaborative process, serving to enhance relationships and explore applications of data to enhance community well-being (Reason, 1994).

Dissemination of Study Findings

The CBPR process engages community members to create a format (e.g., data sheets, booklets) in which to present study findings and identify "influential advocates" (e.g., policy makers, community leaders, organizations) perceived as having power to impact the issue addressed. It is also important to obtain group consensus on the identification of the person(s) responsible for disseminating the study findings and the resources (e.g., financial, professional organizations, professional societies, professional colleagues) needed to facilitate dissemination of study findings (Gaventa, 1993; Smith, 1997). Through collaboration, new networks are established across organizations which cut across traditional boundaries to address social issues. CBPR can bring community-based organizations, public agencies, academic institutions, public and private funding resources, and medical settings together for the advancement of research impacting the client population resulting in service enhancement (Schensul, 1999).

Application of Study Findings to Address Community Well-Being

The CBPR process should facilitate the community understanding of the research issue and application of the knowledge gained to perpetuate community change. The community members should become empowered to become increasingly independent in sustaining the research process and creating and following action plans to enhance community well-being (Park, 1999). When the partnership suggests a course of action to impact policy, decisions regarding the approach should be developed through group consensus on information identifying the most appropriate agent to bring about community change (Citrin, 2000). Themba (1999) suggests community members and research partners choose agents based upon the following:

1. Identification of key persons and/or entities having the power to address the issue and support the community demands.
2. Identification of gatekeepers to key persons and/or entities with power.
3. Identification of the self-interests of the key persons/entities with power.
4. Identification of the incentives for key persons to support the identified actions.
5. Identification of relevant commissions or sub-commissions that engage in community participation that a member has joined or can join.
6. Identification of the most significant strategic power sources for influence (e.g., community organizations, faith-based organizations, human rights organizations, politicians, voters).

ADVANTAGES OF CBPR

CBPR is an approach to health and disability research, based in collaboration intended to increase the knowledge gain and empowerment of researcher and community members. As a collaborative approach, it is designed to ensure equitable participation by both parties through structured interaction throughout the research process. CBPR relies on community participation to identify research issues and ensure research questions are important not only to the researcher for accumulation of knowledge, but also for community members. It ensures that methods are reasonable, authentic, and noninvasive; yielding more effective actions or interventions because of their foundations in community participation. Rhodes and Benfield (2005) identified several advantages of the utilizing the CBPR process found in the literature (see Table 1).

Table 1. Advantages of Community-Based Participatory Research

- Enhances data relevance, usefulness, and use (Integrates knowledge and action for the benefit of all partners)
- Improves the quality and validity of the research by engaging local knowledge and local theory based on the lived experiences of the people involved
- Recognizes the limitations of the concept of value-free science and encourages a self-reflexive, engaged, and self-critical role of researchers
- Recognizes that knowledge is power and thus knowledge gained can be used by all partners involved to direct resources and influence policies that will benefit the community
- Overcomes the fragmentation and separation of the individual from his culture and context
- Aims to increase well-being of communities involved, both directly through examining and addressing identified needs and indirectly through increasing power, control and skills
- Joins partners with diverse skills, knowledge, and expertise to address complex issues
- Strengthens the research, program, and problem-solving capacity of partners
- Creates theory grounded in social experience, and creates better informed and more effective practice guided by such theories
- Increases the possibility of overcoming the understandable distrust of research on the part of communities that historically have been the subjects of such research
- Has the potential to bridge "cultural gaps"
- Involves communities that have been marginalized on the basis of, for example, disability, race, ethnicity, socioeconomic status, gender, and sexual orientation in examining the impact of marginalization and attempting to reduce or eliminate it

Common CBPR Research Methods

Although CBPR does not specify a specific research methodology, it can be infused into many research methodologies. The following section highlights three research methods and briefly describes how these can be applied in the CBPR process. These methods include in-depth interviews, focus groups, and photovoice.

In-Depth Interviews

Individual in-depth interviews are a common data collection methodology. Contingent upon the research goals, the interviews are *unstructured*, *semi-structured*, or *structured*. Unstructured interviews are characterized by questions that emerge during the interview process. Although the research partners may have general research issues or categories, the questions are asked as they are formulated in the natural course of the discussion. Questions are not predetermined. This style of in-depth interviews is conversational and increases the salience and relevance of questions. A weakness of unstructured interviews is that as the discussion progresses with each participant, different information is collected from individuals based on different questions. Although they are less systematic and comprehensive and may result in challenges in the analysis of data, they may be useful for initial exploration or case studies.

Semi-structured interviews provide more structure for the interviewer, with topics and issues to be explored and discussed in advance, and often in outline form. Semi-structured and structured interviews often require an *Interview Guide* to facilitate the interview process. When conducting a semi-structured interview, the sequence of questions is determined by the interviewer. The interviewer may probe for detail and further develop questions during the interview process. The data collection process is more systematic than in the unstructured interview. Because the semi-structured interview remains conversational and situational, gaps in data can be explored and closed. However, interviews may develop in directions jeopardizing comparability among participants, inadvertently omitting important and salient topics.

Structured interviews are often well defined prior to the interview. All interviewees are asked the same basic questions in the same sequence and manner. Questions may be *open-ended*, *closed-ended*, or may comprise a combination of question type. Open-ended questions provide more exploratory, developmental, and contextual data. Data from open-ended questions tend to be more descriptive. For example, an open-ended question could be asked of persons living with HIV/AIDS (PLWHA) in Washington, DC as: "If you could envision an answer to meeting the employment needs of unemployed PLWHA in the Washington DC area, what would that vision be?" Answers are descriptive and complex, providing information on meeting employment needs in the short-and long-term, types of services needed, and root-cause explanations.

Closed-ended questions are characterized by response options that are *fixed*. Participants choose among a list of fixed responses. An example closed-ended question from a structured interview that was implemented among PLWHA who were unemployed was: "Some PLWHA report their infectious disease physician as influential in their decision to return to work; do you believe that your infectious disease physician is influential in your decision to return to work? The response options were: "yes," "no" and "refused to answer." Closed-ended response options simplify the data collection and data analysis because questions can be asked in a shorter period of time and responses are easily aggregated and compared. However, the disadvantage is that participants must respond within the predetermined categories, limiting their response choices; which can distort their authentic experiences and feelings toward the survey issues.

Closed-ended interviews collect data on a topic, by asking individuals questions for the purpose of generating statistics on the group or groups within a community or population the individuals represent. Closed-ended interviews ask questions about a variety of factors that influence, measure, or are affected by health. For example, population-based closed-ended interviews may document and follow health or disability status. Or, closed-ended interviews may provide local data and a baseline for evaluation of intervention efforts. Once a CBPR project has evolved and developed a research methodology to effect change (e.g., individual, community change, organizational, policy), comparing baseline data to intervention implementation or post-intervention follow-up may provide information on the success of intervention.

When applying a CBPR approach to research, the research question, methods of measurement (e.g., interview, questionnaire), participant recruitment, and administration must be agreed upon by the partnership. Rhodes and Benfield (2005) identify items the research partnership will address through research methodology including: (1) How will participants be recruited? (2) What type of compensation will be provided? (3) Who will administer the interviews or questionnaires? And (4) Will interviewers be used or a self-administered questionnaire? Although researchers may have significant experience in interviewee recruitment and questionnaire administration, community partners may provide great insight that may increase recruitment and response rates as well as honesty. The researcher should acknowledge that which seems scientifically sound from a positivist perspective (e.g., reducing bias, threats to reliability and validity) may inhibit responses in a constructivist inquiry.

Focus Groups

Focus group methodology provides the opportunity to more fully investigate participants' responses and reactions to issues and allows new areas of inquiry to emerge. Explicit to focus group methodology is group interaction, through which participants are encouraged to discuss identified issues, talk among themselves, ask questions, comment on each other's perspective, and exchange anecdotes. This methodology can identify pertinent issues and nuances in CBPR that researchers may not otherwise be able to identify (Rhodes & Hergenrather, 2002).

Briefly, focus groups usually are comprised of six to ten participants who are guided through a set of general predetermined open-ended questions outlined in a *focus group moderator's guide,* developed by researcher partners. It may be based in a behavioral theory or allow for theory to explain phenomenon to be developed based on the findings, much like a *grounded theory* approach to research (Glasser & Strauss, 1967). Either way, the guide and line of inquiry delineated in it, should reflect the most meaningful approach and language as agreed upon by the research partners.

In facilitating a focus group study, participants are introduced to the focus group process and informed consent is obtained. The moderator outlines ground rules (e.g., speaking one at a time, respecting opinions, maintaining confidentiality) and participants sit in an informal circle to respond to open-ended questions. Group interaction is an explicit component of focus group methodology. To enhance continuity, the same person should moderate each focus group. The moderator must be skilled and experienced in facilitating group discussion, reminding participants that there are no wrong answers, probing for detail, and affirming opinions. When probing for detail, whether through examples or clarification, further exploration is key to successful qualitative data collection when using focus groups. In most cases, qualitative research requires the researcher to allow the design to emerge more fully during the project's evolution, thus all potential questions cannot be predicted (Sandelowski, Davis, & Harris, 1989). The *moderator's guide* is meant to serve as an outline, but the moderator facilitates the discussion beyond what is written within the *guide*. However, the moderator must keep the discussions focused and the discussion if it deviates from the purpose of the focus group.

Furthermore, besides a moderator, successful focus groups often involve at least one *note taker* who documents participant speaking order, body language, and facial expressions that cannot be captured by audio-recording but may provide important insight during the data analysis and interpretation phases. For each question the moderator asks, the note taker usually writes the question on a separate flip chart sheet and writes participant responses below it. When participants exhaust their responses to the question, the sheet is posted, and the next question is asked. Because anonymity is desired, participant names are not be used. Rather, participants may be assigned numbers that are added to the focus group transcript to track which focus group participant is saying what. It may not be important to know participant names; however, it may be important to attribute certain quotations to certain participants. Perhaps only one participant has a certain perspective about a topic that she or he continues to reiterate. When analyzing the transcripts, it may be important to recognize this and "weigh" findings accordingly.

During the focus group, the note taker may notice a participant who is uncomfortable with a discussion topic or the focus group discussion but does not assert her or his unease or disagreement; these observations should be noted by the note taker. Overall, the note taker is documenting what is going on during the focus group session that may be missed by the audio-recorder and by the moderator who is leading the session. Focus group audiotapes are transcribed verbatim. The first stage of data analysis involves sorting the transcripts into broad content categories. After initial independent organizing of transcripts into broad conceptual categories, the categories would be shared, establishing conceptual themes based upon standard procedures (Morgan, 1998; Rhodes & Hergenrather, 2002). Participant quotations are extracted from transcriptions and observer notes to illustrate themes. When applying a CBPR approach to focus group research, the research question, moderator's guide, and recruitment methods must be developed and agreed upon by the research partners. Data analysis and interpretation should be completed in partnership to enhance collaboration.

PHOTOVOICE

Photovoice methodology provides participants the opportunity to take photographs and present them in group discussion that empowers participants to reflect upon personal and community strengths, create critical dialogue, share knowledge about personal and community issues, and provide a forum for the presentation of participant's lives through self-identified images, language, and context (Streng, et al., 2004).

Photovoice is a qualitative research methodology in which participants photograph potential variables of concern, participate in group discussions regarding the photographs taken, and utilize the findings to impact change. It is an innovative CBPR method of inquiry founded on the principles of constructivism, feminist theory, and documentary photography. Constructivism defines learning through the individual's interactive process of developing and constructing meaning through experiences (Dewey, 1958; Merriam & Caffarella, 1999; Crain, 1992). Feminist theory suggests that power is based in those who have a voice, language, history, and make decisions. In taking photographs, participants have a language through which to voice salient concerns (Maguire, 1987; Smith, 1997, Wang & Buris, 1994). Within the realm of documentary photography, the images photographed by participants are used to address social issues (Strack, Magill, & McDonagh, 2004). Photovoice involves a series of procedures which include (1) identification of research issue; (2) recruitment of participants; (3) introduction of Photovoice methodology by group discussion; (4) obtain informed consent, (5) distribute cameras and providing instruction on camera use; (6) pose an initial research issue as a *photo-assignment* for taking photographs; (7) group consensus on subsequent photo-assignments; (8) weekly photo-discussions of one *photo-assignment* of selected photographs using a Freirian-based (Freire,1973) model of root-cause questioning and discussion represented by the mnemonic "SHOWED;" (8) analysis of study findings; and (9) identifying a plan of action; and (10) the identification of influential leaders, policy makers, and/or organizations with whom to share the study findings.

The process commences with the identification of an issue of social impact, which is presented to a community of those persons the issue impacts. The community further refines the issues and identifies the pertinent themes of the issues, which become session photo-assignments. Photo-discussions typically begin with a review and discussion of the research issue, themes, and photo-assignment of the prior session. Photos are then presented in the method of questioning and discussion known by the acronym **SHOWED** (What do you **S***ee* here? What is really **H***appening* here? How does this relate to **O***ur* lives? **W***hy* does this concern, situation, strength exist? How can we become **E***mpowered* through our new understanding? What can we **D***o*?). Photo-discussion data are analyzed like other qualitative data, through exploring, formulating, and interpreting themes. The participants then create an action plan to study findings with local community leaders, service providers, and policy makers. The photographs serve as the medium to raise awareness among a group of allies, mobilize these allies, and plan for change.

Photovoice expands the representation and diversity of the participant voices that assist to define and improve the social and political realities of the identified issues. As a flexible process that can accommodate a variety of physical and developmental disabilities, Photovoice does not require that community participants be able to read or write. The concept of Photovoice includes understanding that (1) images teach what one perceives as significant in defining a situation; (2) community members have power in defining the images to shape policy; (3) photographs can influence policy makers, programs, and society; (4) emphasis is placed upon the participant's identification of an influential audience for the community people's perspective; and (5) the integration of participant knowledge, skills, and resources within affected populations contributes to policy change (Wang, 1999).

Although a relatively new methodology, photovoice is a flexible method. It has been employed to explore and address with culturally diverse groups and persons with disabilities including communities of PLWHA in Washington, DC, US; Latino adolescents in rural North Carolina, US; Chinese women in the Yunnan Province, China; homeless people in Michigan, US; mothers with learning disabilities, and intergenerational African American women seeking housing solutions (Clark & Zimmer, 2001; Lykes, Blance, & Hamber, 2003; Hergenrather, 2005; Streng et al., 2004; Wang & Pies, 2003).

Applications to Health and Disability Issues

Addressing the health and disability issues of the public will require researchers, clinicians, and organizations to collaborate with communities to gain new understandings of the issues impacting societal marginalization and develop innovative ways to promote change that enhances the well-being of a community. Through CBPR, community members, organizational members, and researchers collaborate to understand and address the complex social, structural, and physical factors impacting behaviors to reduce health and disability disparities (Viswanathan et al., 2004). The inclusion of disabilities and secondary conditions in Healthy People 2010, with a goal of eliminating disparities, reflects the progress of the US government toward recognizing disability as a public health issue (US Department of Health and Human Services, 2000).

In this section, two case studies are presented. The first, HoMBReS, utilizes focus groups to identify and intervene upon the social determinants of sexual health among immigrant Latinos in North Carolina. The second, Windows to Work, utilized photovoice to address the employment-seeking behavior of PLWHA in Washington, DC.

Case Study 1: HoMBReS: Hombres Manteniendo Bienestar y Relaciones Saludables

HoMBReS: Hombres Manteniendo Bienestar y Relaciones Saludables (Men: Men Maintaining Wellness and Healthy Relationships) is an ongoing intervention research project in rural North Carolina (NC) US that was initiated through a partnership of lay community members, community based organization (CBO) representatives, university clinicians, practitioners, and researchers. HoMBReS was initially designed to gather formative data from Latino men on social determinants of sexual health; and explore intervention opportunities that build on assets within the Latino community, using CBPR.

A community health coalition known as Chatham Communities in Action (CCIA) was formed in 1991 as part of the NC Community-Based Public Health Initiative (CBPHI). Because of the rapidly growing Latino community in the region and their early success in diabetes prevention within the African American community, CCIA, with expanding Latino membership, chose to explore Latino health concerns within their local community. A subgroup of CCIA members met with university researchers to develop a plan to explore the healthcare priorities of the Latino community (Margolis et al., 2000; Parker et al., 1998).

The research partnership, which initially was comprised of current members of CCIA, came together first to determine how to further develop and expand the research partnership to include more Latino representation. Local Latino-serving CBOs and interested individuals that were not involved with CCIA were invited to participate in the process. This inclusion required time to build trust and clarify goals. These added members included representatives from the Liga Hispana de Fútbol de_North Carolina (LHFNC; NC Hispanic Soccer League), a local Latino tienda (grocery store), and a farm worker advocacy group. LHFNC is a 9-county Latino soccer league of over 1,600 adult Latino men. The League president along with various other interested League members became involved in the research partnership. The research partners continued to build trust among themselves as research partners through personal relationships, genuineness, respect, and "being there." CCIA representatives and the researchers spent many dinners meeting with League representatives. Although CCIA had a history of working with the university, these relationships could not be assumed or taken for granted; building and maintaining trust and communication always play a paramount role in CBPR.

The expanded research partnership gained consensus on the research aims. This process involved answering two equally important questions. First, the research partners had to ask themselves: "What do we want to know?" Second, the partners had to ask themselves: "Why do we want to know it?" This distinction is important because a CBPR approach recognizes that knowledge for knowledge sake (i.e., the accumulation of scientific knowledge) is important, but the immediate application of knowledge to affect the health and wellbeing of the participating community is equally important. The researchers had many curiosities and theories they wanted to explore but the research partners kept the focus on the practical use of knowledge gain.

In this study, the research partnership chose to explore health concerns of Latino men primarily because the majority of newly-arrived to the US Latinos are male, especially in rural NC. The research partnership had to come to agreement on the research and recruitment design and the roles and contributions of the partners. They decided to use focus groups to explore health priorities. The partnership created, reviewed, revised, and approved the Focus Group Moderator's Guide. The League president recruited focus group participants and two partnership members served as the focus group moderator and the note taker. The note taker was the university researcher who was fluent in Spanish. A Latino-serving CBO hosted the focus groups. A total of 50 men (mean age: 29.9, range: 18-51) participated in 1 of 5 focus groups. Over 80% of participants reported Mexico as their country of origin; other participants reported being from El Salvador, Guatemala, and Honduras.

The first stage of data analysis involved members of a subgroup from the research partnership sorting the focus group transcripts into broad content categories. After the initial sorting process was complete, the analysis team came together to compare broad categories and began interpreting the findings into conceptual domains. Once themes were created, the themes were presented to the research partnership and other community members including LHFNC members for number checking and interpretation. This was done by writing themes on flip charts, which were presented to the research partners and representatives from the soccer league, reviewed, discussed, and revised. Several iterations of this process were completed.

Qualitative data analysis identified 5 themes, including (a) the participants' prioritization of sexual health; (b) the lack of access to accurate and comprehensive HIV and STD information and resources; (c) barriers to accessing health care in the US; (d) the role of hegemonic masculinity in risk behavior; and (e) potentially-effective intervention approaches to health promotion and diseases prevention. This analysis suggested that a Latino soccer league may be an effective social network with which to partner to develop, implement, and evaluate a prevention intervention reaching men inaccessible in traditional venues typically used for intervention delivery.

Findings were disseminated through community and national presentations, report writing, and manuscript development. Because action is a key component of CBPR, the findings also were used for funding proposals and intervention design. All partners had equal access to the findings; for example, CBO representatives used findings for grant preparation, and community members used the findings to advocate for Latino men's health.

The HoMBReS intervention study was designed and funded by the Centers for Disease Control and Prevention (CDC). The goal of this CBPR study is to reduce the risk of HIV and sexually transmitted disease (STD) infection among Latino migrant and seasonal farm workers. The study has four interrelated objectives (see Table 2).

Table 2. Study Objectives of HoMBReS

Objective 1: Develop and implement a lay health advisor (LHA) intervention to reduce STD/HIV risk behaviors among members of an adult male Latino soccer league in central NC.
Objective 2: Evaluate the efficacy of the intervention by comparing Latino soccer league members in the intervention to those in the delayed-intervention control group using self-reported sexual risk behaviors and utilization of STD/HIV counseling, testing and treatment services.
Objective 3: Evaluate the changes experienced by the lay health advisors (LHA) by being trained and serving as lay health advisors.
Objective 4: Assess the feasibility of engaging a Latino soccer league in implementing a lay health advisor intervention designed to reduce STD/HIV transmission among male Latino migrant and seasonal farm workers.

Briefly, HoMBReS is a 3-year quasi-experimental research study based on the natural helper model. The natural helper model has emerged as an important approach in health promotion and disease prevention. Implicit in the approach is the exchange of social support, such as information, advice, tangible aid, and referrals to external resources (Eng & Parker, 2002). From a health and disability perspective, the empirical associations found between social support and health hold substantial potential for translating the health-enhancing effects of social support into social support interventions (Heaney & Israel, 2002). The common feature of natural helper-based interventions is to enlist indigenous members of a given population in channeling health-enhancing social support to individuals and groups (Eng & Parker, 2002).

Important conceptual and methodological distinctions among natural helper-based interventions have been viewed as falling along a continuum (Eng, Parker, & Harlan, 1997). At one end are interventions in which natural helpers serve as paid employees of an agency, such as a paraprofessional or outreach worker, and seek to deliver social support, such as information and assistance to individuals to protect the health of those individuals. At the other end are interventions for which natural helpers have expertise and knowledge that enhance the health and competence of their community through information distribution, assistance and organization of community-building activities within their social networks. This emphasis on natural helpers working within their own social network, defined as person-centered webs of relationships that connect individuals to other individuals or groups (Israel, 1982; Israel & Antonucci, 1987; Rounds & Israel, 1985), is different from that involving an outreach worker, who provides social support to individuals who may or may not be in his or her social network. HoMBReS includes the identification of natural helpers to serve within their naturally-occurring social networks within the Soccer League.

The HoMBReS natural helpers are known as "Navegantes" ("Navigators") who completed 16 hours of training to provide HIV and STD prevention education and prevention information and service and resource referral to their teammates. They serve as: (a) sources of HIV/STD information and referral; (b) opinion leaders to change risky behavioral norms resulting from culturally-infused male gender socialization; and (c) community activists to work with organizations such as the local public health department to better address the needs and priorities of Latino men in culturally-relevant approaches.

This project has been successful in the recruitment and training of a strong cadre of Navegantes because of the initial "buy in" of the LHFNC. Without their history of interest, support, and involvement, the idea for primary HIV and STD prevention and the use of team members as natural helpers would not necessarily have been considered. Had it been considered, the risks would have been higher because buy in would not have been garnered. Less knowledge about whether men would want to participate in a 16-hour, theory-based training and what that training should include would have left more opportunity for misjudgment on the part of the researchers. Instead, the partnership approach has ensured that fewer problems are incurred and when unavoidable roadblocks do occur, creative solutions that have a higher potential for success can be explored because more perspectives and options can be explored.

Case Study 2: Windows to Work: Employment and PLWHA

The *Windows to Work* project was a community-university collaboration in Washington, DC. The project was initiated through a partnership of Whitman-Walker Clinic (WWC) management, George Washington University (GWU) researchers, and persons living with HIV/AIDS (PLWHA) who were unemployed and receiving WWC services. WWC is the leading non-profit provider of HIV/AIDS prevention and treatment services in the Washington DC area and annually provides HIV/AIDS services to more than 6,000 persons.

The partnership utilized a CBPR process to gather exploratory data from PLWHA on the impact of HIV prognosis and disability status, upon their employment-seeking behavior, to create personal and community change. Under the US Americans with Disabilities Act (ADA), a PLWHA meeting defined criteria is provided specific rights as an individual with a disability. This Act defines disability status and discrimination protection, in respect to both the individual and the employment process (ADA, section 3:Definitions, 1990). US federal legislation has mandated the provision of public vocational rehabilitation services in each state and the District of Columbia to address the employment needs of individuals meeting the ADA disability criteria.

Due to the advent of health-enhancing protease inhibitors and highly active anti-retroviral therapy, the increased longevity of PLWHA, the increase in number of PLWHA in the US, PLWHA meeting ADA disability criteria, and increasing numbers of PLWHA on WWC caseloads, WWC management met with university researchers to explore the employment-seeking behavior of PLWHA (CDC, 2004). Upon the success of the initial meeting to initiate research collaboration, several subsequent meetings were held. Although an established history of collaboration existed between the WWC and the university researchers, it could not be taken for granted. The researchers attended several meetings with WWC management teams, PLWHA, WWC case managers, and the WWC internal review board (IRB) to gather input on the significance of the issue. Through the meetings, the partnership was further solidified, trust was built, research issues were clarified, and members were perceived as equitable partners.

Partners agreed that the research issue was important, but wanted to know if the PLWHA community with whom they work perceived employment as an important issue. Participants identified an important key research question as, *"What do we know about the employment interests of PLWHA?"* However, they agreed that understanding how PLWHA defined the word "employment" would be crucial in the response to the question. The expanded discussion led to a research study addressing two questions: *"How is employment defined by PLWHA?"* and *"When PLWHA think about returning to employment, what comes to mind?"* The partnership assisted in refining the research issues and methodology, equitably involving members in developing the project structure, identifying a researcher as the study facilitator, and developing the research proposal for the IRB of approval both the WWC and the GWU (Minkler & Wallerstein, 2003).

The partnership agreed to use photovoice methodology in exploring the employment-seeking behavior of PLWHA. Photovoice methodology provides the opportunity to more fully investigate participants' responses and reactions to issues and allows new areas of inquiry to emerge. Participants are encouraged to discuss issues among themselves, comment on other's perspectives, and exchange anecdotes. Photovoice methodology can identify pertinent issues and nuances that researchers may not otherwise be able to identify (Wang, 1999; Wang & Pies, 2003). The partnership created, revised, and facilitated the Photovoice Moderator's Guide (PMG) to increase the validity of the research study. The PMG introduced methodology, outlined group processes, and discussion format (Streng et al., 2004).

Participants were recruited by flyer postings at the WWC and through WWC case managers. Eleven PLWHA participated in the study; mean age 46.6 (range 33-64); 9 were African American; 8 were male; and 8 completed one or more years of college. They attended an initial meeting, at which the WTW study was described. Participants then engaged in discussion to define the word *employment* by the question, *"When you think about the word employment, what comes to mind?"* During the discussion, the facilitator listed participant responses on flip chart sheets. From the lists, participants identified the first *photo-assignment:* to conceptualize the word *employment*. Participants then engaged in a discussion addressing items impacting their employment-seeking behavior through the question, *"When you think about returning to employment, what comes to mind?"* Participants identified 97 items impacting employment-seeking behavior, which were grouped into five participant-identified *employment constructs.* The constructs became independent discussion topics with corresponding *photo-assignments* topics for five consecutive sessions. Sessions averaged two hours and were audio taped.

Each session concluded with a summary in which participants were provided opportunity through consensus to modify the structure and research methodology, as needed, to ensure the subsequent session aligned with community needs. Commencing with session two, participants arrived 30 minutes early to each session to have the photo-session topic digital photographs downloaded and have their photos in-hand for presentation. Session two, and each subsequent session, was structured with four components (1) a review of the prior session, (2) a presentation of each participant's 1-5 photographs for the *photo-assignment*, (3) a discussion of one *employment construct*, (4) a discussion of the next *photo-assignment* conceptualizing the employment construct addressed.

After each session, the transcript and facilitator notes were reviewed by the researchers for analysis consisting of a detailed reading and rereading of each transcript and corresponding facilitator notes. The data analysis involved members of a subgroup from the partnership consisting of the researchers and WWC management (Green et al., 1995). Participant responses and lines of text were tracked throughout the transcripts and analyses. After initial independent organizing of transcripts into broad conceptual categories, the subgroup shared categories, established conceptual themes, and interpreted individual statements according to standard procedures (Morgan, 1998; Rhodes & Hergenrather, 2002). Once themes were identified, they were presented at the next photovoice session for participant discussion, clarification, consensus and validation.

Through participant photographs and statements, the term *employment* was conceptualized and 19 themes impacting behavior were identified. Themes were grouped into the five participant-identified employment constructs of (a) disadvantages of employment, (b) advantages of employment, (c) persons influencing their decision to work, (d) facilitators to employment, and (e) barriers to employment. Participants utilized the themes to develop an action plan addressing the employment-seeking behavior of PLWHA.

Participants conceptualized *employment* as a multifaceted term defined as a societal expectation that rejuvenates a person, through providing opportunities for career growth and development, while earning income to provide for loved ones and family. To represent this, participants selected a photograph of a tree along a riverbank, with a background of bright blue sky in which the tree is presented as a silhouette. They agreed to describe the photograph by the statement, "Employment for me is like the tree. It is autumn and the tree is becoming dormant. In the spring, it will grow, reach out its branches, and provide shade and a place for birds to nest. I am that tree in the photo. With employment I will grow, develop my skills, and provide for myself and my family."

The first employment construct identified by participants addressed disadvantages to employment. Four themes emerged as disadvantages to employment. Participants identified one theme as "Accepting employment into a workplace that not sensitive to PLWHA." They perceived a person's acceptance by coworkers and employers as contingent upon HIV status. To represent this, the group selected a photograph of a town house, obscured by gruesome Halloween decorations. The house has an iron-fenced yard, exhibiting life-size figures of ghosts and demons. The entrance archway to the yard contains the word "Welcome," which is barely visible with the Grim Reaper situated atop the archway with outstretched arms. The participants represented this by the statement, "You should feel good about work. It's a place that you believe you are welcome. When coworkers find out you have HIV/AIDS, it's scary, like the photo. We could lose our jobs because some people are ignorant."

Another employment construct consisted of important referents, identified as influential in their employment-seeking behavior. Participants identified the theme of "friends," defined as important others who stood by PLWHA throughout their HIV prognosis. This theme was represented by a photograph of two grasped hands. Participants represented the photograph by the statement, "The friendships I have maintained throughout my 24 years of living with AIDS are so important to me. I pray that I'll be able to continue these relationships which help me get through life on a daily basis, despite the obstacles of my prognosis."

The final two sessions addressed personal and community empowerment, providing participants the opportunity to develop an action plan and identify Influential Advocates (e.g., policy makers, community leaders, organizations) impacting the employment of PLWHA, to whom the study findings should be disseminated (Israel et al., 1998). Participants conceptualized an action plan and developed the Employment Decision-making Model (EDM). The EDM is an 11-step model in which the five employment constructs are evaluated to identify influences upon the employment-seeking behavior of PLWHA. It also presents a process through which to identify employment services. Participants utilized the EDM to make informed decisions, which facilitate behavior change. Employment outcomes, influential others, facilitators to employment, and barriers to employment have been identified as items impacting the employment-seeking behavior of PLWHA (Hergenrather, Rhodes, & Clark, 2004, 2005).

The study findings provided an opportunity for participants to raise awareness of their employment concerns. Through consensus, participants decided that the community-university partnership would present the study findings (e.g., photographs, statements, themes, employment decision-making model) in various research and practice settings. Participants identified the importance of a targeted approach in multiple outlets that to date have included national advocates, including representatives from the Department of Labor, the American Medical Association, the Social Security Administration (SSA), the National Rehabilitation Association, the American Public Health Association, HIV/AIDS community based organizations, and the District of Columbia Rehabilitation Services Administration.

The participants played a key role in advising researchers on the relevant issues impacting employment-seeking behavior. They reviewed the methodology, data analyses, employment constructs, themes, and evaluation. Study findings (e.g., data, photos, quotations) were disseminated through community, national, and international presentations, and manuscript development. Study findings identified (1) PLWHA wanted to return to work, (2) PLWHA had limited knowledge of, and access to, employment services, (3) employment was not perceived as an essential component of case management services, and (4) PLWHA receiving SSA services were unaware of the Ticket to Work and Self-Sufficiency (TTWSS) program which could extend benefits up to 48 months (National Archives and Records Administration, 2001; Silverstein, 2002). At the commencement of the study, none of the participants were aware of the TTWSP. At the end of the study, 57.1% of those receiving on SSA were enrolled in the TTWSP.

The CBPR process heightened a sense of awareness of employment-seeking behavior among participants, researchers, and WWC. Participants increased critical consciousness and responsibility, accompanying a gain in power achieved through the acquisition of knowledge, skills, and access to resources (Israel et al., 1998). This CBPR method differs greatly from traditional qualitative research, in which PLWHA would likely be subjects in research studies rather than collaborators in defining the research issue, designing the research methodologies, and instrumental in creating action plans from study findings to enhance both personal and community well-being.

Discussion

In this chapter, the foundations of community-based participatory research (CBPR) were presented. We then described applications of CBPR to the research process, followed by the research methodologies of in-depth interviews, focus groups, and photovoice. Two case studies were provided, demonstrating applications of CBPR process to address the health issues of Latino men in North Carolina and the disability issues of PLWHA in Washington, DC. Researchers who are exploring the application of CBPR will find that it can be infused into numerous research designs. CBPR presents a process for involving those persons impacted most by health or disability issues to be involved in research addressing the underlying causes.

Limitations

In applying CBPR, there are a few limitations researchers should address. First, researchers must be aware of their possible biases on the identified health or disability issue that results from their training or worldview. A researcher must remove his or her bias from the CBPR process to ensure that participants are empowered. Although researchers may be receptive to the opinions of the community members, researchers may align with a preconceived agenda and minimizing the expressed desires the community. Coordinating the "agendas" of the researcher and participants may be challenging at times. Thus, it may be important for a researcher to carefully listen and truly hear what is being communicated.

Second, during the process of involving the community, the researcher may need to choose between working with existing partnerships and assisting in the creation of new partnerships. When using existing partnerships, pre-existing group biases towards and about the health or disability issue may be present. Opinions about potential solutions may cloud the partners' exploration of innovative approaches. Thus, although it is important that the researcher involves the stakeholders of the issue, he or she must recognize that biases exist with power disparities among partners.

Third, because some participants are more vocal than others, researchers should establish guidelines to enable all members to participate equally, even though participants may contribute at different levels and contribute different skills. Establishing group norms, identifying the ground rules from which the group functions, can allow equal communication, keep members respectful of each other, and distribute power to less engaged members of the group (Levi, 2001). Regardless of group dynamics, if the social issue is regarded as personal or sensitive, some members may not participate.

Fourth, when disparities in power among group members become apparent, the potential for "group think" may exist. "Group think" occurs when member's desires to maintain good relationships becomes more important that reaching good decisions. Foundations of group think include structural decision-making flaws in which group members ignore input from outside resources, accept decisions without critical analysis, and outside forces place stress on the group to make decisions (Janis, 1983). Group think may develop in CBPR when there exists a strict research timeline, the researcher aligns with the research agenda of the funding agency, or community members do not have critical analysis skills. In groups of community members having unequal power, group communication is reduced to those powerful members controlling the communication. This is likely to affect group cohesion because individuals with similar status are likely to interact with each other and form alliances (Tolbert, Andrews, & Simons, 1995).

Fifth, it is important to consider the cost and time of the study which may impact the attrition of subjects, staffing changes in partner agencies, and even changes in research staff. CBPR demands a significant amount time on the part of the researcher and research partners. It requires flexibility to schedule around work hours, holidays, weekends, and family and professional obligations. Many times the health concerns of partners and lack of transportation may impact their participation in CBPR.

Finally, in developing the methodology, it is important to consider the size of the study, the type of evaluation, and the researcher's ability to manage the evaluation. Because the partners contribute to determining the research methodology, the researcher must be able to tolerate ambiguity and be willing to be "vulnerable" in sharing power. The researcher must determine how "realistic" is it really to meet the theoretical challenge of power sharing and how to find the balance between empowering participants, moving a project along a reasonable research timeline and not inadvertently silencing or steering the process.

Enhancing Future Research

In working with marginalized communities, CBPR suggests a process to examine the ecologic determinants impacting the well-being of communities, from which to develop action plans pursuing change at the individual, community, and policy levels. Through CBPR, the researcher and community members become co-learners, bridging cultural differences among participants and equitably sharing expertise based in professional and personal knowledge. The collaboration can identify and respond to community needs through developing an interactive research study upholding the tenets of scientific inquiry, rather than a research study base upon a preconceived agenda to enhance community well-being (Levine, Becker, & Bone, 1992; Tanjasiri, Kagawa-Singer, Nguyen, & Foo; 2002).

Collaboration with community members increases the likelihood that the research study would be conducted in a culturally sensitive and educationally appropriate manner and sustained through community interest. Regardless of training or research experience, motivated community members could participate in addressing complex problems in complex situations. Through CBPR, researchers are provided the opportunity to develop community collaborations to identify social issues, enhance community relations, increase the quality and validity of research, generate knowledge through community-researcher dialogue, create action plans, disseminate study findings to reduce disparities, and improve individual and community well-being.

References

Agency for Healthcare Research and Quality. (2002). *Community-based participatory research.* Rockville, MD: US Government printing office.

Americans with Disabilities Act, Pub. L. No. 101-336, 104 Stat. 327 (1990), codified 42 U.S.C. [sections] 12101 et seq.

Arnstein, S. R. (1969). A ladder of citizen participation. *American Institute of Planning Journal, 35,* 216-224.

Brown, D. L., & Tandon. R. (1983). Ideology and political economy of inquiry: Action research and participatory research. *Journal of Applied Behavioral Science, 19*, 277-294.

Centers for Disease Control and Prevention. (1997). *Principles of Community Engagement.* Atlanta, GA, US Department of Health and Human Services.

Centers for Disease Control and Prevention. (2004). *HIV/AIDS Surveillance Report.* 15 (2),1-46.

Chisholm, R. & Elden, M. (1993). Features of emerging action research. *Human Relations, 46*, 275-297.

Citrin, T. (2000). Policy issues in community-based approach. In T. A. Bruce & S. Urange McKane (Eds.). *Community-based public health: A partnership model* (pp. 83-90). Washington, DC: American Public Health Association.

Clark, L., & Zimmer, L. (2001). What we learned from a photographic component in a study of Latino children's health. *Field Methods, 13*(4), 303-328.

Cooper, R. S., Kennelly, J. F., Durazo-Arvizu, R., Oh, H. J., Kaplan, G., & Lynch, J. (2001). Relationships between premature mortality and socioeconomic factors in black and white populations of US metropolitan areas. *Public Health Report, 116*, 464-473.

Cornwall, A., & Jewkes, R. (1995). What is participatory research? *Social Science Medicine, 41,* 1667-76.

Cornwall, A. (1996). Towards participatory practice: Participatory rural appraisal (PRA) and the participatory process. In K. De Koning & M. Martin (Eds.), *Participatory research in health: Issues and experiences* (pp.94-107). London: Zed Books.

Crain, W. (1992). *Theories of development: Concepts and applications.* (3rd ed.). Englewood Cliffs, NJ: Prentice Hall.

Dewey, J. (1958). *Democracy and education.* New York: Macmillan.

Eng, E., & Parker, E. (2002). Natural helper models to enhance a community's health and competence. In R. J. DiClemente, R. A. Crosby & M. C. Kegler (Eds.), *Emerging theories in health promotion practice and research. Strategies for improving public health* (pp. 126-156). San Francisco: Jossey-Bass Wiley.

Eng, E., Parker, E., & Harlan, C. (1997). Lay health advisor intervention strategies: A continuum from natural helping to paraprofessional helping. *Health Education Behavior, 24*(4), 413-417.

Fals-Borda, O. (1991). Some basic ingredients. In O. Fals-Borda & A. Rahman (Eds.), *Action and knowledge: Breaking the monopoly with participatory action research* (pp. 3-12). New York: Apex Press.

Fals-Borda, O. (1997). Participatory action research in Colombia: Some personal feelings. In R. McTaggart (Ed.), *Particpatory action research: International contexts and consequences* (pp. 107-112). New York: State University of New York.

Freire, P. (1973). *Pedagogy of the oppressed.* New York: Herder and Herder.

Freire, P. (1982). Creating alternative research methods: Learning to do it by doing it. In Hall B., Gillette, A., and Tandon, R (Eds.) Creating knowledge: A monopoly? *Participatory research in development.* New Delhi: Society for Participatory Research in Asia.

Freire, P. (1987). *Education for critical consciousness.* New York: Continuum.

Gaventa, J. (1993). The powerful, the powerless, and the experts: Knowledge struggles in an information age. In P. Park, M. Brydon-Miller, B. Hall, & T. Jackson (Eds.), *Voices of Change: Participatory Research in the United States and Canada* (pp.21-40). Toronto, Canada: OISE Press.

George, M. A., Green, L. W., & Daniel, M. (1996). Evolution and implications of P.A.R. for public health. *Health Promotion Education, 3*, 6-10.

Glaser, B., & Strauss, A. (1967). *The Discovery of Grounded Theory: Strategies for Qualitative Research.* Chicago, IL: Aldine.

Green, L. W. (2001). From research to "best practices" in other settings and populations.*American Journal of Health Behavior, 25*,165-78.

Green, L. W., George, M. A., Frankish, C., Herbert, C. , Bowie, W., & O'Neil, M. (1995). *Study of participatory research in health promotion: Review and recommendations for the development of participatory research in health promotion in Canada.* Ottawa: Royal Society of Canada.

Green, L. W., George, M. A., Daniel, M., Franklin, C., Herbert, C., Bowie, W., et al. (2003).Guidelines for participatory research in health promotion. In Minkler, M., and Wallerstein, N. (Eds). *Community-Based Participatory Research for Health.* San Francisco, CA: Jossey-Bass, 419-428.

Habermas, J. (1984). *The theory of communicative action.* Cambridge, MA: Polity Press.

Hatch, J., Moss, N., Saran, A., Presley-Cantrell, L., & Mallory, C. (1993). Community research: Partnership in black communities. *American Journal of Preventive Medicine, 9,* 27-31.

Heaney, C. A., & Israel, B. A. (2002). Social networks and social support. In K. Glanz, B. K. Rimer & F. M. Lewis (Eds.), *Health behavior and heath education: Theory research and practice* (3 ed., pp. 185-209). San Francisco: CA: Jossey-Bass.

Hergenrather, K. C. (2005, February). *Employment-seeking behavior of persons living with HIV/AIDS: A comparison of three research methods.* Paper presented at Coventry University Post Graduate Conference. Coventry, United Kingdom.

Hergenrather, K.C., Rhodes, S. D., & Clark, G. (2004) Employment–seeking behavior of persons living with HIV/AIDS: A theory-based approach. *Journal of Rehabilitation,70*(4), 22-32.

Hergenrather, K.C., Rhodes, S. D., & Clark, G. (2005). The employment perspective study: Identifying factors influencing the job-seeking behavior of persons living with HIV/AIDS. *AIDS Education and Prevention,17(2), 132-144.*

Institute of Medicine. (2003). *Unequal treatment: Confronting racial and ethnic disparities in health care.* Washington, DC, National Academy Press.

Israel, B. A. (1982). Social networks and health status: Linking theory, research, and practice. *Patient Counseling Health Education, 4*(2), 65-79.

Israel, B. A., & Antonucci, T. C. (1987). Social network characteristics and psychological well-being: A replication and extension. *Health Education Quarterly, 14*(4), 461-481.

Israel, B. A., Checkoway, B., Schulz, A., & Zimmerman, M.A. (1994). Health education and community empowerments: Conceptualizing and measuring perceptions of individual, organizational, and community control. *Health Education Quarterly, 21*, 149-170.

Israel, B., Shurman, S., & Hugentobler, M. K. (1992). Conducting action research: Relationships between organization members and communities. *Journal of Applied Behavioral Science, 28*, 74-101.

Israel, B. A., Schulz, A. J., Parker, E. A., & Becker, A. B. (1998). Review of community-based research: Assessing partnership approaches to improve public health. *Annual Review of Public Health, 19*, 173-202.

Israel, B. A., Schulz, A. J., Parker, E. A., & Becker, A. B. (2001). Community-based participatory research: Policy recommendations for promoting a partnership approach in health research. *Education for Health, 14*(2), 182-197.

Janis, I. L. (1983). Groupthink. In H. H. Blumberg, A. P. Hare, V. Kent, & M. F. Davis (Eds.). *Small groups and social interaction,* (pp.39-46). New York: Wiley.

Kidd, S. A., & Kral, M. J. (2005). Practicing participatory action research. *Journal of Counseling Psychology, 52*(2), 187-195.

Klien, D., Williams, D., & Witbrodt, J. (1999). The collaboration process in HIV prevention and evaluation in an urban American Indian clinic for women. *Health Education & Behavior, 26*(2), 239-249.

Levine, D. M., Becker, D. M., Bone, L. R., Stillman, F., Tuggle, M., Prentice, M., et al. (1992). A partnership with minority populations: A community model of effectiveness research.*Ethnicity & Disease*, *2*, 296-305.

Levi, D. (2001). *Group dynamics for teams.* Thousand Oaks, CA: Sage.

Lewin, K. (1946). Action research and minority problems. *Journal of Social Issues, 2*(4), 34-46.

Lewin, K. (1947). Frontiers in group dynamics. *Human Relations, 1*, 143-153.

Lewin, K. (1951). *Field theory in social science*. New York: Harper.

Lincoln, Y. S., & Guba, E. G. (2000). Paradigmatic controversies, contradictions, and emerging confluences. In: N. K. Denzin and Y. S. Lincoln (Eds.), Handbook of qualitative research (pp. 163-188). Thousand Oaks, CA: Sage.

Lykes, M. B., Blance, M. T., & Hamber, B. (2003). Narrating survival and change in Guatemala and South Africa: The politics of representation and a liberatory community psychology. *American Journal of Community Psychology, 31*(2), 79-90.

Maguire, P. (1987). *Doing participatory research: A feminist approach.* Amherst: University of Massachusetts, Center for International Education.

McKnight, J. l., & Kretmann, J. P. (1992). *Mapping community capacity.* Evanston, IL: Center for Urban Affairs and Policy Research, Northwestern University.

Margolis, L. H., Stevens, R., Laraia, B., Ammerman, A., Harlan, C., Dodds, J., et al. (2000). Educating students for community-based partnerships. *Journal of Community Practice, 7*(4), 21-34.

Merriam, S., & Caffarella, R. (1999). Learning in adulthood (2nd ed.) San Francisco:Jossey-Bass.

Metzler, M. M., Higgins, D. L., Beeker, C. G., Freudenberg, N., Lantz, P. M., Senturia, K. D., et al. (2003). Addressing urban health in Detroit, New York City, and Seattle through community-based participatory research partnerships. *American Journal of Public Health, 93*, 803-11.

Minkler, M., & Wallerstein, N. (2003). Introduction to community based participatory Research. In Minkler, M., and Wallerstein, N. (Eds), *Community-Based Participatory Research for Health,* (pp. 3-26). San Francisco, CA: Jossey-Bass.

Morgan, D. L. (1998). Focus groups as qualitative research. In P. Manning, M. Miller, & Maanen J. (Eds.), *Qualitative research methods series 16*. Newbury Park, CA: Sage.

National Archives and Records Administration (2001). The Ticket to Work and Self-Sufficiency Program: Final Rule; Part 411 of Title 20 of the Code of Federal Regulations [20 CFR Part 411]; *Federal Register*, 66, 67370-67442.

Park, P. (1999). People, knowledge, and change in participatory research. *Management Learning, 30*(2), 141-157.

Parker, E., Eng, E., Laraia, B., Ammerman, A., Dodds, J., Margolis, L., et al. (1998). Coalition building for prevention: Lessons learned from the North Carolina community-based public health initiative. *Journal of Public Health Management Practice, 4*(2), 25-36.

Peters, M. & Robinson, V. (1984). The origins and status of action research. *Journal of Applied Behavioral Sciences, 20*, 113-124.

Rahman, A. (1991). The theoretical standpoint of PAR. In O. Fals-Borda & A. Rahman (Eds.), *Action and knowledge: Breaking the monopoly with participatory action research* (pp.13-23). New York: Apex Press.

Reason, P. (1994). Human inquiry as discipline and practice. In P. Reason (Ed.), *Participation in human inquiry* (pp. 40-56). Thousand Oaks, CA: Sage.

Rappaport, J. (1977). *Community psychology: Values, research and action*. New York: Holt.

Rappaport, J. (1990). Research methods and the empowerment social agenda. In P. Tolan, C. Keys, F. Chertok, & L. Jason (Eds.), *Researching community psychology: Issues of theory and methods* (pp.51-63). Washington, DC: American Psychological Association.

Rhodes, S. D., & Benfield, D. (2005) Community-Based Participatory Research: An introduction for the clinician researcher. In Blessing J. D. (Ed.).*Physician Assistant's Guide to Research and Medical Literature.* (2nd ed., pp. 105-118). Philadelphia, PA: F. A. Davis.

Rhodes, S. D., & Hergenrather, K. C. (2002). Exploring Hepatitis B vaccination acceptance mong young men who have sex with men: Facilitators and barriers. *Preventive Medicine, 35,* 128-134.

Rounds, K. A., & Israel, B. A. (1985). Social networks and social support: Living with chronic renal disease. *Patient Education Counseling, 7*(3), 227-247.

Sandelowski, M., Davis, D., Harris, B. (1989). Artful design: Writing the proposal for research in the naturalist paradigm. *Research Nursing and Health, 12*, 77-84.

Schensul, J., (1999). Organizing community research partnerships in the struggle against AIDS. *Health Education & Behavior, 26*(2), 266-283.

Schensul, S., & Schensul, J. (1978). Advocacy and applied anthropology. In G. H. Weber, & G. J. McCall (Eds.), *Social scientists as advocates* (pp.121-126). Beverly Hills, CA: Sage.

Schensul, J., Weeks, M., & Singer, M. (1999). Building research partnerships. In J. Schensul, M. LeCompte, M. Weeks, & M. Singer (Eds.), *Ethnographer's toolkit: Vol. 6. Researcher roles and research partnerships.* Walnut Creek, CA: Altamira.

Sharpe, P., Greany, M., Lee, P., & Royce, S. (2000). Assets-oriented community assessment. *Public Health Reports, 113*, 205-211.

Silverstein, R. (2002). Final regulations implementing the ticket to work and self-sufficiency program (The ticket to work program). *Policy Brief, 4*(1), 1-42.

Sim, J., & Wright, C. (2000). *Research in Healthcare: Concepts, Designs and Methods*. Cheltenham, UK: Stanley Thornes, Limited.

Smith, S. E., (1997). Deepening participatory action research. In S. E. Smith, D. G. Williams, & N. A. Johnson (Eds.), *Nurtured by knowledge: Learning to do participatory action research* (pp. 173-264). New York: Apex Press.

Staples, L. (1997). Selecting and cutting the issue. In M. Minkler (ed.), *Community organizing and community building for health* (pp. 175-194). New Brunswick, NJ: Rutgers University Press.

Steuart, G. W. (1993). Social and cultural perspectives: Community interventions and mental health. *Health Education Quarterly* (Suppl. 1), 99-111.

Stoecker, R., & Stuber, A. (1999). Building an information superhighway of one's own: A comparison of two approaches. *Research in Politics and Society, 7*, 291-309.

Strack, R., Magill, C., & McDonagh, K. (2004). Engaging youth through photovoice. *Health Promotion Practice, 5*(1), 49-58.

Streng, J., Rhodes, S., Ayala, G., Eng, E., Arceo, R., and Phipps, S. (2004). Realidad Latina: Latino adolescents, their school, and a university use photovoice to examine and address the influence of immigration. *Journal of Interprofessional Studies, 18*(4), 403-415.

Tanjasiri, S. P. Kagawa-Singer, M, Nguyen, T. U., & Foo, M. A. (2002). Collaborative research as an essential component for addressing cancer disparities among Southeast Asian and Pacific Islander women. *Health Promotion Practice, 3*, 147-157.

Themba, M. N. (1999). *Making policy, making change: How communities are taking law into their own hands*. San Francisco: Jossey-Bass.

Tolbert, P., Andrews, A., & Simons, T. (1995). The effects of group proportions on group dynamics. In S. Jackson & M. Ruderman (Eds.). *Diversity in work teams: Research paradigms for a changing workplace* (pp.131-159). Washington, DC: American Psychological Association.

US Department of Health and Human Services (2000). *Healthy People 2010: With Understanding and Improving Health and Objectives for Improving Health.* Washington, DC: US Government Printing Office.

US Department of Health and Human Services. (2001). *The Surgeon General's Call to Action to Prevent and Decrease Obesity*. Rockville, MD: US Public Health Services.

Viswanathan, M., Eng, E., Ammerman, A., Gartlehner, G., Lohr, K. N., Griffith, D., et al. (2004). *Community-based participatory research: Assessing the evidence* (Evidence Report/Technology Assessment No. 99). Rockville, MD: Agency for Healthcare Research and Quality.

Wallerstein, N. (1999). Power dynamics between evaluator and community: Research relationships within New Mexico's Healthier communities. *Social Science Medicine, 49*, 39-53.

Wang, C. C. (1999). Photovoice: A participatory action research strategy applied to women's health. *Journal of Women's Health, 8*(2), 185-192.

Wang, C., & Burris, M. A. (1994). Empowerment through photo novella: Portraits of participation. *Health Education Quarterly, 21*(2), 171-186.

Wang, C. C., & Pies, C. A. (2003). Family, maternal, and child health through photovoice. *Maternal & Child Health Journal, 8*(2), 95-103.

Wekerle, G., & Whitzman, C. (1995). *Safe cities: Guidelines for planning, designing, and management.* New York: Van Nostrand Reinhold.

Zax, M., & Specter, G. (1974). *An introduction to community psychology.* Oxford, UK: Wiley.

In: Focus on Disability: Trends in Research and Application ISBN: 978-1-60021-792-0
Editor: Thilo Kroll, pp. 89-108 © 2008 Nova Science Publishers, Inc.

Chapter VI

Peer-Mentoring and Disability: Current Applications and Future Directions

Erin Hayes and Fabricio Balcazar
University of Illinois at Chicago, USA.

Abstract

Peer-mentoring involves a relationship in which two individuals share some common characteristic or experience and one provides needed assistance or support to the other. Research and theory have suggested that peer-mentoring has great potential for providing assistance to individuals struggling with challenging life experiences, while also benefiting the peers who are providing the assistance. Though highly relevant and applicable to the area of disability, peer-mentoring has been incorporated in the disability literature in a very limited way. This chapter will set the context for the construct of peer mentoring in the area of disability from a theoretical stance, and will then review the empirical and intervention literatures related to peer-mentoring and disability. Though limited, such interventions have been applied in employment, hospital, and community-based settings. We discuss the reported benefits and challenges of using peer-mentoring models, as well as how this approach benefits both the mentees who are involved. As demonstrated here, peer-mentoring has much to offer to the area of disability and should continue to be examined in the areas of program development and research.

Introduction

Peer-mentoring involves a relationship in which two individuals share some common characteristic or experience and one provides needed assistance or support to the other (Sherman, DeVinney, & Sperling, 2003). Key to the concept of peer-mentoring is the mentor's ability to understand someone else's situation because of some shared experience or status (Ensher, Thomas, & Murphy, 2001). Through this common understanding, peer-mentors share stories, provide information, and often, once the relationship has become solid enough, challenge mentees in situations where they find that doing so is appropriate. Peer-mentoring is distinguished from the more general concept of "peer-support" in that peer-mentoring involves a purposeful, unidirectional relationship, where the mentor is there to function as a support for the mentee; whereas in peer-support, the interaction tends to focus on mutual support benefiting all individuals involved. This does not mean that peer-mentors do not benefit in the process; however, mentors benefiting is not a primary purpose of the peer-mentor relationship. Peer-mentoring has great potential for providing assistance to individuals struggling with challenging life experiences, such as in cases where someone has acquired a new disability, experienced a health problem, is transitioning to a new school, or is beginning a new career.

Interestingly, the terms peer and mentor can appear paradoxical. A peer can be defined as someone who shares an important characteristic or experience with another person, such as age, race, social class, or disability (Microsoft Encarta, 1999). Further, the term peer implies that the two people share some equal standing, that they are people of equal status, experience, or cohort, and it is assumed that they share equal power. In comparison, a mentor is seen as someone who is more experienced and advanced, someone who serves as a wise and trusted counselor or teacher (Microsoft Encarta, 1999). These contrasting definitions have in part led to peer-mentoring being distinguished from more general mentoring in the research literature, and oftentimes being left out of discussions of the benefits of mentoring (i.e., DuBois, Holloway, Valentine, & Cooper, 2002), as traditional definitions of mentoring involve a relationship between an older, more experienced mentor and a younger and less experienced mentee (Levinson, Carrow, Klein, Levinson, & McKee, 1978; Rhodes, 1994). Peer-mentoring challenges this traditional definition as the relationship actually relies on the amount of shared experiences between the mentor and mentee. Peer-mentors and mentees tend to have had similar types of experiences at relatively similar points in their lives, but peer-mentors have demonstrated more success in terms of dealing with these experiences: this is what qualifies them as being able to serve as mentors. While it is reasonable to assume that there are indeed some cases in which peer-mentoring may not be appropriate, there are also many cases in which peer-mentoring can be and is most appropriate, as the support needed may be the shared experience of someone with whom the mentee can relate in a unique way. This is particularly critical in the case of the disability experience.

As has begun to be demonstrated in the research literature, peer-mentoring has much to offer. Peer-mentoring has been discussed as an effective tool for enhancing academic (e.g., Jacobi, 1991; Topping, 1996), workplace (e.g., Fine & Pullins, 1998), and health outcomes (e.g., Grummer-Strawn, Rice, Dugas, Clark, & Benton-Davis, 1997; Hailey, Lalor, Byrne, & Starling, 1992; Ozer, Weinstein, Maslach, & Seigel, 1997; Thoits, Hohmann, Harvey, & Fletcher, 2000). Though rarely discussed, another context in which peer-mentoring has much potential is the area of disability. There are very few published accounts of peer-mentoring being applied within a disability context (for notable exceptions see the studies reviewed in this paper: Cullen & Barlow, 1998; Hernandez, Hayes, Balcazar, & Keys, 2001; Hibbard et al., 2002; Powers, Sowers, & Stevens, 1995; Vines, 2000; Whittemore, Rankin, Callahan, Leder, & Carroll, 2000), and to date no papers have synthesized this literature, which leaves us at a loss in terms of understanding both the main contributions of, potential for, and limitations of peer-mentoring in the area of disability.

It is important to note that there has been some work done in the area of general (i.e., not peer) mentoring and disability (Campbell-Whatley, 2001; Campbell-Whatley & Algozzine, 1997; Lee, Storey, Anderson, Goetz, & Zivolich, 1997; McDonald, Balcazar, and Keys, in press). Further, though not specifically peer-mentor related, peer-delivered interventions have also been incorporated into practice among individuals with disabilities (Goldstein & Wickstrom, 1986; Odom & Strain, 1984, 1986; Osguthorpe, Eiserman, & Shisler, 1985; Ragland, Kerr & Strain, 1978). While mentoring and peer-interventions have both seemed positive when applied to the area of disability, what is missing is an intersection of these two: What does peer-mentoring have to offer to disability?

The purpose of the current chapter is to review the literature on peer-mentoring and disability and to make recommendations about the multiple potential applications of peer-mentoring to the area of disability. Here we identify peer-mentoring as mentoring by and for people with disabilities: Disability is the shared experience that defines the work presented as peer-mentoring. We will begin by examining two theoretical perspectives that support the use of peer-mentoring in disability, present empirical research that supports the use of peer-mentoring in disability, summarize the few existing published accounts of how peer-mentoring has been applied to the area of disability, and finally, suggest ways in which disability researchers and practitioners can move forward with applying this useful innovation.

Before we begin our analysis of the current research, it is important to make explicit the fact that we acknowledge and value the diversity of ability levels in our society, and recognize the danger of speaking to the broad area of "disability" in a general way. Though its application may be limited to date, it is our belief that peer-mentoring can be applied across multiple disabilities, with necessary supports being a core part of peer-mentor programming. Every person, including each person with a disability, has strengths and challenges, and obviously each of those strengths and challenges would need to be built into a mentoring relationship in order to achieve success. With that said, since this is intended as a more general review of the research conducted in the area of peer-mentoring and disability, we will attempt to bring in research examples from across disability types. We begin by articulating two theoretical perspectives that support the use of peer-mentoring in the area of disability.

Theoretical Perspective: The Ecological Analogy of Community Psychology and the Social-Ecological Model of Disability Studies

As community psychologists who do disability-related research, we have appreciated the call put forth by Dowrick and Keys (2001) for the two fields of Community Psychology and Disability Studies to work together to improve the lives of people with disabilities. As discussed by Dowrick and Keys, these fields have developed many of the same values while evolving in isolation from one another; by pooling resources and combining energies, they can provide much to each other in terms of using research and action to better understand the needs of people with disabilities, and understand how individuals, communities, and structures in our society can best meet these needs. In an attempt to facilitate continued dialogue between these two fields, we will present key theories from each that can be brought together to complement each other and support the use of peer-mentoring among people with disabilities. These concepts include the ecological analogy from Community Psychology, and the social-ecological model of disability from Disability Studies.

Community psychology as a discipline focuses on the intersection between individuals and their environments, and values collaborative research and action as a way to work *with* people and not conduct research *on* them (Dalton, Elias, & Wandersman, 2001). Through four ecological principles, community psychology's ecological analogy offers a framework for understanding context, as well as understanding the values of the community researcher in terms of spelling out the relationship between the researcher and the community (Kelly, 1966, 1967, 1971; Trickett, Kelly, & Todd, 1972; Trickett, Kelly, & Vincent, 1985). Ecology offers support for the importance of peer-mentoring among any group of individuals, specifically through the principles of cycling of resources and interdependence. First, the cycling of resources principle calls attention to the ways in which the resources of a given setting are "defined, distributed, and developed" (Trickett et al., 1985, p. 285), and makes explicit the idea that "persons, settings and events are resources for the development of the community" (Trickett et al., 1985, p. 287). This principle can be put into action by highlighting the potential of members of social settings to serve as resources to those with similar experiences. Peer-mentoring is a form of intervention that utilizes natural resources (peers) to promote the well-being of others; peer-mentors share their experiences and knowledge with mentees in order to help mentees cope with some challenging life event. Individuals are seen as potential resources (peer-mentors), and can be encouraged to develop as such; in addition to benefiting mentees, this can also have a positive effect on peer-mentors as they are identified as positive resources and are encouraged to develop skills related to helping others.

Second, the interdependence principle of ecological theory focuses on the "interactive nature of the system and the manner in which its component parts are coupled" (Trickett et al., 1985, p. 285). Interdependence acknowledges the potential of the setting or environment to have positive effects on individuals, and reinforces the belief that individual success is directly related to appropriate supports and resources found in one's environment. This principle was demonstrated early on in the research and writings of many ecological and community psychologists, including Lindemann (1953), Klein (1987), and Sarason (Sarason, 1972, 1976; Sarason, Levine, Goldenberg, Cherlin, & Bennett, 1966), and has been exemplified since through the work done by other researchers who have documented the positive effects that settings can have on individuals' behavior (e.g., Allison et al., 1999; Campbell, 1998; Duggan, Lysack, Dijkers, & Jefi, 2002; Foster-Fishman & Keys, 1997; Roach, 2002; Schulz et al., 2000; Trickett, McConahay, Phillips, & Ginter, 1985). This work has acknowledged the opportunity that settings have to promote psychological well-being by providing much needed resources to their members (Kelly, Ryan, Altman, & Stelzner, 2000). Specific to peer-mentoring, the addition of a peer-mentor to one's life impacts one's environment in terms of providing additional support, feedback, or guidance, particularly in contexts where resources and such supports may be scarce.

Though not explicitly cited in the disability literatures, it is important to acknowledge that the principles at the foundation of ecological theory are not new to the area of disability. In fact, these principles relate directly to a theoretical perspective within the social-ecological model of disability (see Pledger, 2003; Taylor-Ritzler, 2002). As discussed by Altman (2001), definitions of disability have been put forth at many levels, including legal, administrative, clinical, and research definitions that at times contradict with one another. Altman presents a framework for understanding these definitions and their intersection. Legal and administrative definitions focus on individuals and their categorization of "disabled" or "non-disabled" in order to determine if they are eligible for certain services, benefits, or protections under United States law. Similarly, clinical definitions focus on some pathology within the individual and that individual's prognosis based on "the type of condition and the characteristics of the patient" (p. 100).

In contrast to these individually-based definitions, the social-ecological perspective locates individuals within their social and physical context (Pledger, 2003), and recognizes that there are "multiple factors involved in the relationship between health, functioning, context and the dynamics of conditions that go into the process that is ultimately labeled as disability" (Altman, 2001, p. 100). This position makes explicit that there are socially created disadvantages facing persons with disabilities, and that many physical and contextual barriers limit their community integration. Here, multiple components contribute to disability; these components include individual impairment, but this perspective moves beyond the more individually-focused models to involve environmental components as well, including inaccessible environments and discriminating attitudes. In adopting this definition of disability, we make explicit that an individual's capacity to function in society is the result of both individual ability as well as environmental factors that enable or disable his or her functioning. While we acknowledge the component of individual impairment that contributes to the broad concept of "disability," we advocate conceptualizing how modifying the environment, or increasing a mentee's social support network (by providing a peer-mentor), can positively impact functioning and promote appropriate independence while providing appropriate supports. An attention to environmental contributions to the concept of disability highlights the potential of communities to provide individuals with needed resources.

The two ecological principles presented above, cycling of resources and interdependence, logically complement the ideas presented in the social-ecological model of disability, as they emphasize both the importance of seeing setting members as resources, and the potential of the setting or social environment to have positive effects on individuals. Particular to the area of disability, where environments are often physically, socially, and psychologically inaccessible, this combined perspective highlights the potential of settings to be facilitative and nurturing. Exploring the potential power of peer-mentors is attentive to ecological theories and involves a change in the environment in at least two ways. First, peer-mentoring adds a person (the peer-mentor) to the mentee's social network, and hence, to the individual's social environment. Second, implementing peer-mentoring as an intervention demonstrates how people with disabilities can become a source of change. This social justice perspective shifts traditional conceptions of people with disabilities from passive service receivers to active advocates and resources in their communities.

Taken together, the social-ecological model of disability and the concept of ecology within community psychology offer a guiding perspective and rationale for the utility of examining and using existing resources in order to facilitate individual success in a setting. Here, we have highlighted the potential of peer-mentoring as an existing resource that has much to offer to the area of disability. In fact, we put this perspective forward as an essential strategy in facilitating the quality of life of individuals with disabilities. Ignoring influences of the social environment and focusing only on individual impairments and conceptualizations of disability unfairly burdens individuals to deal with a problem that is complexly embedded within a social context. This limited perspective also negates the potential positive influences that social environments can have in improving the life situations of people with disabilities, as well as the role people with disabilities themselves can play in creating their own supportive environments. We now turn to empirical research that has begun to illustrate the potential of peer-mentoring to create positive changes in the social environments of individuals with disabilities.

Empirical Research: Peer-Mentoring and Disability

In the process of understanding the potential role of peer-mentoring among people with disabilities, it is first important to consider the significance of social support among this population, a group who frequently deals with issues of social isolation. Whether a person is struggling with a long-term developmental disability, a psychiatric disability, or a recently-acquired physical disability, social support has been related to significant gains in terms of health (Carling, 1995), academic outcomes (Stainback & Stainback, 1990), vocational outcomes (Wehman & Moon, 1988), successful independent living (Barone, Trickett, Schmid, & Leone, 1993; Hasazi, Gordon, & Roe, 1985), as well as in the broader process of acceptance of disability and illness (Berkman, 1986; Boschen, Tonack, & Gargaro, 2003; Leach, Frank, Bouman, & Farmer, 1994; Mauss-Clum, & Ryan, 1981). For example, Kemp and Vash (1971) found that among people with spinal cord injury, high amounts of social support minimized functional limitations: specifically, people with quadriplegia who experienced high levels of social support were rated by investigators as being just as "productive" as people with paraplegia.

Building on research that suggests that social support is helpful to people with disabilities, peer-mentoring is a unique type of social support (Hibbard et al., 2002; Sherman et al., 2003) that offers assistance from someone who has successfully faced and negotiated the same situation (Thoits, 1986; 1995, as seen in Sherman et al., 2003). The very act of peer-mentoring offers an alternative to traditional ways of viewing disability as a deficit or a problem in need of treatment: peer-mentoring demonstrates that this marginalized group (a group often seen as "helpless") is indeed an important resource. Due to societal discrimination, disability can often be an isolating and stigmatizing social status (Odom, McConnel & McEvoy, 1992). The particular availability of a peer mentor, however, can challenge social stigma by affirming the strengths and capabilities of individuals with disabilities (including both mentors and mentees). Furthermore, peer mentoring can be an empowering experience for those who have faced discrimination and marginalization (Block, Balcazar and Keys, 2002). The mentoring relationship can provide an example to mentees as to how they can live their lives to the fullest (e.g., become as independent as possible and, as desired, pursue vocational or educational goals). Such a relationship can provide a positive and critical alternative way of looking at the world. For these reasons, peer mentoring has emerged as a central guiding force in many disability-related organizations and services, including the Independent Living movement, where peer-delivered services are central to the philosophy of care (Mathews, Mathews, & Pittman, 1985).

Peer-mentoring has also emerged as a result of key studies investigating what has helped individuals with disabilities succeed (Gulam & Triska, 1998; Hammel, 1999). For example, Hammel worked with participants with traumatic spinal cord injuries to build a conceptual framework for explaining how roles change after injury. Her participants discussed the importance of peer-mentors in each of their new and returning roles, and how they wished more opportunities for peer-mentoring had been made available. They also specifically talked about how "dump and gripe" support groups were not as helpful as experiences shared with peer-mentors who had actually gotten out and accomplished things: "We should get people back who have succeeded in whatever they have chosen in a career – the worker role-model is important" (Hammel, p. 52). Peer-mentors were thought to help individuals with new disabilities begin to formulate how to move on and create new life roles after acquiring their disability.

Two retrospective studies, both in the area of physical disability, specifically investigated the effects of peer-mentoring on adjustment to disability. First, Sable, Craig, and Lee (2000) conducted a single case study where they found positive results for a therapeutic recreation intervention called PATH (Promoting Access, Transition and Health), which included peer-mentoring as a key component. The case report summarized the experiences of a 22-year old rural participant with a recent T-12 complete spinal cord injury as he progressed through the PATH intervention. The case report found positive results for a peer-mentor, whether that person was formally assigned or more informally located within the participant's natural environment, to provide "real-life, practical advice" for coping with spinal cord injury (Sable et al., 354). The researchers also discussed the importance of their intervention being flexible and responsive to the needs of participants, as in some cases when participants felt that peer-mentor support was already found within their existing networks, formal peer-mentors were not assigned.

Second, Sherman et al. (2003) surveyed individuals with spinal cord injury to compare peer-mentoring experiences and the presence of a live-in partner on individuals' adjustment after SCI. Sixty-two participants completed a survey by mail; participants were an average age of 30.3 years (range, 10 to 85 years), and had been injured for an average of 11.65 years (range, 0.33 to 35 years). Forty-eight percent of participants reported currently living with a partner, and 53% reported having had a peer-mentor. Results indicated that past peer-mentoring experiences were associated with higher occupational activity and life satisfaction, whereas having a live-in partner was associated with greater mobility and economic self-sufficiency. Sherman et al. concluded that these two sources of support were both important in their own right, and that peer-mentoring positively compliments the benefits of having a live-in partner. Their results argue for more interventions that use peer-mentor components as this specific type of support can add unique positive benefits above and beyond existing traditional support networks.

Though this line of research is still in its formative stage, and despite the fact that most of the studies discussed above were retrospective in nature and focused only on individuals with physical disability, this research has begun to demonstrate the need for peer-mentoring in the context of all disability types. Specifically, peer-mentoring may have the potential to positively influence the establishment of life roles after the new acquisition of a disability, and in particular, facilitate occupational activity and higher life satisfaction. Next we will examine the limited literature that has begun to apply a peer-mentoring model among individuals with disabilities.

Intervention Research: Applying Peer-Mentoring to Disability

Historically, peer-based interventions have been integral to the core practices among many Centers for Independent Living (CILs). These agencies provide assistance and support to adults with disabilities to live independently in the community (Hayes & Hernandez, in press; Mathews et al., 1985). Here, peers play a significant role as service providers, advocates and role models to consumers of CILs. Specifically, Mathews et al. surveyed disability advocacy groups, rehabilitation programs, members of the National Coalition of Independent Living Programs, and community-based independent living centers, and found that over half (59%) of these organizations offered peer counseling services. As an explanation for the prevalence of peer-approaches, Mathews et al. discussed that peer-interventions remain important because they encourage consumer activism, a core value of CIL's. The perspective that "peers know best" remains in opposition to traditional means of service delivery by highly-trained professionals or "experts." The historic importance of peer-interventions in disability practice is yet another reason to be surprised for the relative lack of peer-mentor and disability research interventions.

Before turning to the specific research on peer-mentoring and disability, it is important to note that there has been some intervention work done in the area of general (i.e., not peer) mentoring and disability. As one example, Lee et al. (1997) examined how mentoring could facilitate positive employment experiences among individuals with severe disabilities. They compared "traditional" job coaching with a situation in which co-workers served as mentors and trained individuals with disabilities as new employees. Lee et al. found that the latter group demonstrated significantly more initiated interactions towards non-disabled co-workers, and also had significantly more reciprocal interactions with non-disabled co-workers than employees who had a more traditional job coach. McDonald et al. (in press) reviewed the characteristics of mentoring studies that seemed to be most effective, and concluded that the concept of mentoring holds much potential for positively influencing a number of outcomes among youth with disabilities.

Further, though not specifically peer-mentor related, peer-delivered interventions have also been incorporated into practices among individuals with disabilities. For example, contact with peers has been demonstrated as important in the social interactions of children with language delays (Goldstein & Wickstrom, 1986) and children with autism (Odom & Strain, 1984, 1986; Ragland et al., 1978). Peer-tutoring has also been found helpful in terms of increasing social acceptance of students with cognitive disabilities (Osguthorpe et al., 1985). Osguthorpe et al. trained fourth through sixth grade students with mental retardation to teach sign language to students without disabilities in an attempt to increase the former students' interactions with their peers. Results indicated that the students with disabilities' interactions with non-disabled students increased significantly, and parents of tutors reported that they demonstrated additional social interactions at home as well. As another positive effect, tutored students reported learning more about their classmates with mental retardation.

The area of general mentoring practice and prior work related to peer interventions and individuals with disabilities have both begun to indicate the potential of this innovation in the area of disability, and provide an empirical basis for further studies on peer-mentoring among this population. We now turn to the intervention research that has been conducted in the specific area of peer-mentoring and disability. These studies can provide information on where peer-mentoring is applicable and how it can best be incorporated among individuals with disabilities. In all of these studies, peer-mentoring was used to help facilitate "success" (although the specific area varied) among individuals with disabilities. As mentioned above, a definition of a peer-mentor study in this context indicates that mentors had a similar disability to mentees, and that because of this disability experience they were paired together so that the mentor could offer support to his or her mentee. Six such studies are presented here, one occurs in a job-training setting, two in a hospital setting, and three in a community setting. It is important to note that one artifact of the fact that this is a new body of literature is that not all articles reviewed focus on the same aspects: some attend to process, others to outcomes. Therefore we will present as much information as possible in the review below; however, as a result of the lack of consistency in the literature this review may seem uneven at times.

Employment Setting

Cullen and Barlow (1998) examined mentoring within an employment-training program for young adults (ages 16-46) with arthritis. Individuals were matched with volunteer mentors who also had the same disability. Contact between the two was often by telephone due to the geographic distance between most mentor and mentee pairs. Cullen and Barlow took a qualitative evaluation approach and administered questionnaires, conducted telephone interviews, and held group feedback sessions among a sample of 36 trainees. Results indicated that mentors were a key source of support, help, advice, and guidance related to employment-readiness. Cullen and Barlow also identified many program limitations, including the fact that mentees at times felt bad about bothering mentors, as they knew they faced similar (health-related) problems. Other program limitations included findings that each mentor worked with too many mentees, the program duration was too short, and having mentor-mentee contacts occur primarily over the phone made it hard to build personal relationships.

Cullen and Barlow (1998) acknowledged the benefits of mentoring but also identified critical limitations related to adding too many roles or responsibilities into the mentor role, and highlighted additional intervention resources (i.e., an additional support person) that could be used to counteract these limitations. A significant limitation of this study however involved the fact that results were not discussed extensively, nor were the analysis strategies specified. The authors highlighted the limited nature of presentation of results as related to the confidential nature of mentor-mentee relationships, and discussed the difficulty of conducting this kind of evaluation work.

Hospital Setting

Two studies highlighted hospital-based programs. Vines (2000) presented a hospital-based peer-mentor intervention for individuals with spinal cord injury. She discussed the need for such programs, especially in a context where lengths of stay continued to shrink for patients with new injuries: patients were in need of additional community reentry supports once they left the hospital environment. Her primarily descriptive article traced the program since its inception, and she discussed program development, including how peers were selected, trained, and matched with new patients. Vines reported that over the three years of the program, 30 mentors were trained and were assigned to see over 150 patients with new spinal cord injuries. Though program outcomes were not presented in detail, Vines did say that follow-up interviews with patients after their hospital discharge reflected a "positive response" (p. 187).

Similarly, Hernandez et al. (2001) discussed a hospital-based peer-mentor intervention for a particular sub-group of people with spinal cord injury, those with violently-acquired injuries. The rationale for the project was based upon the specific needs of those with violently-acquired injuries, as they faced not only a new disability but the social discrimination that comes along with multiple minority statuses. Further, the importance of the hospital as a setting was highlighted because, for this population in particular, the hospital was oftentimes one of the only accessible, safe, supportive settings in their lives (Balcazar, Hayes, Engstrom, & Keys, under review). Hernandez et al. highlighted their program development, and went into more detail about their conceptual framework, participatory action research (PAR). They also discussed the critical need for mentor supervision and how support for mentors was built into the program throughout. Intending to implement the program at four hospitals, they detailed their pilot implementation with the first hospital and discussed plans for the other three sites. Though also a descriptive study, Hernandez et al. did include some preliminary findings from qualitative interviews that had been conducted with mentees. They reported positive preliminary results, as mentees reported positive relationships with their mentors, and reported gaining both emotional support and instrumental support, in that their questions regarding medical issues, sexuality, and local social service agencies were being answered. In addition, mentees had already attained some of their goals, which included things like obtaining hand controls to drive independently, enrolling in school to complete a degree, and working.

Across these two hospital-based programs, a key theme emphasized the importance of mentors serving as a bridge between the hospital and patients, thus having positive impacts on mentees' continued health maintenance. It is important to state that while these two programs self-defined themselves as hospital-based, in each, the hospital served primarily as the point of entry, and mentors followed individuals into the community after their hospital discharge. This long-term relationship seemed to be key to program effectiveness. Because of the descriptive nature of these studies, a significant limitation included the lack of definitive evaluation results. While both studies provided preliminary support for peer-mentoring in the area of disability, and also discussed key supports needed to ensure program success, further evaluation is needed to understand the full potential of this approach.

Community Setting

Three studies focused on community-based programs. Hibbard et al. (2002) presented a community-based peer-support program for individuals and their family members following traumatic brain injury (TBI). Unlike some of the other papers discussed, Hibbard et al. presented information on program development and implementation, but also highlighted evaluation results with both quantitative and qualitative components. Twenty partners (mentees) participated in the quantitative interview and seven participated in the qualitative interview; participants included both individuals with TBI and family members. In general, both groups saw the greatest program impact as being that related to an increase in knowledge about TBI, and in helping individuals cope with the consequences of TBI. Most participants from both groups also reported that the program increased their quality of life, their general outlook, and their ability to cope with sadness and depression. Satisfaction with the program was also high, though was higher in reports from individuals with TBI than for family members. Family members were more conservative in their ratings, and they discussed how they would have liked longer relationships with their peer-mentors, a higher frequency of contacts, and the ability to initiate contacts with their peer-mentors rather than just waiting to be contacted. This study provides preliminary support for peer-mentoring among individuals with newly acquired TBI and their families, but also provides a critical assessment of what mentors should realistically be expected to do, what supports are necessary for their success, and what things may fall beyond the boundaries of a peer-mentoring study.

Powers et al. (1995) tested the impact of mentoring by role models on the self-efficacy, disability-related self-efficacy, community-based self-confidence, and community-based knowledge of 10 participating adolescents with severe physical challenges. While this study was not explicitly identified as a peer-mentor study, it was chosen for inclusion here because the mentors were adults with similar disabilities. The investigators also looked at the impact of mentoring on parents' perceptions of their children's abilities. This was a community-based program but youth were chosen from the school district. Results indicated that youth with mentors had significantly higher levels of disability-related self-efficacy, community-based knowledge, and self-confidence than youth in the control group. Parents of mentored youth also perceived their children to be significantly more competent and to possess significantly more community-based knowledge than the other parents.

Finally, Whittemore et al. (2000) conducted a qualitative investigation as part of a larger study in order to investigate the effects of a peer-mentor study with individuals with myocardial infarction on the peer-mentors themselves. While a little different in focus in that the purpose of this research was to examine the program experience from the peer-mentor point of view, this study is important to include for several reasons. First, this program involved peer advisors to assist people with health impairments. Second, this study provides information as to the nature of the peer-mentor – mentee relationships. Specifically, the ten peer advisors discussed two main characteristics of their relationships with elders: helping, which included giving advice, helping with problem solving, being advocates, and alleviating fears; and mutual sharing, which both helped peers establish rapport and served as a mechanism by which help was given. Peer advisors specifically mentioned their role in mentees' continued health, as they were able to route mentees to the hospital at the first sign of a medical complication. Finally, the study takes an important step by examining how this type of relationship can be helpful for the peers as well as the mentees. They found that peers benefited in three main (unexpected) ways: first, they felt good about helping others, they felt that they were giving back or contributing in return for much of the support they felt they had in their own lives; second, they benefited by being able to talk about their own illness with someone else; and third, they benefited by becoming more aware of their own health behaviors and what they needed to do to stay healthy.

The studies conducted in community settings continue to provide preliminary support for the effectiveness of peer-mentoring in the context of disability. These studies included more evaluation results than those provided in the first two sections, as they provided both quantitative data (though at times with small sample sizes), as well as rich qualitative data that described both the process and outcomes of peer-mentor relationships. Importantly, Hibbard et al. (2002) continued to highlight limitations of peer-mentoring in their study, and pointed out critical steps and boundaries to put in place around peer-mentor relationships in order to facilitate their success. Both Hibbard et al. and Powers et al. (1995) included multiple data sources, and provided a snapshot of peer-mentor effects from both the perspective of mentees and their family members. Finally, Whittemore et al. (2000) included information on how the process was benefiting peer-mentors as well as mentees, an oftentimes overlooked consequence of peer-mentor interventions.

Discussion

Taken together, this groundbreaking work offers much to our understanding of how peer-mentoring can be applied to disability. Specific to the intervention research presented above, these six studies demonstrate preliminary support for the benefits of peer-mentoring in the context of disability. In particular, peer-mentoring has the potential to provide advice and support in terms of helping individuals with long-term disabilities develop "employment potential" (Cullen & Barlow, 1998, p. 390) and disability-related self-efficacy and self-confidence (Powers et al., 1995). Peer-mentoring may also assist individuals with new disabilities in their post-injury community reintegration and continued health management (Hernandez et al., 2001; Hibbard et al., 2002; Vines, 2000; Whittemore et al., 2000). Further, these studies demonstrate that peer-mentoring can be used across a number of settings, including employment training scenarios, hospitals, and the general community.

These intervention studies also bridge practice and the theoretical frameworks presented above. Specifically, two of the studies discussed highlighted the importance of program development, and involving people with disabilities in the development and shaping of the intervention itself (Hernandez et al., 2001; Hibbard et al., 2002). Both of these studies specifically mentioned the principles of Participatory Action Research (PAR) (Balcazar, Keys, Kaplan, & Suarez-Balcazar, 1998; Park, 1993; Whyte, 1991), and how this process helped the needs of individuals with disabilities become a central driving force behind the program at all stages. This is a core concept in the disability rights movement and here is highlighted as important in related programming as well.

The principles of PAR tie strongly into the theoretical perspectives discussed above, including the principles of cycling of resources and interdependence in Community Psychology, and the social-ecological model of Disability Studies. PAR acknowledges and builds on setting members as resources by involving them as integral participants in the action-research process. Participants are not involved in a periphery or token way; rather, they guide the research action agenda and participate in each critical step as active members. Further, this active participant role allows for a fuller examination of participants' life contexts; participants bring their social and physical environments to the table with them, and these environments become critical pieces of the action research process and agenda.

Peer-mentoring is not without its limitations, however, many of which the intervention researchers above carefully considered. Several studies (Cullen & Barlow, 1998; Hernandez et al., 2001; Hibbard et al., 2002; Powers et al., 1995; Whittemore et al., 2000) discussed how peer-mentors need to be supported throughout their relationships with their mentees, both in order to avoid feeling overwhelmed, and in order to make sure mentees are getting appropriate services. Cullen and Barlow (1998) and Hibbard et al. (2002) provided the most explicit discussion of shortcomings within their programs, as they discussed how some mentees reported that the program wasn't long enough to meet their needs, that they could have used more face-to-face contact versus only phone contact, and that in general participants and family members seemed to need more clarification up-front regarding what the program could do for them. As discussed by several of the authors above, re-visiting peer-mentor training models and also making program expectations clear among both mentors and mentees can help in these efforts. We applaud these authors for taking the time to investigate and share their program challenges as well as successes. It is however critical to not see these limitations as a sign of failure of peer-mentoring, but instead to acknowledge the conditions under which mentoring can be more successful. Necessary supports are, as Hibbard et al. (2002) discussed, "a small price to pay for the potential benefits" that programs like this can offer (p. 130).

There is also a need in this work to expand to other types of disabilities. With the exception of the group of individuals with TBI addressed by Hibbard et al. (2002), most of the above studies focus solely on individuals with physical disability and health impairments. There are obviously a number of other disabilities that can provide the context for peer-interventions, including but not limited to individuals with learning, cognitive, and psychiatric disabilities. One reason for the lack of application of peer-mentoring among these disability groups may be a perception that those with cognitive disabilities cannot perform the functions of a mentor. Perhaps the model presented by Hibbard et al. (2002), where both individuals with TBI and family members were involved, offers an example of how these types of programs could be built. In some cases, agency staff can also serve as supports and complement the role of peer-mentors. Future work is vital in these areas as individuals with other types of disabilities and their family members have the potential to benefit from peer support.

In addition, there is much room for continued application of peer-models in the area of health and disability. Four of the six studies discuss the connection between peer-mentoring and health, by explicitly including some health indicator as an outcome or program goal. Specifically, Vines (2000) and Hernandez et al. (2001) discussed how mentors can serve as a bridge between the hospital and patients with new spinal cord injury. Hibbard et al. (2002) talked about mentors helping to increase participants' knowledge about TBI, and helping mentees deal with their mental health issues, particularly in coping with sadness and depression. Finally, Whittemore et al. (2000) discussed specific examples where peer advisors routed their mentees to the hospital at the first signs of a medical complication. Peer mentor models have been demonstrated as successful in past health-related studies among individuals without disabilities (e.g., Grummer-Strawn et al., 1997; Hailey et al., 1992; Ozer et al., 1997). Peer-mentors as an intervention innovation may be particularly key as prior research has found that among individuals with disabilities, other health-related problems are not as well attended to by medical professionals (Blondis, Roizen, Snow, & Accardo, 1993; Santosh & Baird, 1999). Attending to these complications is critical, as research has found that health maintenance and/or pain management are predictive of individuals' functional ability, community integration, and quality of life (Boschen et al., 2003).

There are also implications for future research based on this review. First, it is important to point out the methodological limitations related to the intervention studies above. As mentioned, partly due to the young nature of this body of literature, much of the published work is primarily descriptive in nature. Though some of the work above (i.e., Powers et al., 1995; Hibbard et al., 2002) presented solid evaluation methodology and results that provided both support for and cautions regarding the application of peer-mentoring, this was not the norm. Most of the studies instead talked more briefly about the results of their preliminary evaluation efforts, and did not provide detailed information as to the research design or data analysis (Cullen & Barlow, 1998; Hernandez et al., 2001; Vines, 2000). While program description is critical to understanding how peer-mentoring can be applied to this new context, future work should continue to expand upon evaluation components as well.

In general, future research in this area must continue to gather information regarding how peer-mentoring can be applied across various disabilities and life contexts. While it is difficult to measure and evaluate peer-mentoring because of the individualized nature of each relationship, options include continuing to borrow flexible methodologies from our colleagues in such fields as community psychology and anthropology (e.g., Hibbard et al., 2002). Community-based methodologies may provide more insight into how relationships evolve, what supports mentors need, and how mentees can maximize program benefits.

Program developers and researchers can also continue to be creative in applying more traditional methodologies to understand program outcomes and effects. Specifically, future research should continue to examine the role of the peer-mentor in the socialization of people with disabilities, the effects of expanding social support through the addition of a peer-mentor, how peer-mentors may be used successfully to promote a vision for appropriate independent living, how peer-mentors may be successful in working with parents, caregivers and families to support and promote self-determination among individuals with disabilities, and what other intervention components may be necessary to help introduce someone to living with a disability. Taken together, a more complete understanding of these issues can help build our knowledge around peer-mentoring and disability.

In conclusion, research to date highlights the potential application of peer-mentoring in the area of disability. The work above provides an important first-step in terms of helping begin to understand how to build peer-mentor programs for people with disabilities, including the importance of involving people with disabilities in the process, what mentor- and mentee-related supports are important in programming, and what outcomes can potentially be impacted. Further, peer-mentoring is a way of affirming that the presence of a disability does not mean that the individual's capacity to serve and be helpful to others has been diminished. Future work should continue to investigate the impact and role of peer-mentoring as an important source of social support that can complement the support provided by health care providers, educators, family members, and friends.

Acknowledgements

The authors appreciate the thoughtful comments on earlier drafts provided by our colleagues Katie McDonald and Bianca Wilson. We would also like to thank Thilo Kroll for his helpful guidance, support, and generosity throughout this process. Finally, we would like to thank the peer-mentors and mentees with whom we have worked over the past several years; it is because of their amazing spirit and willingness to share with us that we have been able to begin understanding the strength and potential application of peer-mentor approaches.

References

Allison, K. W., Crawford, I., Leone, P. E., Trickett, E., Perez-Febles, A., Burton, L. M., & LeBlanc, R. (1999). Adolescent substance use: Preliminary examinations of school and neighborhood context. *American Journal of Community Psychology, 27*(2), 111-141.

Altman, B. (2001). Disability definitions, models, classification schemes, and applications. In G. L. Albrecht, K. D. Seelman, & M. Bury (Eds.), *Handbook of Disability Studies* (pp. 97-122). Thousand Oaks, CA: Sage.

Balcazar, F. E., Hayes, E., Engstrom, M., & Keys, C. B. (under review). Peer-mentors as agents of change: A case study of participatory action research. *American Journal of Community Psychology.*

Balcazar, F. E., Keys, C. B., Kaplan, D. L., & Suarez-Balcazar, Y. (1998). Participatory action research and people with disabilities: Principles and challenges. *Canadian Journal of Rehabilitation, 12,* 105-112.

Barone, C., Trickett, E. J., Schmid, K. D., & Leone, P. E. (1993). Transition tasks and resources: An ecological approach to life after high school. *Prevention in Human Services, 10,* 179-204.

Berkman, L. F. (1986). Social networks, support, and health: Taking the next step forward. *American Journal of Epidemiology, 123*(4), 559-562.

Block, P., Balcazar, F. E., & Keys, C. B. (2002). Race, poverty and disability: Three strikes and you are out! Or are you? *Social Policy, 33*(1), 34-38.

Blondis, T. A., Roizen, N. J., Snow, J. H., & Accardo, P. J. (1993). Developmental disabilities: A continuum. *Clinical Pediatrics, 32*(8), 492-498.

Boschen, K. A., Tonack, M. & Gargaro, J. (2003). Long-term adjustment and community reintegration following spinal cord injury. *International Journal of Rehabilitation Research, 26*(3), 157-164.

Campbell, R. (1998). The community response to rape: Victim's experiences with thelegal, medical, and mental health systems. *American Journal of Community Psychology, 26*, 355-379.

Campbell-Whatley, G. (2001). Mentoring students with mild disabilities: The 'nuts and bolts' of program development. *Intervention in the School & Clinic, 36*, 211-216.

Campbell-Whatley, G., & Algozzine, B. (1997). Using mentoring to improve academic programming for African American male youths with mild disabilities. *School Counselor, 44*, 362-367.

Carling, P. J. (1995). *Return to Community: Building support systems for people with psychiatric disabilities.* New York: The Guilford Press

Cullen, L. & Barlow, J. (1998). Mentoring in the context of a training program for young unemployed adults with physical disabilities. *International Journal of Rehabilitation Research, 21*, 389-391.

Dalton, J. H., Elias, M. J., & Wandersman, A. (2001). *Community Psychology.* Belmont, CA: Wadsworth.

Dowrick, P. W., & Keys, C. B. (2001). Community psychology and disability studies. *Journal of Prevention & Intervention in the Community, 21*(2), 1-14.

DuBois, D., Holloway, B., Valentine, J. & Cooper, H. (2002). Effectiveness of mentoring programs for youth: A meta-analytic review. *American Journal of Community Psychology, 30*, 157-197.

Duggan, C. H., Lysack, C., Dijkers, M., & Jeji, T. (2002). Daily life in a nursing home: Impact on quality of life after spinal cord injury. *Topics in Spinal Cord Injury Rehabilitation, 7*(3), 112-131.

Ensher, E. A., Thomas, C., Murphy, S. E. (2001). Comparison of traditional, step-ahead, and peer mentoring on proteges' support, satisfaction, and perceptions of career success: A social exchange perspective. *Journal of Business and Psychology, 15*(3), 419-438.

Fine, L. M., & Pullins, E. B. (1998). Peer mentoring in the industrial sales force: An exploratory investigation of men and women in developmental relationships. *Journal of Personal Selling & Sales Management, 18*(4), 89-103.

Foster-Fishman, P. G., & Keys, C. B. (1997). The person/environment dynamics of employee empowerment: An organizational culture analysis. *American Journal of Community Psychology, 25*(3), 345-369.

Goldstein, H. & Wickstrom, S. (1986). Peer intervention Effects on communicative interactions among handicapped and nonhandicapped preschoolers. *Journal of Applied Behavioral Analysis, 19*, 209-214.

Grummer-Strawn, L. M., Rice, S. P., Dugas, K., Clark, L. D., & Benton-Davis, S. (1997). An evaluation of breastfeeding promotion through peer counseling in Mississippi WIC clinics. *Maternal and Child Health Journal, 1,* 35-42.

Gulam, W. & Triska, J. (1998). Students with special needs: a paradigm for the transition from school to college in the UK. *Journal of Postsecondary Education & Disability, 13*, 29-36.

Hailey, B. J., Lalor, K. M., Byrne, H. A., & Starling, L. M. (1992). The effects of self-reinforcement and peer-reinforcement on the practice of breast self-examination. *Health Education Research, 7,* 165-174.

Hammel, J. (1999). The life rope: A transactional approach to exploring worker and life role development. *Work, 12,* 47-60.

Hasazi, S. B., Gordon, L. R., & Roe, C. A. (1985). Factors associated with the employment status of handicapped youth exiting high school from 1979 to 1983. *Exceptional Children, 51,* 455-469.

Hayes, E. & Hernandez, B. (in press). Peer Support. In G. Albrecht (Ed.), *The Encyclopedia of Disability*. Newbury Park, CA: Sage Publications.

Hernandez, B., Hayes, E., Balcazar, F., & Keys, C. (2001). Responding to the needs of the underserved: A peer-mentor approach. *Psychosocial Process, 14*(3), 142-149.

Hibbard, M. R., Cantor, J., Charatz, H., Rosenthal, R., Ashman, T., Gundersen, N., Ireland-Knight, L., Gordon, W., Avner, J., & Gartner, A. (2002). Peer support in the community: Initial findings of a mentoring program for individuals with traumatic brain injury and their families. *Journal of Head Trauma Rehabilitation, 17*(2), 112-131.

Jacobi, M. (1991). Mentoring and undergraduate academic success: A literature review. *Review of Educational Research, 61*(4), 505-532.

Kelly, J. G. (1966). Ecological constraints on mental health services. *American Psychologist, 21,* 535-539.

Kelly, J. G. (1967). Naturalistic observations and theory confirmation: An example. *Human Development, 10,* 212-222.

Kelly, J. G. (1971). Qualities for the community psychologist. *American Psychologist, 26,* 897-903.

Kelly, J. G., Ryan, A. M., Altman, B. E., & Stelzner, S. P. (2000). Understanding and changing social systems: An ecological view. In J. Rappaport & E. Seidman (Eds.), *The handbook of community psychology.* New York City: Plenum.

Kemp, B. J., & Vash, C. L. (1971). Productivity after injury in a sample of spinal cord injured persons: A pilot study. *Journal of Chronic Disabilities, 24,* 259-275

Klein, D. C. (1987). The context and times at Swampscott: My story. *American Journal of Community Psychology, 15,* 531-538.

Leach, L. R., Frank, R. G., Bouman, D. E., & Farmer, J. (1994). Family functioning, social support and depression after traumatic brain injury. *Brain Injury, 8,* 599-606.

Lee, M., Storey, K., Andersen, J., Goetz, L. & Zivolich, S. (1997). The effect of mentoring versus job coach instruction on integration on supported employment settings. *Journal of the Association for Persons with Severe Handicaps*, *22*, 151-158.

Levinson, D. J., Carrow, C. N., Klein, E. B., Levinson, M. H., & McKee, B. (1978). *The seasons of a man's life.* New York: Ballentine.

Lindemann, E. (1953). The Wellesley project for the study of certain problems in community mental health. In, *Interrelations between the social environment and psychiatric disorders* (pp. 167-185). New York: Milbank Memorial Fund.

Mathews, R. M., Mathews, S. A., & Pittman, J. L. (1985). Peer counseling: Consumer involvement in independent living programs. *Rehabilitation Counseling Bulletin, 28,* 161-166.

Mauss-Clum, N., & Ryan, M. (1981). Brain injury and the family. *Journal of Neurosurgery Nursing, 13,* 165-169.

McDonald, K.E., Balcazar, F. & Keys, C.B. (in press) Youth with disabilities. In. D. DuBois & M. Karcher (Eds.), *Handbook of Youth Mentoring.* SAGE Publications.

Microsoft Encarta. (1999). *Encarta World English Dictionary.* New York: St. Martin's Press.

Odom, S. L., McConnel, S. R., & McEvoy, M.A. (1992). *Social competence of young children with disabilities: Issues and strategies for intervention.* Baltimore: Paul Brookes Publishing Co.

Odom, S. & Strain, P. (1986). A comparison of peer-initiation and teacher-antecedent interventions for promoting reciprocal social interactions of autistic preschoolers. *Journal of Applied Behavioral Analysis, 19*, 59-71.

Odom, S. & Strain, P. (1984). Peer-mediated approaches to promoting children's social interaction: A review. *American Journal of Orthopsychiatry, 54*(4), 544-557.

Osguthorpe, R., Eiserman, W. & Shisler, L. (1985). Increasing social acceptance: Mentally retarded students tutoring regular class peers. *Education and Training of the Mentally Retarded, 20*, 235-240.

Ozer, E. J., Weinstein, R. S., Maslach, C., & Seigel, D. (1997). Adolescence AIDS prevention in context: The impact of peer educator qualities and classroom environment on intervention efficacy. *The American Journal of Community Psychology, 25,* 289-323.

Park, P. (1993). What is participatory research? A theoretical and methodological perspective. In P. Park, M. Brydon-Miller, B. Hall, & T. Jackson (Eds.), *Voices of change: Participatory research in the United States and Canada* (pp. 1-19). Westport, CT: Bergin & Garvey.

Pledger, C. (2003). Discourse on disability and rehabilitation issues: Opportunities for psychology. *American Psychologist, 58,* 279-284.

Powers, Sowers & Stevens (1995). An exploratory, randomized study of the impact of mentoring in the self-efficacy and community-based knowledge of adolescents with severe physical challenges. *Journal of Rehabilitation, 61,* 33-41.

Ragland, E. U., Kerr, M. M., & Strain, P. S. (1978). Behavior of withdrawn autistic children: Effects of peer social initiations. *Behavior Modification, 2*(4), 565-578.

Rhodes, J. (1994). Older and wiser: Mentoring relationships in childhood and adolescence. *The Journal of Primary Prevention, 14*, 187-196.

Roach, M. J. (2002). Community social structure as an indicator of social integration and its effect on quality of life for persons with a spinal cord injury. *Topics in Spinal Cord Injury Rehabilitation, 7*(3), 101-111.

Sable, J., Craig, P., & Lee, D. (2000). Promoting health and wellness: A research-based case report. *Therapeutic Recreation Journal, 34*(3), 348-361.

Santosh, P. J., & Baird, G. (1999). Psychopharmacotherapy in children and adults with intellectual disability. *Lancet, 354*(9174), 233-242.

Sarason, S. B. (1972). *The creation of settings and the future societies.* San Fransisco: Jossey-Bass.

Sarason, S. B. (1976). Community psychology, networks, and Mr. Everyman. *American Psychologist, 31*(5), 317-328.

Sarason, S. B., Levine, M., Goldenberg, I., Cherlin, D. L., & Bennett, E. M. (1966). *Psychology in community settings: Clinical, educational, vocational, social aspects.* New York: Wiley.

Schulz, A., Williams, D., Israel, B., Becker, A., Parker, E., James, S. A., Jackson, J. (2000). Unfair treatment, neighborhood effects, and mental health in the Detroit metropolitan area. *Journal of Health & Social Behavior, 41*(3), 314-332.

Sherman, J. E., DeVinney, D. J., & Sperling, K. B. (2004). Social support and adjustment after spinal cord injury: Influences of past peer-mentoring experiences and current live-in partner. *Rehabilitation Psychology, 49*(2), 140-149.

Stainback, W. & Stainback, S. (1990). *Support networks for inclusive schooling: Interdependent integrated education.* Baltimore: Paul Brookes Publishing Co.

Taylor-Ritzler, T. (2002). *Conceptual Approaches in the Assessment of Parenting with Intellectual Disability*. Unpublished manuscript, University of Illinois at Chicago.

Thoits, P. A. (1986). Social support as coping assistance. *Journal of Consulting and Clinical Psychology, 54*(4), 416-423.

Thoits, P. A. (1995). Stress, coping, and social support processes: Where are we? What next? *Journal of Health and Social Behavior, Spec No,* 53-79.

Thoits, P. A., Hohmann, A. A., Harvey, M. R., & Fletcher, B. (2000). Similar-other support for men undergoing coronary artery bypass surgery. *Health Psychology, 19*(3), 264-273.

Topping, K. (1996). Reaching where adults cannot: Peer education and peer counselling. *Educational Psychology in Practice, 11*(4), 23-29.

Trickett, E.J., Kelly, J.G., & Todd, D. (1972). The social environment of the high school: guidelines for individual change and organizational development. In S. Golann & C. Eisdorfer (Eds.), *Handbook of community mental health* (pp. 361-390). New York: Appleton -Century -Crofts.

Trickett, E. J., Kelly, J. G., & Vincent, T. A. (1985). The spirit of ecological inquirty in community research. In E. C. Susskind & D. C. Klein (Eds.), *Community research: Methods, paradigms, and applications.* New York: Praeger.

Trickett, E. J., McConahay, J. B., Phillips, D., & Ginter, M. A. (1985). Natural experiments and the educational context: The environment and effects of an alternative inner-city public school on adolescents. *American Journal of Community Psychology, 13*(6), 617-643.

Vines, C. L. (2000). Promoting community reentry: The TIRR PEERS program. *Psychosocial Process, 13*(4), 185-187.

Wehman, P. & Moon, M. S. (1988). *Vocational rehabilitation and supported employment.* Baltimore: Paul Brookes Publishing Co.

Whittemore, R., Rankin, S. H., Callahan, C. D., Leder, M. C., Carroll, D. L. (2000). The peer advisor experience: Providing social support. *Qualitative Health Research, 10*(2), 260-276.

Whyte, W. F. (1991). *Participatory action research.* Newbury Park, CA: Sage.

In: Focus on Disability: Trends in Research and Application ISBN: 978-1-60021-792-0
Editor: Thilo Kroll, pp. 109-121 © 2008 Nova Science Publishers, Inc.

Chapter VII

THE PREVALENCE OF COMPLEMENTARY AND ALTERNATIVE MEDICINE PRACTITIONER USE BY PEOPLE WITH PHYSICAL DISABILITIES

Matthew J. Carlson[1,2,*] and Gloria Krahn[2]
[1]Portland State University, USA;
[2]Oregon Health & Science University, USA.

ABSTRACT

Objectives: Estimate the annual prevalence and determine symptoms and reasons for CAM practitioner use among insured adults with physical disabilities.

Sample: 830 individuals randomly selected from disability organizations (51%), a purposive sample from disability publications, websites, and provider practices (40%), and a snowball sample (9%).

Data: Panel survey data collected in 2000 and 2001.

Methods: Cross-sectional, bivariate analysis of the 2001 survey.

Results: CAM practitioners were used by 19% of the sample. CAM use was more prevalent among women than men (24% vs. 10%), in the Western US (30%) compared to the Midwest (20%) Northeast (14%), and South (10%) and among prior users (62%) compared to non-users (8%). Common symptoms treated were pain (80%), decreased functioning (43%), and lack of energy (24%). Common reasons for using CAM practitioners included lifestyle choice (67%) and because they are more effective (44%).

Conclusions: People with physical disabilities use CAM modalities at similar or higher rates than the general population, for similar symptoms, and for reasons similar to the general population.

* Correspondence concerning this article should be addressed to: Matthew J. Carlson, Ph.D., Dept. of Sociology, PO Box 751, Portland OR, 97207, Phone (503) 725-9554, Fax (503) 725-3957, carlsonm@pdx.edu.

The dramatic growth of Complementary and Alternative Medicine (CAM) use in the United States over the past several decades has spurred interest among health care providers and researchers, who are beginning to recognize the growing impact of CAM on health care delivery [1-3]. The most common CAM modalities include practices such as massage, chiropractic services, acupuncture, relaxation, naturopathic medicine, herbal supplements, and religious or spiritual practices. The available historical evidence suggests that both the lifetime prevalence of CAM therapy use, as well as the annual number of visits to CAM practitioners have been steadily growing over the past few decades [4-6]. Current estimates based on nationally representative surveys indicate that between 9% and 19% of the U.S. population visit CAM practitioners during the course of a given year [4,7-10].

Surveys of the general population typically find that rates of CAM practitioner utilization are higher for people in poor health, with chronic conditions, and/or with low functional status [4,7,9-12]. Likewise, samples drawn from populations of people with disabling conditions or in clinical settings tend to report higher levels of CAM practitioner use than in the general population. Among the highest estimates were derived from two separate studies conducted with patients from rheumatology clinics. In these studies, more than 40% of those with fibromyalgia had visited a CAM practitioner, and more than 25% of arthritis patients regularly used chiropractors. Both of these estimates were based on geographically specific samples. This is more than double the rate of practitioner use found in studies of the general population [13,14]. Two other studies of individuals with disabilities recruited from outpatient rehabilitation facilities reported estimates more similar to studies conducted with the general population. In one study, approximately 20% of the sample consulted a CAM practitioner and 9% visited a chiropractor [15]. In the other only 29% reported any CAM use (including self-administered use) and 14% reported using a chiropractor [16]. The rates of CAM practitioner use in the former study and the rates of chiropractic use in both studies were higher than some national estimates, but were similar to others [4,10,11].

The symptoms for which people seek CAM practitioners are fairly consistent across studies. Back and neck problems, chronic pain, arthritis, fatigue, depression and anxiety are among the most commonly cited symptoms for which CAM providers are consulted. This is consistent across both nationally representative and local clinical samples [4,9,16-18]. The reasons persons choose to use CAM either as an adjunct or an alternative to traditional Western medicine are less consistent across studies. Several studies based on clinical samples suggest that many individuals, particularly those with difficult to treat illnesses characterized by chronic pain, back pain, fatigue or depression seek out CAM practitioners because they were dissatisfied with conventional treatment and wanted faster and/or more complete amelioration of symptoms [14,18]. In addition, the desire to have increased involvement in health-care decision-making is often cited as is the desire to have better communication with providers [18,19]. However, a recent study conducted on a representative sample of U.S. adults compared several values and attitudes about CAM practitioner use along with health status and satisfaction with conventional providers and treatments. Individuals in poor health were more likely to use CAM, but after controlling for health status, the strongest predictor of CAM use was philosophical congruence with CAM [17]. Two specific philosophical approaches or values examined in that study were related to CAM use. The first was a holistic approach to health. That is, the mind, body, and spirit are related and health care providers should take all three into account. The second value related to CAM use was a belief in the importance of spiritual or religious factors in health. Contrary to expectations, in the aforementioned study, dissatisfaction with conventional medicine was not associated with CAM use [17]. Current trends associated with increasing CAM use are especially salient for people with disabilities. Their dual status as a vulnerable population and as heavy users of care has put them at risk of poor access and made them especially vulnerable to changes in health care delivery and financing [20]. Since CAM treatments represent a rapidly growing proportion of the medical care obtained by Americans, especially those with chronic health conditions, understanding the patterns of utilization and the reasons behind CAM use is important. Although most surveys suggest that CAM use, like use of medical care in general, is higher among people with chronic illness and disabilities, there are currently no estimates of CAM use derived from a nationally representative sample of people with disabilities.

Very few studies have examined the impact of insurance status on CAM use. What little is known suggests that the uninsured are less likely to use cam [8], that most individuals pay out-of-pocket for CAM services [4], and that individuals in managed care are half as likely to use chiropractic services, but equally likely to use other CAM services [10]. Because all of the studies were conducted using data that is several years old, they may not reflect current trends in insurance coverage of CAM modalities. More recent data suggest that in 2000, 70% of employee sponsored insurance covered chiropractic care, 17% covered acupuncture, and 12% covered massage [2]. Public insurance coverage for CAM is undoubtedly much lower.

There are several reasons why a national survey of CAM practitioner use among insured people with disabilities represents a substantial addition to the literature. First, virtually all estimates of CAM use among people with disabilities come from local clinical samples. Because CAM use varies dramatically by region, estimates of CAM use obtained from local populations can provide only a limited picture. Second, because people with disabilities are more likely to use traditional health services than the general population, estimates of CAM use derived from clinical settings may be biased and overestimate its use. Third, there is no current information about the influence of insurance type (e.g., fee-for-service vs. managed care) on CAM use. Finally, much of what we know about why people use CAM practitioners, either as an alternative or an adjunct to traditional Western medicine, has been learned from either clinical samples or from samples of the general U.S. population. Very little is known about the reasons people with disabilities use CAM practitioners and whether those reasons differ from the general population.

This study provides estimates of CAM practitioner use derived from a national survey of insured individuals with one of 4 physically disabling conditions: cerebral palsy, multiple sclerosis, arthritis, and spinal cord injury. The objective of this research is to address the following questions:

1. What is the prevalence of CAM practitioner use among people with physical disabilities?
2. For what conditions and symptoms do adults with physical disabilities consult CAM practitioners?
3. For what reasons do people with disabilities report using CAM?

METHODS

Sample

Data from this study come from the second and third waves of a three-year longitudinal national survey of insured adults with the following conditions: cerebral palsy (CP), multiple sclerosis (MS), spinal cord injury (SCI) or arthritis (rheumatoid or osteoarthritis). The larger study was designed to assess the health care experiences of people with disabilities enrolled in fee-for-service or managed care in commercial health plans, Medicare or Medicaid. Data were collected using a mail-return survey. For approximately 5% of the sample who required assistance filling out the survey, surveys were administered by telephone.

Collecting a nationally representative sample of people with disabilities is a difficult and resource intensive task for which traditional methods of recruitment are not effective. A multi-modal approach including both random and purposive sampling strategies was undertaken in order to identify a representative sample of insured adults with disabilities. In the first stage, individuals were recruited using a random sample of mailing lists of national organizations for individuals with MS, CP, SCI or arthritis. Survey recruitment packets with informed consent forms were sent to 12,000 individuals and 571 consented to participate in the survey. This group made up 51% of the final study sample. In stage two, a purposive sampling strategy was employed by recruiting participants using notices in national and local publications, listserves and notices on organizational websites. This group made up 29% of the final sample. The remainder of the respondents (20% of final sample) were recruited through referrals from clinical centers or physicians specializing in the target conditions, fliers posted in libraries and independent living centers, and through word of mouth of those already participating. Through these procedures, a total of 1114 persons were identified to whom surveys were mailed out. Of these, 942 surveys (85%)were returned. The final sample consists of 830 (75%) people who met study criteria. The informed consent process used in this study was approved by the MedStar Institutional Review Board in Washington, D.C.

Measures

CAM use was assessed in years 2 (2000) and 3 (2001) of the three-wave study. The estimates reported in the current study were derived from a cross-sectional analysis of data collected in 2001. CAM practitioner use was assessed by asking respondents how many times they obtained alternative medical treatment from a professional in the past 12 months. The response options included "relaxation therapy," "acupuncture," "massage therapy," "herbal or naturopathic medicine," "chiropractic treatment" and "other." Additionally, a binary variable indicating prior use of CAM practitioners was created that identified anyone who reported visiting a CAM practitioner in the 2000 survey.

The survey included a symptom checklist by which respondents could identify all of the symptoms for which they consulted CAM practitioners. Based on a review the literature, the symptoms included were "pain," "decreased functioning," "lack of energy," "depression," "insomnia," "anxiety," "infection," and "other." In addition to the symptom checklist, the survey included a checklist of commonly cited reasons people use CAM practitioners. Options included "fits my lifestyle/philosophy", "more effective in reducing symptoms", "better communication with my provider", "easier to access than traditional medical care", "less expensive than traditional medical care", and "other". Satisfaction with CAM practitioners was assessed using a single item with a five-category response option ranging from Very Dissatisfied to Very Satisfied.

Health status was measured using a categorical measure of general health status as well as the number of limitations reported in one of 6 activities of daily living (ADLs) including bathing, dressing, eating, toileting, transferring, and getting around inside the home. The survey instrument included sociodemographic, health insurance and health status variables.

Analysis

All data were analyzed using SPSS for Windows 11.0. Bivariate analyses were conducted to estimate use of CAM modalities by each disability group. Chi-square tests were used to ascertain significant differences in CAM practitioner use across demographic and disability groups. The same procedures were used to examine symptoms and reasons for which CAM practitioners were used.

RESULTS

Sample Characteristics

Sample characteristics are reported in Table 1. As would be expected from a sample of people with disabilities, a substantial proportion of the population reported fair/poor health (29%) and more than 3 ADL limitations (19%). Of the four condition-types sampled, arthritis made up nearly half of the sample (48%), followed by SCI (19%) and MS (19%). The smallest proportion of the sample were individuals with CP (14%). More than half of the sample were women (68%). Income was evenly distributed, with approximately 25% of the sample in the lowest, and 25% in the highest income groups. The region in which respondents lived was also relatively evenly distributed. Approximately 26% of the sample resided in each of the three regions: West, Midwest, and South, and 21% in the Northeast. Half (51%) of the respondents had fee-for-service insurance. The majority of respondents were covered by private insurance (52%), the rest were covered by Medicare (42%) and Medicaid (6%). Only 20% of the respondents had reported CAM use in the 1999 survey.

CAM Use

As shown in Table 2, CAM practitioner use was reported by 19.2% of the sample, and was consistent across all disability types except spinal cord injury. Only 13.7% of people with SCI reported any CAM use, which was considerably lower than the average. Estimates of CAM practitioner use are similar to Eisenberg et al.'s recent study (1998) [4], and substantially higher than both the Robert Wood Johnson Access Survey (1994) [10] and the Medical Expenditure Panel Survey (1996) [8,11], see Table 3.

Table 1. Sample Characteristics

	N	%
All respondents	830	100
Age (n=827)		
Age 18-50	405	49.0
Age 51-89	422	51.0
Health Status (n=827)		
Excellent / Very Good	251	30.4
Good	337	40.7
Fair / Poor	239	28.9
Disability Severity (n=825)		
0 ADL Limitations	506	61.3
1-3 ADL Limitations	164	19.9
4-6 ADL Limitations	155	18.8
Condition Type (n=830)		
Arthritis	400	48.2
CP	112	13.5
MS	157	18.9
SCI	161	19.4
Gender (n=829)		
Male	265	68
Female	564	32
Payer Source (n=796)		
Private	410	51.5
Medicare	335	42.1
Medicaid	51	6.4
Income Level (n=798)		
< $20,000	207	25.9
$20,000-$40,000	240	30.1
$40,001-$60,000	157	19.7
>$60,000	194	24.4
Region (n=699)		
West	184	26.3
Midwest	181	25.9
Northeast	148	21.1
South	186	26.6
Health Plan Type (n=818)		
Fee for Service	418	51.1
Managed Care	400	48.9
Prior CAM use (n=830)		
Yes	174	20.9
No	656	79.1

Table 2. CAM practitioner use in the past 12 months by respondent characteristics and disability type.

	Percent Visiting CAM Practitioners				
	Total	CP	MS	SCI	Arthritis
All respondents	19.2	19.6	20.4	13.7	21.0
Age					
Age 18-50	20.5	20.5	22.4	12.7	25.7
Age 51-89	18.0	17.9	18.8	14.0	18.6
Health Status (n=827)					
Excellent / Very Good	14.7	21.8	8.8	11.8	15.1
Good	22.0	20.0	23.4	17.0	23.3
Fair / Poor	20.5	11.8	23.7	12.9	22.0
Disability Severity (n=825)					
0 ADL Limitations	19.4	***18.6***	20.0	***20.8***	18.9
1-3 ADL Limitations	24.4	***46.7***	17.9	***4.5***	28.4
4-6 ADL Limitations	14.2	***13.5***	25.9	***8.2***	20.0
Gender (n=829)					
Male	***10.2***	12.7	***8.9***	***8.5***	***11.3***
Female	***23.6***	26.3	***25.0***	***20.9***	***23.2***
Income Level (n=798)					
< $20,000	17.9	19.6	21.2	***14.0***	17.6
$20,000-$40,000	20.4	24.0	9.8	***26.3***	22.2
$40,001-$60,000	22.9	28.6	31.4	***3.4***	25.3
>$60,000	17.0	8.3	21.2	***8.5***	22.2
Region (n=699)					
West	***30.4***	34.4	32.4	25.0	***30.7***
Midwest	***20.4***	18.8	24.4	15.4	***21.7***
Northeast	***14.2***	13.8	15.4	12.5	***14.3***
South	***12.4***	5.9	10.0	5.2	***21.1***
Payer Source (n=796)					
Private	20.2	16.9	27.8	11.1	22.0
Medicare	18.8	20.7	15.5	17.5	20.0
Medicaid	17.6	20.0	10.0	16.7	20.0
Health Plan Type (n=818)					
Fee for Service	17.5	14.0	17.1	15.6	19.4
Managed Care	21.3	23.3	25.7	11.8	22.3
Prior CAM use (n=830)					
Yes	***62.1***	***63.6***	***48.8***	***69.6***	***65.9***
No	***7.9***	***8.9***	***10.3***	***4.3***	***8.3***

All shaded cells are significantly different at the .05 level.

Table 3. Comparison of current estimates with other national estimates of past-year CAM practitioner use

	Current Estimates: 2001	Eisenberg 1997	RWJF ACESS 1994	MEPS 1996
CAM Modality	%	%	%	%
Any Pracitioner	19	19	9	5
Chiropractic	7	7	7	4
Massage	11	7	3	2
Acupuncture	1.5	.9	.4	1
Relaxation	1.5	1	1.3	NA
Naturopathic/ Homeopathic	1.5	1.8	NA	.4
Other Practitioner	2	>1*	NA	NA

* Did not ask about "other" CAM provider, but included 10 other categories for which CAM practitioner use was sought.

As expected, gender, region and prior CAM use was strongly associated with past-year use of CAM practitioners, with women using CAM more often than men, and persons in the West and Midwest using CAM more than those in the Northeast or South. The difference between prior users and prior non-users was rather striking: 62% of individuals who had reported using CAM practitioners in 2000 also reported CAM in 2001 compared to only 7% of prior non-users. However, health status and income were not associated with increased CAM practitioner use, while disability severity was only associated with CAM use by the SCI group, and then with greater use by those with less severe ADL limitation. Insurance type was not significantly related to CAM use, but there was a trend toward more CAM use among those with private insurance compared to those with either Medicare or Medicaid. Additionally, individuals enrolled in managed care plans were only slightly more likely than those in fee-for-service to use CAM.

As reported in Table 4, the most common symptoms for which CAM practitioners were consulted included pain (80%), decreased functioning (43%), and lack of energy (24%). There was little variation across disability groups in these reported symptoms with few exceptions. For all 4 groups, pain and functioning were the two most commonly cited reasons for CAM use. However, a substantial proportion of those with CP (32%) and SCI (32%) listed "other" and among those with MS, 19% indicated "anxiety" as one symptom for which a CAM practitioner was used.

By far the most common reason for using CAM practitioners was congruence with lifestyle or philosophy (67%), which was considerably higher than the proportion indicating that they used CAM because it was more effective in treating their symptoms (44%). Only 14% and 9%, respectively, reported that they used CAM because they had better provider communication, or it was easier to access than traditional medicine. See Table 5.

As in prior research of CAM, most respondents were satisfied or very satisfied with their CAM providers - 89% of the sample, across all disability categories, reported being satisfied, or extremely satisfied with their CAM provider. This is not particularly surprising given that the population essentially is self-selected into CAM use.

Table 4. Use of CAM for symptom relief by disability type, among those reporting at least 1 CAM utilization in past 12 months

	CP	MS	SCI	arthritis	All respondents
Symptoms	%	%	%	%	%
Pain	68.2	65.6	86.4	86.7	79.9
Decreased functioning	68.2	53.1	45.5	57.8	43.4
Lack of Energy	13.6	18.8	18.2	30.1	23.9
Depression	9.1	9.4	13.6	15.7	13.2
Insomnia	9.1	9.4	13.6	13.3	11.9
Anxiety	0.0	18.8	13.6	10.8	11.3
Infection	4.5	3.1	4.5	7.2	5.7
Other	31.8	22.6	31.8	3.6	15.2

Table 5. Reasons for obtaining alternative medical treatment by disability type, among those reporting at least 1 CAM utilization in past 12 months (n=159)

	CP	MS	SCI	Arthritis	All respondents
Reasons	%	%	%	%	%
Fits my lifestyle	77.3	59.4	68.2	66.7	66.9
More effective	40.9	59.4	40.9	40.5	44.4
Better communication with provider	9.1	9.4	18.2	15.5	13.8
Easier to access than traditional	13.6	15.6	18.2	3.6	9.4
Less expensive	4.5	18.8	22.7	2.4	8.8
Other	18.2	18.8	27.3	23.8	22.5

Note: categories are not mutually exclusive.

DISCUSSION

CAM practitioner use in a national sample of people with disabilities was similar to other recent estimates obtained from a nationally representative sample [4]. In both studies, 19% of the respondents reported visiting a CAM practitioner in the past 12 months. However, rates of CAM use for both of these studies were substantially higher than those reported in the Robert Wood Johnson Access to Care Survey (10%) [10] or the Medical Expenditure Panel Survey (9%) [8,11]. Differences in reported rates of practitioner use across surveys may occur for several reasons: differences in sampling frames, differences in definition of CAM use, differences in definition of "disability". Because the current study includes only insured individuals, it is possible that estimated CAM use was higher than in the general population which would include some uninsured individuals. Nevertheless, rates from the current study were not higher than Eisenberg et al.'s study, which included uninsured individuals in the sample.

Another explanation for differences in reported CAM use across studies is that Eisenberg et al.'s study focused on CAM use, whereas the other national studies included CAM use only as part of a broader survey [9]. However, the current study also assessed CAM practitioner use as only one relatively small component of the overall survey. Differences may also be due to survey modality (e.g., face to face vs. telephone interviews and mail surveys). It has been suggested that the telephone surveys used in Eisenberg et al.'s study may underrepresent low SES participants, which could inflate use of CAM practitioners [9]. Because income was not reported in either the MEPS or the RWJ Access survey, it is difficult to assess the impact of income differences on CAM use reporting, but it should be noted that the present study included a relatively highly educated and high income sample and no significant differences in CAM use by income were reported.

Another factor complicating the comparison of CAM use across surveys is the variability in definitions of CAM as well as time periods considered. One way to ensure consistency is to examine rates of CAM practitioner use rather than self-administered or practitioner use, with the latter measure regarded as less reliable. Even these estimates, however, are highly variable based on the number and types of providers included. Different surveys include different types of CAM practitioners, making direct comparisons difficult. Table 3 compares past-year estimates of CAM practitioner use from the current survey with the 3 major recent national surveys. A glance at the table shows at least two obvious reasons for differences across surveys. First, not all categories of CAM practitioners are represented in all surveys. Both the current survey, as well as Eisenberg et al.'s 1998 survey included more categories of CAM practitioner use, as well as an "other" category or categories. Second, several of the CAM modalities represented, especially massage therapy, had higher rates of use in both the current and the Eisenberg et al. study.

The individual characteristics associated with CAM use in the current study differed from previous studies in several notable ways that reflect the heterogeneity among people with physical disabilities. As with other studies, gender and region were related to CAM use, and there was a trend toward fewer people in very good or excellent health visiting CAM providers. There were no differences in CAM use between income groups, or by insurance type. It is possible that income differences were mitigated by insurance status. Prior studies showing strong income associations in CAM use have not typically controlled for insurance status. It may be that as with other kinds of health utilization, income differences are partially explained by insurance status. Based on prior research we would have expected low income and managed care to be associated with lower rates of use, and there is certainly reason to believe that private insurance would be more likely to cover CAM than public insurance [10]. Nevertheless, as stated at the outset, insurance companies are expanding coverage of CAM modalities, which could explain both the relatively high rates of CAM use and the lack of income differences found in the current study.

It was somewhat surprising, however, that having more functional limitations did not appear to be associated with CAM practitioner use as has been found in other studies of the general population [21]. In fact, rates of use were lower for persons with the most limitations. It is possible that within the population of people with physical disabilities there are ceiling effects in the relationship between disability and CAM practitioner use, or that the relationship is with degree of pain (or some other condition) rather than disability status per se. For example, although the differences were not statistically significant, persons with spinal cord injuries were the least likely to report CAM use, and those with SCI who reported greater ADL limitations were the least likely of any group to use CAM. Correlates of CAM use for persons with disabilities is not clearly determined. It is possible that physical access to CAM practitioner offices are no better for persons with mobility impairments than conventional medical clinics.

The symptoms for which people with disabilities seek CAM practitioners are fairly consistent across studies. Nearly all studies that identify specific symptoms report pain, especially back pain as the principal reason for consulting a practitioner. Given that chronic pain is one of the most difficult to treat conditions in conventional medicine, findings from both the current survey and other similar surveys support the hypothesis that CAM practitioner use is driven, in part, by patients' desire to obtain more effective treatments for pain than can be provided by traditional medicine. On the other hand, the majority of CAM users reported that they used CAM because it was more congruent with their lifestyle, not that it was more effective.

"Symptoms" may reflect the motivation for seeking professional help, while the "reasons" for CAM practitioner use may reflect the choice in type of help sought. The most common reason for CAM choice was congruence with lifestyle. This finding is further supported by the fact that in the current survey, the largest difference in CAM use was among prior-users compared with prior non-users. Taken together these findings suggest that value and attitudinal differences may be the principal drivers of CAM use for the disabled and that these are consistent over at least relatively short periods of time. A recent study that compared several theories of CAM use, including dissatisfaction with the effectiveness of traditional medicine and philosophical congruence, found that values and attitudes were much stronger predictors of CAM use than dissatisfaction [17]. The importance of dissatisfaction with traditional medicine on the use of CAM among people with disabilities should not be discounted however. More than 40% of the sample indicated that they believed CAM use was more effective than conventional medicine in treating their symptoms.

The current study has some limitations that may affect generalizability and bear consideration. As mentioned at the outset, identifying a nationally representative sample of people with disabilities is a difficult task. Typical methods of identifying patients including stratified random sampling, or random digit dialing are ineffective. Any other sampling method used presents difficulties in generalizability. More than half of this sample was randomly selected from the target populations. Among those recruited for the study, the response rate was very high, nonetheless, the initial recruitment yielded only about 5% of the total target population. The other purposive sampling techniques were effective, but it is more difficult to judge their representativeness. Some portion of this sample, less than 10% was generated from clinical samples. This strategy too yields a bias, albeit a more predictable one. Another bias comes from using mail-return surveys in that responders tend to be those for whom the topic is more salient. Nevertheless, because this survey was about health care in general, and not CAM use in particular, there is no reason to believe that responders were more interested in, or used CAM more than non-responders. Likewise, because such a small proportion of the population came from clinical samples, this survey is likely more representative of people with disabilities than prior research conducted wholly in clinical settings.

Another important limitation is that this survey was conducted only on the insured population and many of the respondents indicated that insurance covered their therapy. It is highly likely that a sample of people with disabilities that included uninsured respondents would have yielded lower or higher rates of CAM use. Therefore the findings of the current research is generalizable only to insured populations.

Finally, the extent to which respondents could identify the types, the symptoms, and the reasons for CAM use were limited to the closed-ended format available in a mail-only survey. Given this limitation, every attempt was made to create response options congruent with large national surveys, in order to enhance comparability.

People with physical disabilities appear to use CAM practitioners at rates similar to, or higher than, the general population. Use seems to be for similar symptoms and for the same reasons as the general population. Results from the current survey suggest that CAM treatments represent a substantial proportion of the medical care obtained by Americans with chronic health conditions and highlight the need for more consistent regulation as well as integration with traditional medicine. More work is needed that includes uninsured populations as well as evaluations of the relative impact of individual characteristics, health care access and satisfaction, and values and attitudes on the utilization of CAM practitioners among individuals with physical disabilities.

Acknowledgements

This study was made possible by grants from the US Department of Education, National Institute on Disability and Rehabilitation Research (Grant No. H133B70003, H133B990019, H133B980022). We gratefully acknowledge the participation of respondents to the survey who provided information about their health status and health care, including CAM use.

References

[1] Spencer J, Jonas W. And now, alternative medicine...*Archives of Family Medicine.* 1997;6:155-156.

[2] Bodeker G, Kronenberg F. A public health agenda for traditional, complementary, and alternative medicine. *American Journal of Public Health.* 2002;92(10):1582-1591.

[3] Silenzio VMB. What is the role of complementary and alternative medicine in public health. *American Journal of Public Health.* 2002;92(10):1562-1564.

[4] Eisenberg DM, Davis RB, Ettner SL, et al. Trends in alternative medicine use in the United States, 1990-1997. *JAMA.* 1998;280(18):1569-1575.

[5] Hurwitz EL, Coulter ID, Adams AH, Genovese BJ, Shekelle PG. Use of chiropractic services from 1985 through 1991 in the United States and Canada. *American Journal of Public Health.* 1998;88(5):771-776.

[6] Kessler RC, Davis RB, Foster DF, et al. Long-term trends in the use of complementary and alternative medical therapies in the United States. *Annals of Internal Medicine.* 2001;135:262-268.

[7] Eisenberg DM, Kessler RC, Foster C, Norlock FE, Calkins DR, Delbanco TL. Unconventional medicine in the United States—prevalence, costs, and patterns of use. *New England Journal of Medicine.* 1993;328(4):246-252.

[8] Druss BG, Rosenheck RA. Association between use of unconventional therapies and conventional medical services. *JAMA.* 1999;282(7):651-656.

[9] Bausell RB, Lee WL, Berman BM. Demographic and health related correlates of visits to complementary and alternative medical providers. *Medical Care.* 2001;39(2):190-196.

[10] Paramore LC. Use of alternative therapies: Estimates from the 1994 Robert Wood Johnson Foundation National Access to Care Survey. *Journal of Pain and Symptom Management.* 1997;13(2):83-89.

[11] McFarland B, Bigelow D, Zani B, Newsom J, Kaplan M. Complementary and alternative medicine use in Canada and the United States. *American Journal of Public Health.* 2002;92(10):1616-1617.

[12] Ong CK, Petersen S, Bodeker GC, Stewart-Brown S. Health status of people using complementary and alternative medical practitioner services in 4 English counties. *American Journal of Public Health.* 2002;92(10):1653-1656.

[13] Pioro-Boisset M, Esdaile JM, Fitzcharles MA. Alternative medicine use in fibromyalgia syndrome. *Arthritis Care and Research.* 1996;9(1):13-17.

[14] Rao JK, Mihaliak K, Kroenke K, Bradley J, Tierney WM, Weinerger M. Use of complementary therapies for arthritis among patients of rheumatologists. *Annals of Internal Medicine.* 1999;131(6):409-416.

[15] Krauss HH, Godfrey C, Kirk J, Eisenberg DM. Alternative health care: It's use by individuals with physical disabilities. *Archives of Physical Medicine and Rehabilitation.* 1998;79:1440-1447.

[16] Wainapel SF, Thomas AD, Kahan BS. Use of alternative therapies by rehabilitation outpatients. *Archives of Physical Medicine and Rehabilitation.* 1998;79:1003-1005.

[17] Astin JA. Why patients use alternative medicine: Results of a national study. *JAMA.* 1998;279(19):1548-1553.

[18] Elder NC, Gillcrist A, Minz R. Use of alternative health care by family practice patients. *Archives of Family Medicine.* 1997;6:181-184.

[19] London AS, Foote-Ardah CE, Fleishman JA, Shapiro MF. Use of alternative therapists among people in care for HIV in the United States. *American Journal of Public Health.* 2003;93(6):980-987.

[20] Dejong G, Palsbo SE, Beatty PW, Jones GC, Kroll T, Neri MT. The organization and financing of health services for persons with disabilities. *The Milbank Quarterly.* 2002;80(2):261-301.

[21] Hendershot GE. Mobility limitations and complementary and alternative medicine: Are people with disabilities more likely to pray? *American Journal of Public Health.* 2003;93:1079-1080.

HEALTH EDUCATION AND PROMOTION

In: Focus on Disability: Trends in Research and Application ISBN: 978-1-60021-792-0
Editor: Thilo Kroll, pp. 125-150 © 2008 Nova Science Publishers, Inc.

Chapter VIII

DEVELOPMENT AND EVALUATION FOR A TRAINING AND SUPPORT PROGRAMME FOR PARENTS OF CHILDREN WITH DISABILITIES OR CHRONIC CONDITIONS

L.A. Powell and J.H. Barlow
Interdisciplinary Research Centre in Health, Coventry University, UK.

INTRODUCTION

The authors developed a Training and Support Programme (TSP) for Parents and their Children with Disabilities or Chronic Conditions. The impetus for this development arose from our experiences of working with parents of children with juvenile idiopathic arthritis (Barlow, Harrison, & Shaw, 1998). We found that parents were the most psychologically distressed group that we had worked with. We set ourselves a goal of developing an intervention that would help to alleviate parental distress whilst at the same time being of benefit to children. Other factors that influenced development and the nature of the Programme were our expertise in the field of self-management (JB), massage and training (LP), and our combined interest and practice in the field of complementary and applied medicine (CAM).

This Chapter describes the development of the TSP and its subsequent testing. The Chapter commences with an overview of the literature regarding parental well-being in the context of caring for children with disabilities or chronic conditions followed by a description of the Programme itself and an overview of a series of evaluation studies. The term 'parent' is used to refer to the main carer (e.g. mother, father, grandparent, foster parent).

BACKGROUND

Caring for Children with Disabilities and Chronic Conditions

Although the number of children under the age 5 years is set to decline over the next decade, the proportion of children with chronic conditions, long standing illness and disability is on the increase. The reasons for this are primarily the advances in medical care, treatment, and technology. A chronic disease is a 'medically diagnosed ailment with a duration of six months or longer which shows little change or slow progression' (Williams, 1997, p312). Prevalence estimates for chronic diseases of childhood range from 5% to 40% of children (Newacheck & Halfon, 1998; Perrin & MacLean, 1988), and encompass conditions such as asthma, cancer, chronic fatigue syndrome (CFS), diabetes and juvenile idiopathic arthritis (JIA). Lenton *et al.*, (2001) maintain that the number of children suffering from one or more chronic diseases is underestimated.

Disability is a term used to refer to impairments, activity limitations and participation restrictions (ICF, 2002). Since the Office of Population Censuses and Surveys (OPCS) in 1985 to 1986 on disability among children in private households, there have been few research studies to indicate the prevalence of disabled children in the UK (Office for National Statistics, 2004). Hence, the number of carers of children with disabilities or chronic conditions is unknown. In 1999-2000 the predominant disability among severely disabled children and adolescents were autism spectrum and behavioural disorders. Data from the General Household Survey (GHS 1990-2000) and the Family Fund Trust's register of applicants suggest that the rates of severe disability were consistently higher for boys than for girls under the age of 17 years. The highest prevalence rates of severe disability in children and adolescents were among those from semi-skilled manual backgrounds.

PARENTS' STRESS, HEALTH AND WELL-BEING

Despite the uncertainty regarding the precise numbers of children living with a disability or chronic condition, there is a growing body of evidence to suggest that caring for children with disabilities is a source of psychosocial distress (Dyson, 1997; Hintemair, 2000). For example, parents of children with multiple disabilities report higher levels of stress relating to their children compared with parents of children without disabilities (Dyson, 1997; Sloper & Turner, 1993).

Caregiving stress is often associated with the many physical and emotional demands imposed on parents caring for medically fragile children (Kuster & Merkle, 2004). Parents of children with disabilities have to balance time-consuming and complex treatment regimes with other aspects of family life and work commitments. In some cases, parents are often 'caregiving' across the lifecycle of their disabled child and this, in turn, can have a cumulative effect on parents' own health (Kelly & Kropf, 1995). Parental stress usually results from an inability to control the situation and their emotions, lack of self-efficacy (confidence) that they can take care of their child and disappointment that correlates with the child's health condition. Eiser (1993) argued that parents, particularly mothers, are unable to cope with the situation and thus experience more anxiety and depression in comparison with mothers of healthy children.

In relation to their child's condition, parents report many sources of stress leading to anger, frustration and a sense of isolation. For example, Scorgie, Wilgosh & McDonald (1996) found that dealing with health professionals was a source of stress for parents of children with disabilities. Similarly, Barlow, Harrison & Shaw (1998) report that delay in obtaining treatment, lack of information and lack of opportunity to discuss their child's condition were stressors experienced by parents of children with juvenile idiopathic arthritis. Moreover, parents felt a constant need to vigilantly monitor their child's health status for changes in symptoms or side effects of treatments. Support for these qualitative findings was provided by a study of families attending outpatient clinics at a regional hospital (Barlow, Wright, Shaw, Luqmani & Wyness, 2002). Mothers exhibited poorer physical function, poorer general health perceptions, and greater anxious and depressed moods when compared to UK normative data.

Not surprisingly, the time around diagnosis is considered to be critical for families, with parents reporting high levels of anxiety and stress (Rahi, Manaras, Tuomainen & Hundt, 2004). In a study of parents' perceptions of the diagnosis of cerebral palsy in their children, Baird, McConachie & Scrutton, (2000), found that the time of diagnosis was related significantly with later self-reported depression. A review of adjustment and coping among parents of children with cancer concluded that emotional distress (e.g. anxiety, depression) is greater among parents of newly diagnosed children with cancer or children who are in treatment when compared with normative data (Grootenhuis & Last, 1997). Although emotional distress remained heightened one year after diagnosis there was a decrease over time. However, parents continued to experience loneliness, uncertainty, symptoms of post-traumatic stress, fear of relapse and worry about children's future infertility. In a study on parental response to their child's health condition, (Fraley, 1990), parents reported feelings of helplessness, frustration, depression, hope that the child may get better, sadness and self-blame, in almost all the stages of their child's life. In addition, parents experienced high levels of stress at specific times in their child's life such as surgery, and the emergence of a new medical problem. Thus, although the time of diagnosis is a critical one, for well-being, parents remain vulnerable to distress throughout their child's life.

Breslau, Staruch & Mortimer (1982) examined the impact of child disability on psychological distress among 369 mothers of children (aged 3-18 years) with cystic fibrosis, cerebral palsy, myelodysplasia or multiple physical disabilities, compared with those of 456 randomly selected mothers of non-disabled children (aged 3-18 years). They found that mothers of children with disabilities were significantly more depressed and anxious and showed evidence of greater maternal distress. Level of psychological distress was independent of the type of disability suggesting that this finding could be generalisable across childhood conditions. Interestingly, the critical factor affecting maternal responses was found to be the impact of the condition on the child's functioning, particularly in terms of the level of daily care the child required. This finding is echoed in an investigation of the psychological health of mothers of children with a congenital anomaly (Merlo & Barnett 2002), which showed that the amount of daily care needed and number of hospitalisations, significantly predicted greater presence and severity of psychological and psychosomatic problems. Similarly, Pimm (1996), reports that the areas parents find most difficult to cope with are children's physical dependency, lack of mobility, communication difficulties, behaviour and supervision.

Abbeduto, Seltzer, Shattuck, Krauss, Orsmond, Murphy, (2004), argue that factors influencing the process of adjustment and adaptation include the child's age at diagnosis, the nature of the disability and its restrictions, as well as the family's ability to cope with the burdens and their available resources (Raina, O'Donnell, Schwellnus & Rosenbaum et al., 2004). For example, Witt, Riley and Coiro, (2003) have found that mental illness in parents of disabled children was significantly related to poverty and financial burdens in general. Thus, parents that experience burden in other aspects of their lives are more likely to develop later depression, or stress-related disorders. Lack of social support has also been a strong predictor of stress, depression and inability to cope with daily demands (Witt, Rile & Coiro, 2003). Rahi et al., (2004) suggests that families need emotional support from health professionals, relevant information, educational services and support groups.

Although mothers assume the primary burden of care, research has shown that chronic conditions of childhood or the birth of a child with disabilities also impacts on fathers and other family members. For example, Dyson, (1997) found that fathers of school-aged children with disabilities experienced as much stress related to their children, as did mothers. In a review of the literature on fathers' experiences of parenting children with disabilities, Hornby (1993) found several common themes: these included fathers' negative feelings towards professionals involved in children's care and stress related to children's care. These results supported those of earlier studies of school age children, (e.g. Hagborg, 1989) in which investigators also found no difference between fathers and mothers in terms of stress. The results of these studies demonstrate that both fathers and mothers can have similar experiences related to caring for children with disabilities or chronic conditions and experience greater degrees of stress than mothers and fathers of non-disabled children.

Potential Mediators of Parental Distress

Several potential mediators of parental distress have been identified. One such mediator is self-efficacy. Self-efficacy was introduced by Bandura (1977) to explain the effects of self-referent thought on psychosocial functioning. Self-efficacy refers to;

> 'beliefs in one's capabilities to organise and execute the course of action required to produce given attainments' (Bandura, 1977, p3).

Once formed, self-efficacy beliefs influence not only the courses of action pursued, but also the effort expended, perseverance in the face of difficulties, the nature of thought patterns (i.e. encouraging or self-deprecating) and the amount of stress experienced in demanding situations (Bandura, 1977). Strategies shown to enhance self-efficacy are mastery experience, role modelling, persuasion and reinterpretation of physiological and affective states (Bandura, 1977). These strategies can be incorporated, either singly or in combination, into interventions. Development of the TSP drew on the theoretical precepts of self-efficacy with particular emphasis on mastery experience, role modelling, and persuasion.

Feeling that they have a skill or competence that can assist in their child's care is important for parents. However, given the range of health and social care professionals who can be involved in the care of children with disabilities, parents can begin to doubt their own ability to develop caring skills. Indeed, in a survey of over 400 parents of young children with disabilities, Bailey, Blasco & Simeonsson (1992) found that both parents' needs included to know how to teach their child about the condition and its management, and to feel more of a part of their child's care. Although parents acknowledged the important role played by health professionals in their children's treatment and care, parents wanted to feel more included and useful.

Several studies in the field of childhood disability have noted the importance of parental self-efficacy and skill enhancement in relation to children's care. Breslau, Staruch, & Mortimer (1982) suggested that easing the daily burden of care and enabling mothers to participate more fully in their child's treatment regime as well as employment and other activities outside the home, might protect mothers from the risk of psychological distress. Following a study of 365 mothers, Silvers, Bauman and Ireys (1995) concluded that the distress experienced by mothers of children with disabilities could be reduced by interventions promoting skill-building and emotional validation. Support for the importance of improving parental coping ability is provided by Florian and Findler (2001) who found that self-mastery, self-esteem, and family network size were the main predictors of mothers' psychological wellbeing and marital adaptation. Furthermore, parenting self-efficacy has been found to be a significant predictor of maternal perceptions of child adjustment (e.g. Wanamaker & Glenwick, 1998) and self-efficacy for managing the child's condition has been shown to mediate the impact of children's ill health on maternal wellbeing (Barlow & Cullen, 2002).

The Training and Support Programme

The evidence that parents of children with disabilities may be at risk of poor psychosocial well-being and doubt their own ability to cope with the demands of their children's care accords with theoretical models of stress, suggesting that cognitive appraisal and coping mechanisms may play a mediating role in the stress process. The aim of the Training and Support Programme (TSP) was to provide parents with training in a simple intervention that could be easily applied in the home environment, and which would enhance their perceived ability to contribute to the care of their child and enhance their psychological well-being. In addition, we aimed to develop an intervention that also could have beneficial effects for the child. We decided on an intervention based on positive touch applied via simple massage techniques that could be easily learned by parents in a short programme (8 weeks).

Massage

There are currently numerous forms of 'touch-based therapies' that include an element of massage including Therapeutic Massage, Aromatherapy, Reflexology, Touch Therapy, Rolfing and Shiatsu. Massage is an extension of touch and although the oldest and most mastered of touch therapies (Field, 1995), it remains one of the many under-appreciated techniques within CAM (Eisner 1997). Generally, massage is considered to improve circulation of blood and lymph to help eliminate waste products (Arnould-Taylor, 1997), dissolve soft adhesions, reduce swelling, and, soothe the peripheral and central nervous system (Field 1995).

The majority of studies have explored the immediate physiological effects of massage on the receiver. The physiological benefits of providing massage for premature babies and children with or without a health condition are well documented (e.g. Field, 2000). More recently, there is evidence of benefits for the individual giving massage in terms of improvements in psychological well-being and enhanced self-esteem (Field, Hernandez, Quintino, Wheeden, Schanberg & Kuhn *et al,* 1998). Cody (1995) compared the effects of two maternal interactions: infant massage and reading (control group) on hospitalised premature infants and their mothers. Not only did the massaged infants gain weight, the mothers who massaged their babies reported a greater sense of wellbeing, increased self-esteem and showed an increase in positive perception of their babies. Goldstein-Farber (1998) noted that when mothers were used as therapists, the mothers' own levels of depressive symptoms decreased.

Cullen, Field, Escalona & Hartshorn (2000) assessed the effectiveness of massage therapy given by fathers to their children. Fathers became more expressive and showed more enjoyment, warmth and acceptance during interactions with their infants, suggesting that massage techniques are an effective way for fathers to develop more positive interactions with their infants. Consequently, we hypothesised that teaching parents the art of massage may be beneficial to parents of children with disabilities.

Despite the generally positive nature of research on massage, there are a number of caveats that need mentioning. The underlying mechanisms for the effects of massage remain unknown, thus, it is not clear which particular massage techniques are most suited to which health needs. The majority of research is short-term (i.e. immediate effects). The longer-term benefits of massage have been neglected. Further, contra-indications and safety issues have rarely been investigated. Research on the effects of massage on pre-term and/or low birth-weight infants and children with various health conditions is limited by the small sample sizes, few random clinical trials and the use of varying massage techniques (Vickers, Ohlsson, Lacy & Horsley, 2001; Ernst 1994).

In order to understand the effects of massage, research has focused on factors that are clinical in nature (e.g. changes in vagal, chemical and hormonal activity). However, other factors, such as improved parent: child interactions and enhanced recognition of parent: baby cues, may have contributed to the noted improvements in babies healthy growth and development. Anecdotally, giving massage is considered to make mothers feel good and facilitate the bonding process between parent and child (Auckett, 1981). Schneider McClure (1982), (founder of the International Association of Infant Massage (IAIM)), suggests that massage for infants is a means of gentle, warm communication that allows parents to engage and relax their children in a mutually, pleasurable interaction. Further, massage provides a model for becoming more sensitive to subtle cues of babies and offers a technique for eliciting positive reactions. However, interventions involving massage have primarily targeted parents and babies. There is no documented evidence exploring the value of providing parents of children with disabilities instruction in massage techniques for use in the home environment.

The Training and Support Programme

The TSP was designed for parents and in no way aims to treat children or offer a cure; it was purely designed to enable parents to contribute to their child's well-being and to enhance their psychological well-being.

The TSP comprises eight weekly sessions. The first is a telephone consultation between parent and massage therapist, which allows discussion of the Programme, the child's health, medical history and medical diagnoses and enables parents to be open about their fears and expectations without having to 'talk over the child.' During sessions 2 to 8, one therapist works with one parent-child dyad, training the parent in simple massage. The Programme can be tailored to the unique needs of each dyad and the therapist works with the same parent and child throughout the whole 8-week Programme providing continuity of care and the opportunity for parents to discuss their feelings about the TSP.

Each parent is provided with a Training Pack, which provides information on the massage techniques learned during the sessions and photographs of parents using the massage techniques on their children to demonstrate movements and hand positions. The Training Pack includes a list of contra-indications ensuring that parents know when they should not use the massage with their child.

The TSP is based on an ethos of inclusion rather than exclusion therefore the Programme is open to parents of children with a diverse range of disabilities and chronic conditions ranging from colic in babies to teenagers with multiple disabilities and health problems. Support for a non-categorical approach is provided by studies showing that there are more pronounced differences within rather than between disease categories (Stein & Jessop, 1989).

Therapist Training and Quality Assurance

Therapists are recruited through adverts in professional therapy journals or by word of mouth. Therapists are interviewed prior to commencing on the TSP. Criteria include a recognised massage qualification, appropriate insurance, a minimum of two years practical experience, and a check through the Criminal Records Bureau. Therapists are required to attend a Training Day, led by Dr Powell at Coventry University. The aim of the Training is to ensure consistency in delivery, massage techniques, and completion of documentation to accompany the TSP and the research. Therapists are supported through Programme by the Research Team, and attend an annual review held at Coventry University. Dr Powell conducts regular quality assurance visits in order to provide one-to-one support and training to therapists, to ensure that the TSP is delivered to the required standards and to meet with parents and children.

Pilot Testing of the TSP (Previosly Known as the Touch Therapy Programme)

Early pilot work based on interviews with parents showed that both parents and children with a range of disabilities enjoyed the TSP (Barlow & Cullen, 2000). Immediately after completing the 8-week Programme, parents reported benefiting in terms of having something positive to offer, feeling more confident in their own abilities and feeling closer to the child. Children were reported to have improved sleep patterns, more relaxed muscles and improved bowel functioning. Many parents found it hard to think about their own needs and tended to focus entirely on their children. Thus, it was difficult to get parents to talk about how they felt after completing the TSP and some parents queried why our questionnaires were about their own health and well-being rather than their child's.

For many parents, touch had become extremely utilitarian (i.e. limited to dressing, feeding, toileting the child) and sometimes children experienced negative touch as part of their treatment, (e.g. insulin injections for diabetic children and intensive physiotherapy). Parents reported that the application of the skills learned on the TSP enabled them to spend quality time with their children. After the Programme, touch assumed a new meaning in that the massage was pleasurable for both giver and recipient. Some parents found touch gave them an alternative way of communicating with their child. The latter was particularly apparent among parents of children with autism (Cullen & Barlow, 2002a, 2002b). In addition, parents valued the opportunity to learn a practical skill and perceived the TSP as acceptable, useful and enjoyable (Cullen & Barlow, 2002a.)

Process Evaluation

At this stage of development and testing of the TSP, we felt we had sufficient evidence to warrant a larger process evaluation incorporating standard questionnaire measures of parental psychological well-being. A process evaluation was set up that included both quantitative and qualitative methods. The TSP was evaluated quantitatively in terms of parental self-efficacy and well-being, and perceptions of three aspects of children's well-being. Data were collected by questionnaires mailed to participants before they commenced the TSP and after completion. In addition, parents completed Home Record Sheets to document their progress at home during the week following each session and therapists completed Monitoring Forms after each session.

Ninety-nine parents were recruited from a range of sources including the local media and voluntary and health service organisations working for parents and children with disabilities. Seventeen parents failed to complete the follow-up assessment. Comparisons between these non-responders and those who completed all measurements showed no differences on study variables. Eighty-two parents and their children completed the study.

The majority of parents were mothers (85%) who were married or living with a partner (87%), White European (91%), had educational qualifications (91%) and a mean age of 37 years (SD 7, range 23-65). Children (mean age 6 years, range 0-16) presented with a diverse range of disabilities including cerebral palsy, autism, global developmental delay and learning disability, epilepsy, muscular dystrophy and rare conditions and syndromes.

The results revealed statistically significant improvements in parents' self-efficacy in their ability to carry out massage, parents' self-efficacy for managing children's psychosocial well-being, and in levels of anxious mood at the end of the Programme (Cullen & Barlow, 2004). In addition, parental reports of children's sleeping and eating showed significant improvements. Analysis of qualitative data showed that initially some children were wary of receiving massage from their parents. It is likely that many children in our sample had treatments that they experienced as painful or distressing. However, children quickly became accustomed to the therapists, the clinic setting and the experience of receiving massage. Children soon began to enjoy receiving massage. Indeed, several began to take the initiative and requested extra massage sessions at home. This occurred even where children's speech was limited: children indicated their desire for massage non-verbally by taking the bottle of oil to their parent. Importantly, parents found giving massage to be an enjoyable experience that provided them with 'quality time' with their children. Such pleasurable outcomes were reinforcing and encouraged some parents to continue with the massage. One benefit reported by many parents was the improvement in children's bowel movements, this was particularly the case among children who had suffered from constipation prior to the TSP. One parent commented about the whole TSP experience:

> *"... what an enjoyable experience it has been for my son and me. Thank-you for giving us the opportunity to learn massage properly."*

A Controlled Study

Given the encouraging results of the process evaluation, we designed a controlled study in order to examine the outcomes of the TSP in a more systematic way. Our earlier pilot work had shown that failure to offer the TSP to members of the Control Group resulted in high rates of attrition. Thus, a controlled study design with an intervention and a waiting-list control group was used (i.e. all parents received the intervention). Waiting-list controlled designs are often used in evaluations of health education interventions. In addition, TSP therapists have their own client list and are not always able to take on TSP participants at short notice. A pragmatic approach was adopted whereby after returning the baseline questionnaire to the Research Team, participants either commenced the TSP as soon as possible (Intervention Group) or were allocated to a waiting list (Control Group) and received the intervention after 8 weeks.

Parents were recruited through charities and child development centres. Fifteen parents expressed an interest in the study but felt they could not commit to an 8-week programme.

Reasons given included child's admission to hospital, personal circumstances and parents' own ill-health. Of the remaining 100 who completed the baseline questionnaire and attended the TSP, five parents failed to complete the follow-up assessment.

The sample comprised 95 parents (49 in the Intervention Group, 46 in the Waiting-list Control Group) who attended the TSP with their children. Data were collected by self-administered questionnaires at baseline (before commencing the TSP), and at 8-week follow-up. The majority of parents were mothers (88%) who were married or living with a partner (84%), white European (94%) and had formal educational qualifications (92%). Parents' health problems included congenital heart condition, myxadaema, high blood pressure, back problems, epilepsy, diabetes, myotonic dystrophy, and multiple sclerosis.

The TSP demonstrated statistically significant positive effects on parents' anxious mood, self-efficacy for managing children's psychosocial well-being, self-efficacy in giving massage therapy, and perceptions of children's sleeping and eating (See Table 1).

Table 1. Means (standard deviation) on study variables at baseline and 8-week follow-up

	Baseline		**Change scores**		**p values for**
	Intervention n = 49	**Control** n = 46	**Intervention** n =49	**Control** n = 46	**change scores**
Parental self-efficacy (PSE) Mean (SD) (Range 7 - 49) ↑ = better	33.9 (9.1)	32.9 (8.9)	4.1 (9.0)	-0.1 (6.2)	0.004
Parental self-efficacy for massage Mean (SD) (Range 1 - 7) ↑ = better	5.5 (1.7)	5.4 (1.8)	0.7 (1.9)	0.0 (1.5)	0.005
Anxious mood Mean (SD) (Range 0 - 21) ↑ = worse	9.5 (4.2)	9.9 (4.6)	-1.7 (3.0)	0.4 (2.7)	0.030
Parents' perception of child's eating difficulty Mean (SD) (Range 0-10) ↑ = worse	3.8 (3.4)	4.2 (3.6)	-1.0 (1.7)	0.5 (1.7)	< 0.001
Parents' perception of child's sleeping difficulty Mean (SD) (Range 0 -10) ↑ = worse	4.5 (3.1)	4.3 (3.3)	-1.6 (2.9)	-0.0 (2.4)	0.004

Although levels of psychological distress among parents, particularly mothers, declined after attending the TSP, they remained higher than published norms. The relatively high levels of distress accords with the general literature reporting the potential burden on parents of caring for a child with disabilities (e.g. Sloper & Turner, 1993), and supports the original rationale underlying development of the TSP intervention. The results of this study support the suggestion that interventions aiming to provide parents with skills training and self-efficacy may mediate maternal well-being (Silvers et al., 1995, Wanamaker & Glenwick, 1998). In addition, the TSP helps parents to feel more involved in their children's care, thus meeting one of the main needs expressed by parents of young children with disabilities who participated in the survey conducted by Bailey et al., (1992).

The immense diversity of children's disabilities requires some comment. Parents were caring for children with a diverse range of disabilities; some being relatively minor and short-lived (e.g. colic), whilst the majority appeared to be long-term and in some cases multiple, life-threatening or with the potential to adversely influence the child's quality of life (e.g. cerebral palsy, muscular dystrophy, autism). Not all children had problems with mobility, sleeping or eating. Thus, there was a floor effect in operation in the assessment of these features making it more difficult for the study to detect change. This difficulty may be overcome by adopting a parent-generated approach to assessment of children whereby each parent identifies key areas of children's functioning that they would like to see improve. Hence, children with primarily physical conditions may aim to improve mobility whereas those with psychological disorders or learning difficulties may choose to focus on communication, an area that appeared to improve for a number of families. Furthermore, the effectiveness of the TSP could be evaluated within specific conditions to reduce variability.

The significant improvement in perceptions of children's sleep is important both for the child and their parents. Improved sleep among children could lead to more restful nights for parents, who in turn may feel better able to manage their child's care. Furthermore, both quantity of sleep and sleep patterns have been found to affect behavioural adjustment, daytime functioning and mental and language development in children (Bates, Viken, Alexander, Beyers, & Stockton, 2002; Dearing, McCartney, Marshall, & Warner, 2001). In addition, successful interventions aimed at improving sleep for children with intellectual disabilities have been shown to reduce stress and increase perceived control and satisfaction with child's sleep among mothers (Wiggs & Stores, 2001).

A number of caveats need mentioning. The sample size for our controlled study was relatively small and a pragmatic approach was adopted whereby parents either attended the TSP immediately or were allocated to a waiting-list. A randomised, controlled study will be necessary to confirm the findings reported here. However, attaining an adequate sample size is a difficulty faced by many researchers in the field of interventions for children with long-term health conditions or disability and their families (Barlow & Ellard, 2004). A non-categorical approach can be useful in this regard. However, as noted in our study, not all children had problems with mobility thus floor effects were in operation for some respondents and it is more difficult to detect a significant change over time. Longer-term assessments are needed to determine whether parents continue to use massage over one, two, or three years, for example, and to determine whether benefits reported here are maintained, whether benefits attenuate over time or whether additional benefits emerge. For example, changes in depressed mood may take longer than 8-weeks to manifest.

Overall, findings from the controlled study suggested that wider implementation of the Programme was warranted. The next section reports findings from a longer-term follow-up (i.e. 12 months) and two implementation studies that focused on parents of children with cerebral palsy, and parents of children with ataxia respectively.

A Twelve-Month Follow-up

The overall purpose of the twelve-month follow-up was to address the longer term maintenance of massage by parents and their longer term psychological well-being. The aims were:

1. to compare adherers (those who continued to massage their children) and non-adherers (those who discontinued to massage their children) on measures of psychological well-being and self-efficacy;
2. to examine whether the benefits of attending the TSP reported immediately after the Programme were maintained at 12-month follow up among adherers;
3. to document reasons for non-adherence.

Ninety-nine questionnaires were sent to parents 12-months after completion of the TSP. Eighty-two questionnaires were returned giving a response rate of 83%. The sample comprised 76 mothers, 4 fathers and 2 grandmothers with a mean age of 38 years (SD 8.08).

Thirty-six (44%) of parents were continuing to use massage at 12-months. There were no differences in baseline scores on study variables or parents' characteristics between adherers and non-adherers. Thus, none of these variables or characteristics appeared to be risk factors for non-adherence. adherers had higher self-efficacy and better psychological well-being than non-adherers. Moreover, within group comparisons over time, showed that the benefits noted immediately after the TSP, were maintained only among those parents who continued to massage their children at home (Williams, Cullen & Barlow 2005). In contrast, there were significant decreases on self-efficacy and increased psychological distress among parents who had discontinued massage.

It should be noted that over half of the parents participating in this study did not continue to use the massage after the Programme had ended. The fact that parents reported that the main reason for them no longer using the massage was due to time constraints reinforces the findings of earlier work which suggested that one of the negative effects of caregiving was reduced leisure time (White-Means, 1993). This suggests that parents may need additional support in terms of incorporating massage into their daily routines and the provision of booster sessions. We have explored the latter by offering all past participants the opportunity to attend a Refresher Day where they can meet with therapists again to update their massage skills. However, our experience of Refresher Days was that although many parents expressed an interest in attending, in practice, the majority did not avail themselves of this opportunity. This appeared to be due to other family commitments, holidays, travel or the child being too ill to attend. Refresher Days, therefore, do not appear to be a feasible or effective way of offering this support. As an alternative, we are now considering running 'advanced' programmes and workshops for those parents who wish to recap and extend their skills.

In conclusion, this follow-up study suggests that the benefits the TSP are maintained among those parents but only among those who continue to practie massage.

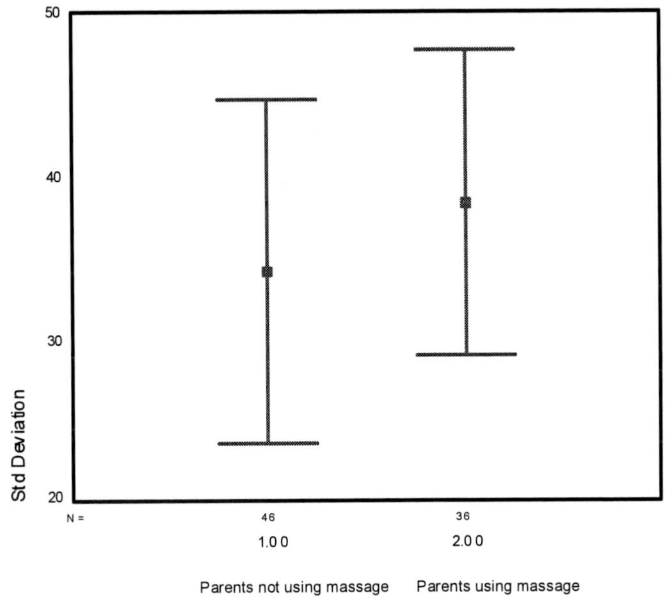

Figure 1. Mean scores and standard deviations for carers' self-efficacy in managing children's psychosocial well-being.

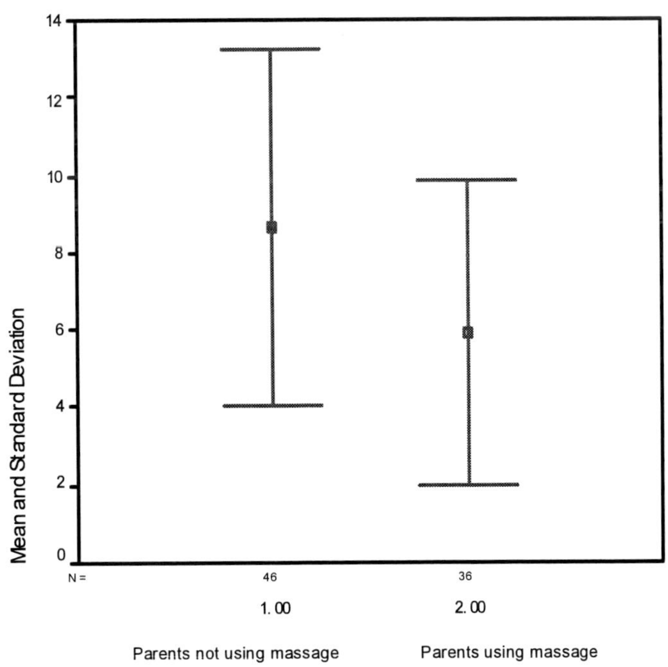

Figure 2. Mean scores and standard deviations for carers' levels of anxiety at follow-up.

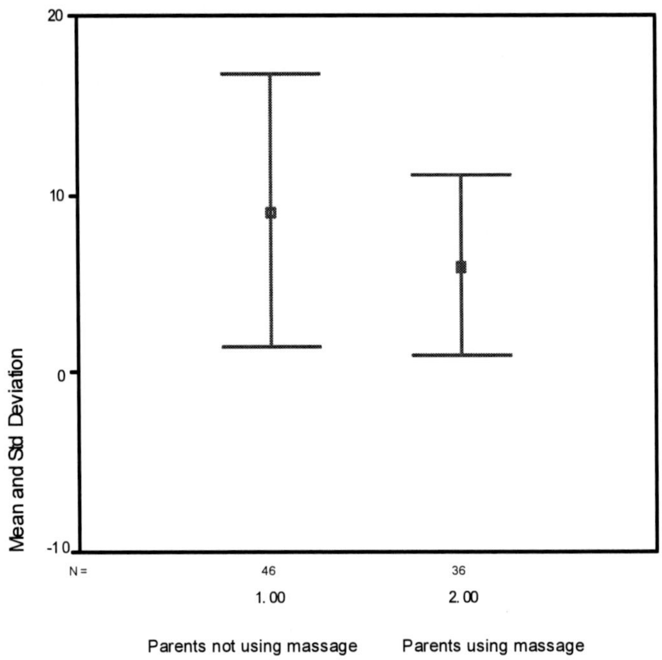

Figure 3. Mean scores and standard deviation for carers' self-efficacy to massage their child at follow-up.

IMPLEMENTATION STUDIES

Given that the TSP may need adapting to better meet the needs of specific participants, the following two studies aimed to evaluate the impact of implementing the TSP among two specific groups: parents of children with Cerebral Palsy (CP), and parents of children with Ataxia. Implementation studies are useful in that they are more flexible than randomised controlled trials where adjustment of recruitment or programme delivery violates a trial protocol thus rendering data unusable. An implementation study allows for adaptation of the programme to match available resources and to better meet the needs of participants.

Study 1: Implementation of the TSP for Parents of Children with Cerebral Palsy

Approximately 1 in 400 children are affected by Cerebral palsy (CP) and the number of people with CP requiring service support is growing (Scope, 2004). Cerebral Palsy affects physical functioning and can have a pervasive impact on children's 'quality of life' in terms of family, education and social integration / relationships. Depending on the type of CP, the control of movement and balance may be affected (Scope, 2004). Problems with walking, feeding, using hands and manual dexterity, and talking may occur. Constipation may result from difficulties in eating, drinking and swallowing. On occasions, co-morbidity may be present including visual and hearing impairments, perception and learning difficulties, and epilepsy (Scope, 2004). Although there is no cure, it is suggested that early treatment can ease the effects of CP.

A literature search of PsychInfo and Medline databases for the years 1996 to 2004 found five studies relating to the use of a complementary therapy (acupuncture, acupressure, and massage) among children with CP conducted in China (2), Russia (1), USA (2) and the UK (1). Three of these studies were reported in English. Hernandez-Reif *et al.* (In Press), studied the effects of massage versus reading on children with cerebral palsy. Twenty children received either 30 minutes of massage or 30 minutes of reading twice a week for 12 weeks. Children who received massage had reduced spasticity, gained more muscle flexibility and motor function and enhanced positive social interaction. In a single case study, Emly (1993) found that daily abdominal massage helped to relieve the constipation of a young man with quadriplegic cerebral palsy (QCP). Stewart (2000) discussed the therapeutic benefits of massage for children with QCP and, notes from her own experience of giving massage, that children with QCP smiled more often and appeared more relaxed.

In our study, 70 parents (3 couples) and 67 children with CP completed the TSP. The majority of parents received one telephone consultation with the therapist and 7 sessions of massage tuition. However, there were some exceptions. We adjusted the programme format for four families, who had to travel a long distance to the therapists. These families completed the TSP in three or four longer sessions.

The study used a pre-test post-test design. Quantitative data were collected by self-administered questionnaires mailed to parents at two points in time: baseline (immediately pre-TSP), and 4-month follow-up. To ensure that the TSP met participants' needs, the first 10 parents to complete the TSP were invited to participate in an exit interview. In addition, parents completed Home Record Sheets and therapists completed Monitoring Forms.

There were only 3 non-responders at 4-month follow-up; an insufficient number for statistically testing for differences between responders and non-responders. However, an inspection of their data revealed no observable differences.

The majority of parents were mothers (88.6%), were married or living with a partner (87.2%), White European (80.0%) and 64 (91.4%) had educational qualifications. Parents had a mean age of 39 (SD = 9) years. A total of 25 (35.7 %) parents reported health problems including: endometriosis, back problems, chronic fatigue, cancer, arthritis, anaemia, epilepsy, asthma, diabetes, and psoriasis. Twenty-six (37.1%) parents were working either full or part-time, 27 (38.6%) described themselves as homemakers, 13 (18.6%) were unable to work due to their children's ill-health, 4 (5.7%) were full or part time students, 3 (4.3%) were retired (due to their child's or own ill health), 2 (2.9%) were unemployed, 2 (2.9%) undertook voluntary work, 5 endorsed the "other" category, and 27 (38.6%) had reduced their working hours to care for their child.

Of the 67 children (mean age 6.38 years, SD 4.09) who received the TSP, 64 had a main diagnosis of CP and 3 had Global developmental Delay, mean age at diagnosis was 10 months (SD 8) and 32 children had co-morbid conditions. These included visual impairment, epilepsy, autism, hydrocephalus, asthma, gastro oesophageal reflux, chronic rhinitis, and chronic lung disease.

Results showed that parents had improved significantly at 4-months in terms of anxious and depressed moods, perceived stress, generalised self-efficacy, parental self-efficacy for managing their children's psychosocial well-being and satisfaction with life. These results were supported by the qualitative findings showing that most parents enjoyed giving the massage and some felt calmer after giving it. Parents reported an improvement in their own sleep patterns as a result of the improvement in their child's sleeping patterns. For example, parents reported that their children were sleeping longer and woke less often during the night.

"We've noticed a massive difference in sleep. It definitely induces deeper sleep, and that is without a shadow of a doubt as well ... nine times out of ten he'll only wake me once if he's had a massage in the night, while if he hasn't had a massage he can wake me up to seven."

However, in contrast to our previous work, this study did not find a significant improvement in parental self-efficacy for giving their child massage. This may be because a number of parents of children with CP have already acquired skills they can use to help their child, such as physiotherapy or conductive education exercises. Thus, they may have already felt confident about learning a new skill before they started the TSP.

In addition to supporting quantitative findings, the interview data provide further insight into the perceived benefits of the TSP. Parents reported changes in their child's physical condition including improvements in musculoskeletal problems, bladder control, bowel movements, feeding, physical size, breathing, and circulation.

"My daughter used to have strong muscle spasms, which woke her up, these seem to be less strong."
"My sons hands are now relaxed and open, before they were clenched fists."
"My son suffers with constipation, he found the massage very soothing."
"My sons circulation in his feet is better during the massage, they go from being cold to warm, I am hoping this progresses to longer lasting effects the longer I do the massage."

One other study has suggested that massage decreases muscle spasticity in CP (i.e. Hemandez-Reif et al. - In press) and this may contribute to some of the improvements noted by parents in our study. Similarly, improved bladder control and bowel movements are in keeping with the results of the single case study by Emly (1993), who found that abdominal massage improvement constipation in a male with QCP. The improvement in bowel movements noted in our study may have assisted children's appetite and eating. Clearly these issues are worthy of further, systematic exploration in future studies and do suggest that simple non-invasive techniques, such as massage, can be of value for families caring for children with disabilities.

Parents noticed changes in their child's emotional well-being and behaviour. Children were reported to be calmer, happier, more alert and aware of themselves. Some children were reported to have a better attention span, increased confidence and improved behaviour. Finally, some parents noticed improvement in children's non-verbal communication such as more smiles, eye contact and gestures. Smiling is important for the formation of relationships and, among infants, serves to initiate interchanges that are both rewarding and affective, and that help with bonding and attachment (Oakley and Jenkins, 1996). Thus, smiling is part of a shared experience of positive emotions. In the context of the TSP, increased smiling could act as reinforcement for parents encouraging them to continue with the massage.

In terms of implementation of the Programme, parents were satisfied with the delivery of the sessions; they liked the therapists and felt the massage techniques were well taught. The parents who had 7 X 1-hour massage sessions were happy with the length of and number of the sessions. Of the parents who had 3 or 4 longer massage sessions, one was happy with the length and number, whereas another felt she would have preferred shorter, more frequent sessions. Regarding the Training Pack, most parents found it helpful whereas a few parents felt that it was unnecessary and one expressed a preference for a video.

Three couples took part in the TSP and their data were used as two separate participants in the analysis. However, it is possible that there may be some confounding between the questionnaire answers, if for example, parents discussed the questionnaire whilst filling it in.

In conclusion, parents of children with CP found the TSP beneficial. Indeed, the improvements that parents reported regarding their children's well-being and functioning, extended our previous findings and were over and above what may be expected from such a simple intervention and certainly warrant further exploration in the future.

Study 2: Training Parents of Children with Ataxia

A literature search failed to identify any published studies examining the use of massage or any other complementary therapy among children with ataxia. We expanded the search to identify any studies reporting the use of complementary therapies in people with ataxia regardless of age. Only one study was found. Guuercio, Chittum & McMorrow (1997) examined the effects of relaxation training and biofeedback on ataxic tremor in one adult. The participant was taught relaxation techniques before biofeedback was introduced. Once proficient in relaxation, these skills were used as a foundation for biofeedback training. The results of this study showed that the participant learned to decrease the amount of tremor experienced and thus was able to perform routine tasks such as feeding with less assistance than previously required.

The aim of our study was to pilot the TSP among parents of children with Freidreich's ataxia (FA). The word "ataxia" means no co-ordination and is given to a number of neurological disorders in which parts of the nervous system that control balance and co-ordination, wear out prematurely. Friedrich's Ataxia is the most common type of inherited ataxia which produces symptoms before the age of 20 and is the easiest one to recognise. It is however, still very rare and has a prevalence of approximately 1 in 50,000. The mean age of onset for FA is 10-12 years, however, onset can be as early as 18 months or as late as 30 years. Curvature of the spine is quite common and varies in severity. The feet may be high-arched from an early age. Weakness of the limbs is a common feature and as the symptoms of FA are progressive, independent walking becomes more and more difficult with age. About two-thirds of people with FA have an abnormal electrocardiogram which reflects a change in the heart muscle, although this rarely causes symptoms apart from occasional palpitations that are controllable by drugs. Diabetes is also more common in people with FA, with an incidence rate of 10% and about one tenth of people with FA have hearing loss. A similar number develop a loss of visual acuity or changes in colour vision. Some individuals have jerky eye movements, but these movements by themselves do not usually interfere with vision.

There is currently nothing that can be done to stop the symptoms of FA occurring or progressing. However, it is possible to relieve some of the symptoms, such as muscle spasms, with medication. Much research into treatments has focused on determining the normal functioning of the frataxin protein in an effort to find ways of compensating for its shortage in FA. People with FA generally require long-term medical care and/ or monitoring by a number of health professionals including, general practitioners, consultant neurologists, speech and language therapists, occupational therapists and physiotherapists.

The low prevalence of FA poses logistical difficulties for implementing interventions such as the TSP where parent: child dyads need to be linked with a TSP therapist in their geographical location. Participants in our study, were all parents of a child with either FA or Ataxia Telangiectasia (AT). All participants were identified and contacted by Ataxia UK. Parents interested in the study then contacted the Research Team, thus preserving the confidentiality of membership lists.

A total of 39 parents expressed an interest in the TSP. Twelve failed to return the baseline questionnaire. Reasons for non-completion were travel difficulties (4), lack of time (3), children viewed as 'too old' for such an intervention (2). All 27 parents (17 mothers, 10 fathers) who commenced the TSP completed the study and 24 children (13 males and 11 females) received the Programme.

A self-administered questionnaire was mailed to all participants at baseline and at 4-month follow up. Exit interviews were conducted with a sub-sample of 10 parents to ensure the TSP was meeting parents and children's needs and to gain more in-depth understanding about parents' experience of the TSP. In addition, parents completed Home Record Sheets and therapists completed Monitoring Forms.

Parents had a mean age of 41 years (range 25-58 years); nine (33%) parents reported health problems; these included back problems, depression, anxiety, thyroid problems, diabetes, anaemia and heart conditions, (5 had co-morbid conditions); 13 worked either full or part time, 15 parents had reduced their working hours or given up work to care for their child and 23 (85%) had educational qualifications.

Twenty two children had a primary diagnosis of FA (14 of these children had co-morbid conditions including scoliosis, developmental delay, heart problems, learning difficulties and Chronic Fatigue Syndrome); 2 children had a primary diagnosis of Ataxia Telangiectasia; 21 (88%) had siblings, 16 (67%) attended mainstream school, only 5 (21%) had received complementary therapy before the TSP.

Results showed that the sample of 27 parents had improved significantly at 4-months in terms of anxious and depressed moods, perceived stress, generalised self-efficacy, satisfaction with life, and current health. These results were supported by the qualitative findings showing that most parents enjoyed giving the massage and felt calmer after giving it. They reported that their relationship with their child was 'closer' and both parent and child enjoyed having 'quality time' together doing something that was not only enjoyable but also beneficial. One parent found that she had become more accepting of her child's condition following the TSP. Several parents had developed a social network through serendipitous meetings with other families attending the TSP in one location. This was an unexpected bonus for the families involved and serves to demonstrate the importance of making contact with similar others not only for parents but also for children. The improvement in psychological well-being noted here is in keeping with previous studies of parents of children with diverse disabilities (Cullen & Barlow, 2004).

> *"I feel more involved with his medical care and the treatment for his ataxia, because we've got something we can do now and it gives us time together. I love giving my son the massage and I think it really does him good which makes me feel better about things then to."*
>
> *"For me, I think it has really helped me come to terms with the diagnosis of my son having ataxia cos I think I was struggling with that to begin with."*
>
> *"We met with other families who had sessions the same day, either before or after us, and we got chatting and went for lunch a couple of times, so it was good to know them, not only for us, but also for my daughter as it made her realise she wasn't also alone and that there were other young children around who had ataxia."*

Although no statistically significant changes in children's functioning were noted, emotional benefits for children were described qualitatively during interviews in terms of greater relaxation, calmness and improved sleep (e.g. deeper sleep and longer periods of sleep). Some parents felt that their children's mobility, balance, alertness, energy, and activity levels had improved. For example, one boy had begun to ride an adult tricycle. Such changes in physical activities are important as they offer children with ataxia a means of developing their independence and reduce reliance on parents and other family members. In turn, this can lead to increased confidence and choice for children and young people. Several parents reported that children's circulation had improved and their 'jumping legs' (a typical characteristic of FA) had eased somewhat. Approximately half of the parents reported improved communication, especially where children had difficulty with verbal communication (e.g. slurred speech). Perhaps most importantly, children were observed to be happier and smiled more often. Figures 4, 5 and 6 show at what stage in the TSP parents perceived changes in their child's alertness, mobility and verbal communication, respectively.

In terms of measurements, this implementation study identified a number of additional dimensions that are important in the context of ataxia, such as 'jumping legs', stiffness, balance, alertness, energy, activity level, and circulation. These dimensions need to be included in any future studies.

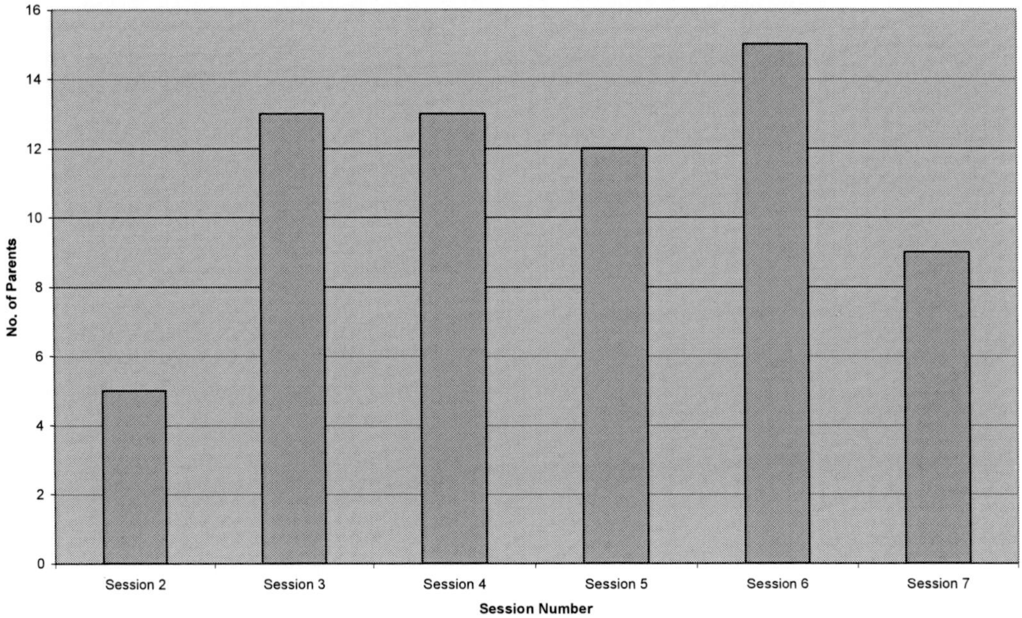

Figure 4. showing at what stage in the TSP parents perceived changes in their child's alertness.

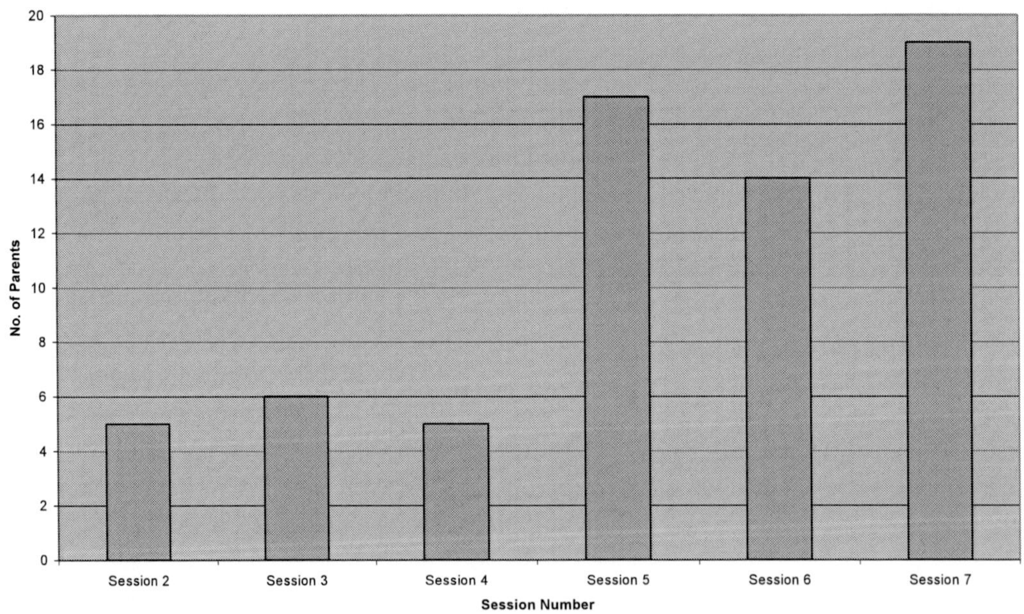

Figure 5. showing at what stage in the TSP parents perceived changes in their child'smobility.

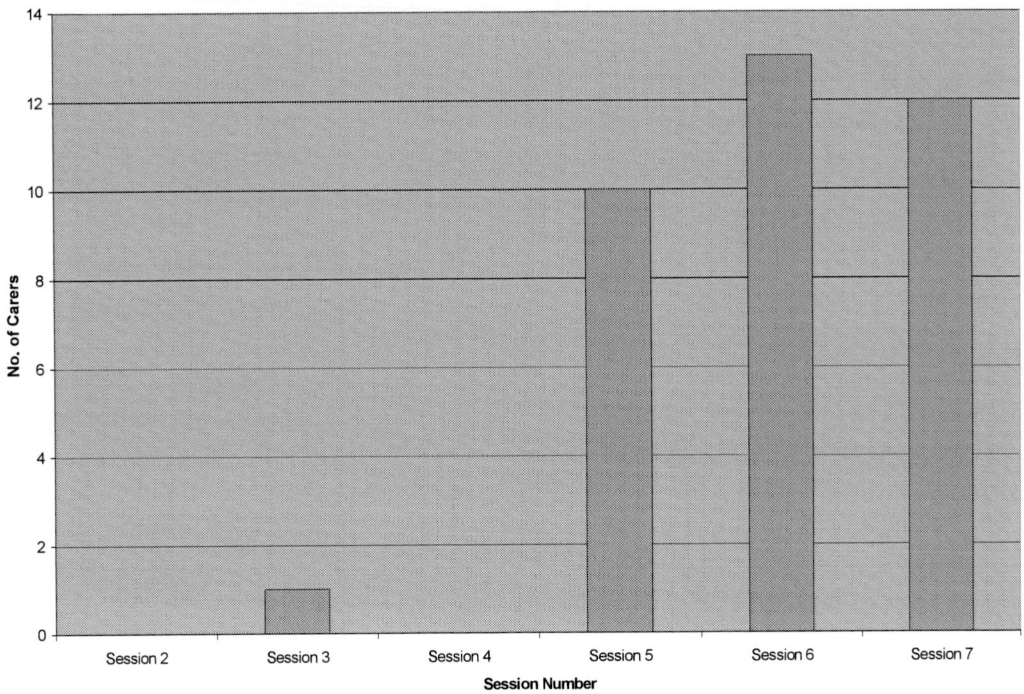

Figure 6. showing at what stage in the TSP parents perceived changes in their children's verbal communication.

A strength of the study was collection of data from questionnaires based on standard measures and interviews. Results of the qualitative analysis confirmed and extended the questionnaire findings. In addition, positive measures such as satisfaction with life were included. It is important that interventions enhance positive dimensions as well as reduce psychopathology. Finally, there are few, if any, published data on the psychosocial aspects of caring for a child with ataxia. Equally, studies of complementary and alternative medicine in the area of ataxia are relatively rare. Results of this study, although based on a small sample size, suggest that further studies in this area are warranted.

Common Issues to Emerge Across Studies

There are a number of limitations to our studies that need mentioning. Although we consistently find a number of statistically significant improvements over time on both parental well-being and parental perceptions of children's functioning, a randomised, controlled trial is necessary to confirm that such changes are in fact due to the intervention. This raises issues of general concern to all researchers working in the field of child and family health. Given the relatively low prevalence of many childhood conditions, it can be extremely difficult to recruit samples of sufficient size for randomisation. Interventions such as the TSP, have the additional logistical problem of matching family to therapist by location. Implementation studies allow the format of interventions to be adjusted with no loss of data, thus, in our implementation studies we adjusted the format of the TSP delivery to assist with parents' travel difficulties. This would not have been possible in a randomised controlled trial where such adjustments would have rendered the data unusable. However, some families decided that travel to the TSP venue was 'too much' and thus declined to participate. As more therapists are trained in TSP delivery, this problem should ease somewhat. Nonetheless, alternative means of Programme implementation may need to be considered such as 1-day regional workshops. Additionally, a longer-term follow-up is needed to confirm whether the reported benefits of the TSP are maintained over time, and to determine whether parents maintain massage.

It is recognised that the samples on which our evaluations have been based are largely female, probably because mothers tend to assume the primary burden of care (Gonyea, 1995) and male carers are usually at work during the day, when the TSP is offered. Thus, further investigation of the psychosocial well-being and needs of fathers attending the Programme appears warranted. By conducting a study based solely on the experiences of male carers, information could be gleaned to encourage more male carers to take part in the Programme. It is also necessary to identify reasons, other than work, why fathers and male carers do not attend the Programme with their child and from this it may be possible to adapt the Programme to better suit their needs and make it more appealing to them.

The levels of psychological distress found among parents of children with disabilities or chronic conditions who enrol on the TSP appear to be consistently and significantly higher than norms and are a cause for concern. The high levels of distress provide unequivocal support for the original rationale underlying development of the TSP intervention and are in keeping with the general literature reporting the potential burden on parents of caring for a child with disabilities (Sloper & Turner, 1993). The results of this study suggest that interventions such as the TSP may be one way of alleviating the distress suffered by many parents and warrant wider implementation in order to reach greater numbers of families living with childhood illness or disability.

In terms of measurements, there was a high level of variability among children's functioning. Not all children had problems with non-verbal communication for example, and therefore floor effects were evident in some cases. This means that it is harder to detect statistically, significant changes on these dimensions. Our two studies focusing on specific conditions (CP and FA) serve to illustrate that variability can be great even within diagnostic categories.

At policy level, there is an increased emphasis on the importance of ascertaining user views. In the UK, the NHS Plan (Department of Health, 2000) emphasised the need to provide users with a greater say in how services are delivered. Furthermore, the Children's Taskforce and the Children's National Service Framework will ensure that children with illness or disabilities are cared for not only in terms of their medical, social and educational needs but also in the light of their own views and decision-making (Department of Health, 2002). Thus, there is a general move towards including children's views as a vital part of research. We intend to include children's views in our future work.

CONCLUSION

The significant improvements observed across the studies reported here on parental well-being and children's functioning are both heartening and inspiring. A key strength of the studies is the collection of data using different methods. Thus, the qualitative analyses supported and extended the questionnaire-based findings showing that parents and their children benefited from taking part in the TSP and learning simple massage skills that could be used in the home environment. Parents valued the opportunity to spend 'quality time' with their children and to be more involved in children's care. The wealth of changes reported by parents regarding their children's well-being and functioning were more extensive than may be expected from a simple intervention and certainly warrant further systematic investigation in a randomised controlled trial. Finally there are few published data focusing on the psychosocial aspects of caring for a child with disabilities. Equally, studies of complementary and alternative medicine in the area of children with disabilities are relatively rare. Thus, we felt that our studies have extended the knowledge base and have illustrated that a simple intervention can have a wide-ranging and positive impact on the live of families living with childhood disability or chronic illness.

REFERENCES

Arnould-Taylor, W. (1997) *Principles of Physical Therapy*, Cheltenham: Stanley Thornes.

Abbeduto, L., Seltzer, M.M., Shattuck, P., Krauss, M.W., Orsmond, G. & Murphy, M.M. (2004). Psychological Well-Being and Coping in Mothers of Youths with Autism, Down Syndrome, or Fragile X Syndrome. *American Journal on Mental Retardation, 109* (3), 237-254.

Baird, G., McConachie, Scrutton, D. (2000). Parents' Percetpions of disclosure of the diagnosis of cerebral palsy. Archives if Disabled *Child*, *83*, 475-480.

Bandura, A. (1977). Self efficacy: Toward a unifying theory of behavioral change. *Psychological Review*, *84*, 191-215.

Barlow, J., Williams, R. B. & Wright, C. (1996). The Generalised Self-Efficacy Scale in People with Arthritis, *Journal of Health Psychology, 6* (2), 205-217.

Barlow, J.H, Shaw, K. & Wright, C.C. (2000). Development and preliminary validation of a self-efficacy measure for use among parents of children with juvenile idiopathic arthritis. *Arthritis Care & Research. 13*, (4), 227-236.

Barlow, J.H., & Cullen, L.A. (2000). Coming Together Through Touch: The Experiences of Parents of Children With Disabilities Learning the Principles of Massage. *Early Child Development and Care, 161*, 93-105.

Barlow, J.H., & Cullen, L.A. (2002). Increasing touch between parents and children with disabilities: preliminary results from a new programme. *Journal of Family Health Care, 12* (1), 7-9.

Barlow, J.H., Harrison, K. & Shaw, K. (1998). The experience of parenting in juvenile chronic arthritis, *Clinical Child Psychology & Psychiatry*, *3*, (3), 445-463.

Barlow, J.H., Turne,r A. & Wright, C.C., (2000). A Randomised Controlled Study of the Arthritis Self Management Programme in the UK. *Health Education Research: Theory & Practice, 15* (6), *665-680.*

Barlow, J.H., Wright, C.C. & Krol,l T. (2001). Overcoming perceived barriers to employment among people with arthritis. *Journal of Health Psychology. 6*, (2), 205-217.

Barlow, J.H., Wright, C.C., Shaw, K.L., Luqmani, R. & Wyness, I.J. (2002). Maternal stressors, maternal wellbeing and children's wellbeing in the context of juvenile idiopathic arthritis. *Early Child Development & Care. 172*, (1) 89-98.

Bates, J. E., Viken, R. J., Alexander, D. B., Beyers, J., & Stockton, L. (2002). Sleep and adjustment in preschool children: sleep diary reports by mothers relate to behavior reports by teachers. *Child Dev, 73*(1), 62-74.

Bond, C. (2002). Baby massage: a dialogue of touch. *Journal of Family Health Care. 12* (2), 44-45.

Breslau, Staruch & Mortimer, (1982), Psychological Distress in Mothers of Disabled Children, *American Journal of Disabled Children, 136*, Aug, 682-686.

Brooks, R.B. (1994). Children at Risk: Fostering Resilience and Hope, *Amer. J. Orthopsychiat. 64* (4), October, 545-553.

Bryan, D., & Herjanic, B. (1980). Depression and suicide among adolescents and young adults with selective handicapping. *Exceptional Education Quarterly, 1*(2), 57-65.

Cohen, S., & Williamson, G. (1988) Perceived stress in a probability sample of the United States. In S. Spacapan & S. Oskamp (Eds.), *The Social Psychology of Health* (pp. 31-67). Newbury Park: Sage.

Crawford, J. R., Jenry, J. D., Crombie, C., & Taylor, E. P., (2001). Brief report: Normative data for the HADS from a large non-clinical sample, *British Journal of Clinical Psychology, 40*, 429-434.

Cullen LA & Barlow JH (2004) A training and support programme for caregivers of children with disabilities: an exploratory study Patient Education and Counselling 55 : 203-209

Dearing, E., McCartney, K., Marshall, N. L., & Warner, R. M. (2001). Parental Reports of Children's Sleep and Wakefulness: Longitudinal Association with Cognitive and Language Outcomes. *Infant Behaviour and Development, 24*, 151-170.

Department of Health. (2002). *Listening, Hearing and Responding. Department of Health Action Plan: Core Principles for the Involvement of Children and Young People.* London: HMSO.

Diener, E, Emmons, R.A., Larson, R.J. & Griffin, S. (1985) The Satisfaction with Life Scale. *Journal of Personality Assessment, 49,* 71-76.

Dyson, L. L. (1996) The experience of families of children with learning disabilities: parental stress, family functioning, and sibling self-concept. *Journal Learning Disabilities, 29* (3), 280-286.

Dyson, L.L. (1997). Fathers and mothers of school-age children with developmental disabilities: Parental stress, family functioning and social support, *American Journal on Mental Retardation, 102* (3) 267-279

Eiser, C. (1993). *Growing up with a chronic disease: The impact on children and their families.* London: Jessica Kingsley Publishers.

Emerson, E., Robertson, J. & Wood, J. (2004) Levels of Psychological Distress Experienced by Family Parents of Children and Adolescents with Intellectual Disabilities in an urban Conurbation, *Journal of Applied Research in Intellectual Disabilities, Jun, 17* (2), 77-84.

Emly, M. (1993). Abdominal massage. *Nurs Times, 89*(3), 34-36.

Field, T. (1995). Massage Therapy for Infants and Children, *Developmental & Behavioural Pediatrics. 16*, (2), April, 105-111.

Field, T. (2001). *Touch*, Cambridge MIT Press.

Florian, V. & Findler, L. (2001). Mental health and marital adaptation among mothers of children with cerebral palsy. *American Journal of Orthopsychiatry, 71*, (3), 358-367.

Fogel Schneider, E., (1996). The power of touch: Massage for infants, *Infants and Young Children, 8*, (3), 40-55.

Fraley, A.M. (1990). Chronic Sorrow: A parental response. *Journal of Paediatric Nursing, 5* (4), 268-273.

Grootenhuis, M. A., & Last, B. F. (1997). Adjustment and coping by parents of children with cancer: a review of the literature. *Support Care Cancer, 5*(6), 466-484.

Hintemair, M. (2000) Children who are hearing impaired with additional disabilities and related aspects of parental stress. Exceptional Children, *66*, 327-332.

Kavale, S. (1996). *Interviews: An introduction to qualitative research interviewing*. London: Sage Publications.

Kelly, T. B. & Kropg, N. P. (1995) Stigmatized and perpetual parents: Older parents caring for adult children with life-long disabilities. Journal of Gerontological Social Work, *24* (1-2), 3-16.

Koegel, R.L., Schreibman, L., Loos, L.M., Dirlich-Wilheim, H., Dunlap, G., Robbins, F.R. and Plienis, A.J. (1992). Consistent health profiles in mothers of children wit autism. *Journal of Autism and Developmental Disorders*, *22*, 205-216.

Kuster, P.A. & Merkle, C. J. (2004) Caregiving stress, immune function, and health: Implications for research with parents of medically fragile children. Issues in Comprehensive Pediatric Nursing, Oct-Dec, *27* (4), 257-276.

Lenton, S., Stallard, P., Lewis, M., & Mastroyannopoulou, K. (2001). Prevalence and morbidity associated with non-malignant, life-threatening conditions in childhood. *Child: care, health and development, 27*(5), 389-398.

Middence, K. (1994). The effects of chronic illness on children and their families: An overview. *Genetic, Social, & General Psychological Monographs*, *20*, 309-326.

Moorey, S., Greer, S., Watson, M. et al., (1991), The factor structure and factor stability of the Hospital Anxiety and Depression Scale in patients with cancer, *British Journal of Psychiatry, 158*, 255-259.

Newacheck, P. W., & Halfon, N. (1998). Prevalence and impact of disabling chronic conditions in childhood. *American Journal of Public Health, 88*(4), 610-617.

Ong, L. C., Afifah, I., Sofiah, A., & Lye, M. S. (1998). Parenting stress among mothers of Malaysian children with CP: predictors of child- and parent-related stress. *Ann Trop Paediatr, 18*(4), 301-307.

Perrin, J. M., & MacLean, W. E., Jr. (1988). Children with chronic illness. The prevention of dysfunction. *Pediatric Clinics of North America, 35*(6), 1325-1337.

Pimm, P. L. (1996). Some of the Implications of Caring for a Child or Adult with cerebral palsy. *British Journal of Occupational Therapy, 59*(7), 335-340.

Rahi, S.J., Manaras, I., Tuomainen, H. & Hundt, G.L. (2004). Meeting the needs of Parents Around the Time of Diagnosis of Disability among their children: Evaluation of a novel programme for information, support, and liaison by key workers. *Pediatrics, 114* (4), 477-482.

Raina, P., O'Donnell, M., Schwellnus, H., Rosenbaum, P., King, G., Brehaut, J., Russell, D., Swinton, M., King, S., Wong, M., Walter, S.D. & Wood, E. (2004). Caregiving Process and Caregiving Burden: Conceptual models to guide research and practice. *Biomedical Central Pediatrics, 4* (1), 1-13.

Rusy, L. M. & Weisman, S. J. (2000). Complementary therapies for acute paediatric pain management. *Pediatr Clin North Am. 47* (3), 589-99.

Scafidi, F. A., Field, T. & Schanberg, S. M., (1993), Factors that predict which preterm infants benefit most from massage therapy, *Development & Behavioural Pediatrics, 14*, (3), 176-180.

Scorgie K, Wilgosh L, & McDonald L, (1996), A qualitative study of managing life when a child has a disability, *Developmental Disabilities Bulletin, 24*, (2), 68-89.

Silvers, E.J., Bauman, L.J., & Ireys, H.T. (1995). Relationships of self-esteem and efficacy to psychological distress in mothers of children with chronic physical illnesses. *Health Psychology, 14*, 333-340.

Sloper, & Turner, (1993). Risk and resistance factors in the adaptation of parents of children with severe physical disability. *Journal of Child Psychology & Psychiatry, 34*, 167-188.

Wanamaker, C.E. & Glenwick, D.S. (1998). Stress, coping, and perceptions of child behaviour in parents of preschooloers with cerebral palsy. *Rehabilitation Psychology, 43* (4), 292-312.

Wiggs, L., & France, K. (2000). Behavioural treatments for sleep problems in children and adolescents with physical illness, psychological problems or intellectual disabilities. *Sleep Med Rev, 4*(3), 299-314.

Wiggs, L., & Stores, G. (2001). Behavioural treatment for sleep problems in children with severe intellectual disabilities and daytime challenging behaviour: effect on mothers and fathers. *Br J Health Psychol, 6*(Pt 3), 257-269.

Williams, P. D. (1997). Siblings and pediatric chronic illness: A review of the literature. *International Journal of Nursing Studies, 34*, 312-323.

Witt, W.P., Riley, A.W. & Coiro, (2003). Childhood Functional status, family stressors, and psychosocial adjustment among school-aged children with disabilities in the united States. *Arch. Pediatr. Adolescence Med, 157*, 687-695.

Young, R., Brewer, N., & Pattison, C. (2003). Early behavioural abnormalities in children with Autistic Disorder. *Autism, 7*, 125-143.

Zigmond, A.S. & Snaith, R.P. (1983) The Hospital Anxiety and Depression Scale. *Acta Psychiatrica Scandinavica, 67,* 361-70.

In: Focus on Disability: Trends in Research and Application ISBN: 978-1-60021-792-0
Editor: Thilo Kroll, pp. 151-162 © 2008 Nova Science Publishers, Inc.

Chapter IX

Ley-Led, Self-Management for People with a Long-Term Health Condition: UK Results

A.P. Turner, J.H. Barlow and C. Heathcote-Elliot
Interdisciplinary Research Centre in Health, Coventry University, UK.

Background

The number of people in the world living with a long-term health condition (LTHC) is set to rise dramatically as a consequence of increasing life-expectancy and an ageing population. The burden of meeting the needs of this growing number of people will fall upon already over-stretched health care services that are struggling to cope with the demands of acute care let alone the needs of those with a LTHC. LTHCs are expected to become the main cause of death and disability in the world by 2020 (Murray & Lopez, 1996) contributing approximately two thirds of the global burden of disease (Sullivan, Ramsey & Lee, 2000) Mental health problems account for nearly a third of the long-term disability affecting the world's population now and comprise five of the top 10 causes of disability (ref).

The treatment of LTHCs is emerging as the largest cause of health care expenditure in many countries throughout the world and is responsible for approximately 70% of all health care costs in the US (Lorig et al. 1999). In the UK, one in three people have a LTHC or disability (Office for National Statistics, 2000) and approximately 17.5 million people are reported to be living with a LTHC at any one point in time (Department of Health, 2001). LTHCs include non-communicable diseases such as asthma, diabetes, arthritis and heart disease, mental health disorders such as depression, and certain communicable diseases such as HIV infection and AIDS. The United Nations, the World Health Organization and 37 countries have proclaimed the years 2000-2010 as the Bone and Joint Decade. This global initiative is intended to improve the lives of people with musculoskeletal disorders, such as arthritis, and to advance understanding and treatment of musculoskeletal disorders through prevention, education and research.

Since LTHCs have become a principal medical problem, it is important that healthcare systems, which were originally developed for treating acute disease, respond to the unique challenges involved. For example, patients would benefit not only from shorter waiting times for referral to specialists but also from being treated by the same GP and specialist who are familiar and knowledgeable about their LTHC. There are several differences between an acute illness and a LTHC including diagnosis and prognosis which are usually accurate in acute illnesses and uncertain in LTHCs. Probably the most important differences though are that there is no cure for many LTHCs and that patients with LTHCs develop an understanding and knowledge of their condition which is complementary to that possessed by their health care team. Following onset of a LTHC, the individual has to accept that the remainder of his or her life may comprise a sustained interaction with health care providers, many of whom are ill equipped to manage effectively the patient's problems. Many patients with LTHC experience episodes of exacerbation and remission in which symptoms can vary in intensity and duration. The key to effective management is to improve the individual's quality of life facilitating pleasurable and independent living.

Self-Management in LTHC

Over the last decade in the UK there has been a shift away from paternalistic models of healthcare that placed patients as the passive recipients of care (Barlow, Wright, Sheasby, Turner, & Hainsworth, 2002). The more active involvement demanded by many patients coincides with the realities of having a LTHC, whereby responsibility for day-to-day disease management gradually shifts from health care professionals to the individual. Thus, it is not surprising that the role of self-management interventions in facilitating adaptation is the subject of increased academic, public and political interest. Indeed, a recent review of LTHC self-management interventions found that the largest proportion of studies was published in the 1990s (Barlow et al. 2002).

Clark et al. [12] suggest that successful self-management requires sufficient knowledge of the condition and its treatment, performance of condition management activities and application of the necessary skills to maintain adequate psychosocial functioning.

Thus, self-management can be described as follows:

> 'Self-management refers to the individual's ability to manage the symptoms, treatment, physical and psychosocial consequences and life style changes inherent in living with a chronic condition. Efficacious self-management encompasses ability to monitor one's condition and to effect the cognitive, behavioural and emotional responses necessary to maintain a satisfactory quality of life. Thus, a dynamic and continuous process of self-regulation is established.' [13].

How Self-Management Education Differs from Patient Education

Traditional patient education, the content of which is determined by health providers, teaches patients disease-specific information and technical skills (e.g. blood glucose monitoring in diabetes and management of inhalers in asthma). Bodenheimer et al (2002) maintain that self-management complements traditional patient education. The provision of information is an important part of self-management, however, self-management differs because of its focus on the patient's own agenda, improving problem solving skills, and improving confidence (self-efficacy) to use those skills in coping with a broad range of consequences of living with a LTHC. In group-based self-management, the course leader acts as guide or model sharing similar characteristics with participants (e.g. having a LTHC). This approach is in contrast with patient education typically delivered by a health professional (see Table 2). Bodenheimer et al. believe that only 'true' self-management interventions include patient focused goals (goal setting). In their review of arthritis and LTHC self-management interventions, they found that interventions which included goal setting tended to demonstrate more improvements than those without a goal setting component.

Self-management may be one means of bridging the gap between patients' needs and the capacity of health and social care services to meet those needs. A diverse range of approaches have been employed in attempts to improve physical and psychosocial well-being among people with a LTHC. Self-management interventions can be group-based, individualized, or a combination of both (Barlow et al. 2002) and include computer-assisted programmes (e.g. Horan, Yarborough, Besigel, & Carlson, 1990), mail-delivered programmes (e.g. Fries, Carey, & McShane, 1997), telephone contacts (e.g. Rene, Weinberger, Mazzuca, Brandt, & Katz, 1992) and individual and group education programmes (e.g. Simeoni, Bauman, Stenmark, & O'Brien, 1995).

A review by Barlow et al. (2002) found broad similarities in the type of self-management approaches developed for people with LTHCs, particularly in terms of course content. However, there was also considerable variation and it is acknowledged that there will always be disease-specific management tasks. A diverse range of self-management components was identified. These were broadly classified as providing information, drug management, symptom management, dealing with psychosocial consequences, lifestyle (including exercise), social support, communication and other self-management strategies such as career planning, goal setting and accessing support services.

The most effective interventions utilize cognitive and behavioural modification, in addition to providing information (Lorig, 1995). Examples of self-management interventions encompassing these techniques and which have an established evaluation record are the disease-specific, lay-led Arthritis Self-Management Programme (ASMP) and the generic Chronic Disease Self-Management Course (CDSMC), both developed at Stanford University by Professor Kate Lorig. Few interventions have dealt with more than one disease or with the problems of co-morbidity (Lorig et al. 1999). The CDSMC recognizes the common issues faced by many people with a LTHC.

It has been estimated that people aged 60 years and older have, on average, 2.2 LTHCs (Hoffman, Rice, & Sung, 1996) and therefore have to manage these diseases and their consequences simultaneously. Equally, there are many generic skills that are needed. Analyses of self-management tasks faced by people with three of the most common LTHCs presenting in primary care (i.e. arthritis, asthma and diabetes) show that there are many commonalties (Barlow, Hearnshaw & Sturt, 2003). Tasks include making lifestyle changes (e.g. exercise, diet, giving up smoking), dealing with the psychological distress, and communicating effectively with health professionals.

Table 1. Comparison of Traditional Patient Education and Self-management Education

	Traditional Patient Education	**Self-management Education**
What is taught?	Information and technical skills about the disease	Skills on how to act on problems
How are problems formulated?	Problems reflect inadequate control of disease	The patient identifies problems he/she experiences that may or may not be reflected by disease
Relation of education to the disease?	Education is disease-specific and teaches information and technical skills related to the disease	Education provides problem-solving skills that are relevant to the consequences of chronic conditions in general
What is the theory underlying the education?	Disease-specific knowledge creates behavior change, which in turn produces better clinical outcomes	Greater patient confidence in his/her capacity to make life-improving changes (self-efficacy) yields better clinical outcomes
What is the goal?	Compliance with the behavior changes taught to the patient to improve clinical outcomes	Increased self-efficacy to improve clinical outcomes
Who is the educator?	A health professional	A health professional, peer leader, or other patients, often in settings

(Bodenheimer et al. 2002, p. 2471)

The content and format (see Table 1) of the ASMP and CDSMC are essentially the same, differing only in respect of the provision of arthritis information in the former. The course comprises six, weekly sessions, each lasting approximately two hours, delivered by pairs of lay leaders, most of whom have a LTHC themselves. The course is multi-component and topics include: disease information, an overview of self-management principles, exercise, cognitive symptom management (e.g. distraction, visualisation and guided imagery), dealing with depression, nutrition, communication with family and health professionals, and contracting. The last of these involves the setting of realistic goals to be achieved during the forthcoming week. Goals should be personally relevant, achievable, but at the same time challenging, have proximal outcomes and depend largely upon a person's own efforts. Participants report back to their group on their achievements at the next weekly session. The format of the course is largely interactive, with short 'lecturettes' to introduce topics, group discussion, problem solving, role plays and mastery experience (i.e. trying out the skills introduced on the course). Course format and content is guided by a manual to ensure consistency of content. The use of a structured manual has methodological and outcome advantages. It helps to ensure a consistent standard of content delivery by lay tutors who often do not come from an education or training/counseling background.

Table 2. Summary of effect sizes for Barlow et al. research studies

	ASMP					CDSMC	
	Barlow et al.1997 (N=62)	Barlow et al. 1999 (N=89)	Barlow et al. 1998 (N=117)	Barlow et al. 1998 (N=112)	Barlow et al. 2000 (N=544)	Wright et al. 2003 (N=185)	Barlow et al. 2004? (N=171)
Outcome measure							
Self-efficacy (pain)	0.51	0.45	0.53	0.51	?	0.43	0.51
Self-efficacy (symptoms)	0.45	0.35	0.43	0.36	?	0.38	0.43
Cognitive symptom management	0.55	0.47	0.76	0.75	?	0.44	0.44
Communication with physician	0.35	0.21	0.24	0.39	?	0.33	0.30
Fatigue (VAS)	-0.19	-	-0.26	-0.20	?	-0.27	-0.34
Pain (VAS)	-0.23	-0.21	-0.27	-0.22	?	-0.09	-0.11
Anxiety	-	-	-0.18	-0.19	?	-0.19	-0.16
Depression[1]	-0.23	-	-0.14	-0.21	?	-0.18	-0.25

[1]Measured by HADs apart from Barlow et al. (1997) which uses CES-D.

Table 3. Format and content of Lorig's self-management course

Format	Content
• Lay-led	• Guide imagery
• 6 weekly 2.5 hour sessions	• Exercise
• Group	• Nutrition
• Interactive	• Dealing with depression and anger
• Goal-setting	• Communicating with health professionals
• Problem solving	• Relaxation
• Role modeling	• Breathing exercises

SELF-EFFICACY ENHANCEMENT

The course is set within the framework of self-efficacy theory (Bandura, 1991). Perceived self-efficacy relates to a person's belief that they can utilise the motivation, cognitive resources and behaviours to meet narrowly defined situations (Bandura, 1991). A person's self-efficacy determines what they will try, how hard they will try and for how long they will try. Both the ASMP and the CDSMC aim to enhance perceived ability to control various aspects of arthritis through four major efficacy-enhancing strategies: skills mastery, modeling, persuasive communication and reinterpretation of symptoms.

Skills mastery is considered to be the most potent efficacy enhancing strategy. This involves learning and practising appropriate behaviours. New behaviours should be broken into smaller, manageable ones to ensure that each is successfully executed. It is important that course participants set their own written goals in the form of a contract. Personal goals serve to provide greater incentive for task accomplishment. Making a contract and receiving feedback provide an opportunity for participants to monitor progress.

Modelling is a technique whereby a realistic, positive, role model who is successfully managing aspects of their life serves as a source of inspiration to course participants. In the context of the ASMP, this role model is represented by the course leaders who themselves have arthritis. Course participants also act as models when encouraged to share their knowledge and strategies for overcoming disease-related problems.

Persuasive communication is most effective when it involves encouraging participants to attempt a little more than they are currently doing. Evidence suggests that group members can influence a member who is reluctant to initiate a course of action. Persuasion is most effective when used in combination with other techniques.

Reinterpretation of physiological symptoms is the final type of efficacy enhancing strategy. Participants are taught to distinguish between physiological disease-related symptoms such as pain, fatigue, muscle soreness of their arthritis and similar symptoms that can arise from therapeutic exercise for example.

Review of Findings from Evaluations of the ASMP and the CDSMC: Non-UK

Worldwide evidence for the effectiveness of the ASMP has been accumulating since the early 1980s. Randomised controlled studies have shown that, after attending the ASMP, participants report improvement across a range of health status variables including pain, depressed mood and visits to physicians (Lorig, Lubeck, Kraines, Seleznick and Holman, 1985). In an exploratory study, Lenker, Lorig and Gallagher (1984) compared participants who reported improvement in at least one health status variable with those who showed no improvement and found that the former group was distinguished by a belief that they could do something to cope with the consequences of arthritis. Subsequent courses were modified to include efficacy-enhancing strategies and resulted in greater improvements in health status outcomes compared to earlier versions (Lorig and Gonzales, 1992), moreover improvements have been sustained over 4 years (ref). Sustained improvements are critical in the context of managing LTHCs. Results from Australia (Simeoni, et al. 1995) and Sweden (Lindroth, Bauman, Barnes, McCredie, & Brooks, 1989) have shown broadly similar improvements.

Evidence for the CDSMC is less extensive and predominantly US based. A randomized controlled trial involving nearly 1000 heart disease, lung disease, stroke and arthritis patients showed that, at 6 months, there were significant improvements on aspects of physical and psychological health status, and health service utilisation (e.g. hospitalisations) (ref). Despite worsening disease, benefits remained evident at 2-year follow-up (Lorig, Ritter, Stewart, Sobel, Brown, Bandura, Gonzalez, *et al.,* 2001a). A non-randomised, 1-year, follow-up study of the CDSMC based on patients recruited through Kaiser Permanente (a non-profit health maintenance organization), found improvements on health behaviours, self-efficacy and health status (Lorig, Sobel, Ritter, Laurent, & Hobbs, 2001b). Similar improvements have recently been reported among US Hispanics (Lorig et al. 2003).

UK Findings

Barlow and colleagues have been evaluating the impact of the ASMP and the CDSMC for participants and tutors for the last 10 years. The course has been evaluated among a range of populations and delivery settings including voluntary organizations, adult education and community settings. In the 1980s, the ASMP was delivered in the UK by Arthritis Care, the leading UK arthritis charity, which is responsible for providing information and services for people with arthritis and campaigning on their behalf for improved health, employment and social rights. In 1998 following the success of the ASMP, the Long-Term Medical Conditions Alliance (LMCA) initiated a project called “Living with Long-term Illness’ (Lill) using the generic CDSMC. The CDSMC has since been adopted as the foundation of the Department of Health's Expert Patient Programme (EPP) that is being rolled out across primary care in England and by the Welsh Assembly in Wales. The CDSMC is subject to an ongoing national RCT. Table 2 provides an overview of the studies conducted and published to date by Barlow and colleagues.

Table 2 shows consistency across all the studies in terms of statistically significant improvements in several outcomes such as self-efficacy, cognitive symptom management and improved communication with physician. The improvement in self-efficacy is important, as it is the theoretical framework upon which the course is based, and studies show that self-efficacy mediates outcomes in self-management (Barlow, Williams and Wright, 1999). However, differential improvements were found particularly for fatigue, pain and exercise outcomes. US studies of the ASMP and CDSMC consistently report significant increases in exercise, as do the UK studies of the ASMP. Thus, failure to find a significant change in exercise in the UK CDSMC study (Wright et al. 2003) was unexpected. In order to gain an insight into this unexpected finding, interviews were conducted with participants and course tutors. Some participants believed that exercise was not appropriate for them because of their severe physical limitations, a view that was echoed by several tutors. Overall, tutors appeared to be concerned about encouraging all people with LTHCs to take up exercise, because of the impaired physical functioning of a few. An observation study found that tutors' goal setting preference influenced participants' own choice of goals (Mcfarland et al). As described above, the key to successful goal setting is choosing goals which are personally relevant. As role modeling is a key aspect of the lay-led CDSMC, further examination of the issue of tutors' exercise beliefs and preferences for their own self-management behaviours and the impact of these on course delivery appears warranted. Greater acknowledgment of existing beliefs may be called for if the CDSMC is to motivate participants with severe physical limitations to begin gentle exercise.

The fact that there are differential outcome effects across the ASMP and CDSMC course may be expected. Although LTHCs can lead to similar psychosocial consequences and need for adaptation, the underlying nature and pattern of symptoms can be quite distinct. Pain is the primary symptom in arthritis and is commonly the reason why the patient seeks medical help (ref). Table 2 shows that the ASMP was successful in reducing this important outcome in ?/? studies. The significant reduction in pain among the Intervention Group at 12 months, which was not evident at 4 months, may suggest that greater use of self-management strategies and increased perceptions of control may take longer than four months to impact on this important aspect of the arthritis experience (Barlow, Turner & Wright, 2000). The CDSMC, which comprised a heterogeneous sample of participants, did not lead to a reduction in pain. The mean pain scores of participants attending the CDSMC were considerably lower than participants attending the ASMP, (i.e. 6 and 3 on a 10 cm VAS respectively), suggesting that pain is not a particularly important problem for many of this group of participants. From a statistical perspective low baseline scores suggest a floor effect (i.e. scores are already at their lowest) and therefore there is little scope for improvement.

The lack of change in health care use in several of the UK studies contrasts with US studies, which consistently show a reduction. This difference may be due to the differences in health care delivery between the two countries, which is free at the point of delivery in the UK. There was no change in the use of healthcare resources at four months in the ASMP RCT study. However, by 12 months the Intervention Group reported a small but significant decrease in visits to GPs to discuss arthritis. The importance attached to reducing health care visits may be misplaced. A more worthwhile, patient-focused outcome would be an improvement in the level of satisfaction and usefulness of the medical encounter rather than a reduction in encounters *per se*. In addition, frequency of hospital visits may not reflect severity of the patient's condition, but rather the typical operating procedures of each clinic (e.g. regular 6 monthly check-ups).

The course to date is primarily marketed and delivered to participants whose primary LTHC is of a physical rather than psychological origin. For most participants' their psychological problems are connected to their physical illness. At baseline, ASMP and CDSMC participants show elevated levels of psychological distress compared to population norms. Half of the female arthritis participants were in the 'at risk' category (ref). In the CDSMC study (ref), 46% and 58% of males were 'at risk' on depressive and anxious moods, respectively, compared with normative values of 8% and 26% (Crawford *et al.*, 2001). The corresponding percents for females were 39% and 64%, compared with normative values of 13% and 38%. No significant changes were found at 4-month follow-up for male participants on depressive and anxious mood states, respectively. However, significant reductions were found for female participants on depressive and anxious mood states. Eighteen percent and 19% of women moved from 'at clinical risk' to 'not at risk' categories on depressed and anxious mood, respectively, compared with 8% and 8% who moved in the opposite direction. A sub group analyses of participants whose primary LTHC was depression (N=13) and found that 12 months after attending the course depressed participants reported a 20% reduction in depression, a 24% reduction in anxiety, a 45% reduction in fatigue and a 25 % increase in self-efficacy.

The finding that the course has the potential to reduce anxiety and depressed mood is interesting and highlights its possible usefulness in the treatment of sub-clinical anxious and depressed participants. The course is considered to be primarily an educational and self-management intervention, rather than a therapy based intervention. However, the difference appears to be more semantic than real when one considers the description of *self-management therapy* offered by Rehm & Rokke () writing in the *Handbook of Cognitive Behvioural Therapies.*

> "Self-management models stress the notion of the person in the person by situation interaction. The therapeutic skills represent individual differences that are relatively consistent across time and place. They are generalized skills that the person may apply as the strategy to similar situations. Generalised application to actual life situations is the central focus of self-management therapy procedures. Such therapies attempt to sample situations from real life, bring them into the therapy office for practice and then send the individual out to apply the strategies in everyday life". (p137.)

Rehma and Rokke () suggest that, generalized, low self-efficacy has a role in the development and maintenance of anxious and depressed mood. In anxiety it is equated with a lack of confidence in one's ability to cope with novel and threatening situations and in depressed mood it is similar to Seligman's concept of learned helplessness. Rehem and Roke argue that, theoretically, Bandura's model of self-efficacy has a potential role in reducing anxiety and depression.

Future Research

Recruitment

"Imagine throwing a party and no one came"

Brady (2003) stated that despite compelling reasons for people with LTHC to benefit from self-management courses many are choosing not to attend. Less than 1% of eligible US citizens have attended the ASMP. Similar difficulties in recruiting participants has also been found in the UK context. Considerable effort is expended on recruitment and it is a major concern for tutors who describe the burden of marketing the course as the least enjoyable aspect of their role (ref). Bancroft et al. () conducted a small-scale study looking at the issues of non-attendance (participants who had registered for the course and who did not attend any sessions) and non-completion (participants who attended < 3 sessions). The main reason for non-attendance and non-completion centered around the timing (either too early or too late), location (too far away and/or unknown) and restricted or no free parking at the venue. Provision of clear directions, a map and details of free parking and transportation may assist. In addition, discussion of travel to course venue could be included in the first session, thus enabling participants to share transport. The other main reason for non-attendance and non-completion was that of illness of the participant or family/friend. Interventions for people with LTHC will have a proportion of participants who have a disease flare that coincides with course delivery. Allowance for illness should be made at the recruitment stage by exceeding the maximum number (16) of participants permitted to attend. Chronicity of problems is predictive of programme completion among people with emotional, coping and interpersonal problems (Tasca et al. 1999).

The Arthritis Foundation in the US found that barriers to participation also included course venue and timing issues. Other factors included inadequate marketing and uncertainty regarding course benefits among health professionals, which meant that they were reluctant to refer patients. Suggestions for improvement included, free transport for participants, waiving course fees, tailoring marketing message for different age groups, targeting media outlets and providing alternative delivery modes. Evidence from the pilot stage of the EPP in the UK (Kennedy et al., 2004) would also suggest that recruiting participants onto courses is a difficult and onerous task. In addition the authors suggest that primary care leads found it difficult to persuade health care professionals, particularly general practitioners, of the benefits of user-led initiatives.

Sample Bias

Whilst effectiveness data from the USA and the UK are encouraging, several important questions remain. Participants are predominantly, self-referred, white, female and educated. The low attendance rates for men found in our studies (usually < 30%) is a concern and warrants further investigation. Evidence from patient support group studies tends to show that men prefer the emphasis to be on education and information, rather than provision of emotional support (refs). Both the ASMP and the CDSMC are emotionally supportive environments, which may deter men from attending and lead to greater attrition compared to women. Tutors should consider that male participants may be unwilling to receive or provide emotional support and would rather focus on the more practical aspects of the course such as problems solving and goal setting. One of the main criticisms often leveled at studies which have examined the effectiveness of self-management courses is selection bias. The majority of studies are based on volunteers, who, by the act of enrolling on an educational intervention demonstrate that they are already motivated to make changes in their lives and are likely to be extremely receptive to the idea of self-management and improving health behavior. There is a sense in which all study participants, regardless of the nature of the study intervention, are volunteers who chose to take part in research (Barlow, 2002). Self-selection, or volunteering, could be deemed essential in pragmatic studies that aim to emulate how an intervention will operate outside of the research setting. Nonetheless, the potential for bias towards improvement in self-referred samples is acknowledged Large scale, UK nationwide ASMP and CDSMC studies involving General Practice referred patients are currently collecting data and will go some way to assessing whether benefits extend to patient samples.

Interest and motivation to self-care may differ between white, well-educated participants and participants from minority ethnic groups and those from socially disadvantaged backgrounds. There is evidence from the UK and the United States showing that existing health care providers fail to deliver services equitably both in terms of access and outcomes. In particular minority ethnic groups experience a number of areas of disadvantage. Only one study has evaluated the CDSMP in a non-white, UK population (ref?). Results show that Bengali participants in Tower Hamlets, London report increases in self-efficacy and symptom management by white participants after attending a culturally modified version of the CDSMC . It is important that the nationwide implementation of the CDSMC addresses inequities in access. A failure to do so is likely to widen rather than attenuate health inequalities. This point has been taken up the EPP who propose that:

In the UK, the Department of Health (December, 2003) have recently emphasized the importance of widening choice and access to health care among disadvantaged, ethnic groups. The Government aims to improve the lives of all people with LTHC by extending the availability of the CDSMC. At the moment it appears that the success of this aim will be severely limited if the CDSMC does not attract interest from ethnic minority participants. Cultural beliefs and practices of minority ethnic groups need to be understood if appropriate and effective self-help interventions are to be offered. One way of achieving this would be to recruit lay tutors from these communities who could act as effective role models for their peers.

Alternative Delivery Modes

"If you cant take Mohammed to the mountain, take the mountain to Mohammed"

Web-enabled and written self-management interventions address problems of inappropriate course location and timing by allowing participants to access courses at a time and location which is convenient to them. Lorig has recently shown that a mail-delivered version and a web-enabled version of the ASMP (the Healthier Living with Arthritis Program) were as effective as original group-based versions in increasing self-efficacy and improving health outcomes. One difficulty with developing web-enabled self-management tools is that those groups who would derive most from this mode of delivery (e.g. the elderly, those with the highest level of functional limitations) are least likely to have access to the internet. For example a recent survey in the UK found that only 15 per cent of adults aged 65 and over had accessed the internet in the three months prior to the survey compared to 83 per cent of 16-24 year olds (http://www.statistics.gov.uk/CCI/nugget.asp?ID=914).

Furthermore, those individuals from the most socio-economically disadvantaged backgrounds are less likely to ready have access to the internet http://www.statistics.gov.uk/statbase/ssdataset.asp?vlnk=6937&More=Y

Source - Family Expenditure Survey (April 1998 to March 2001); Expenditure and Food Survey (April 2001 onwards).

CONCLUSION

The science fiction film *Logan's Run* (1976) recognized the relationship between ageing and infirmity and proposed a novel approach to dealing with the problem – no-one was allowed to live after their thirtieth birthday! As radical euthanasia seems a long way of in the future, today's healthcare policy must find a more humane and sensitive solution to deal with the predicted rise in the number of people with LTHCs. Interventions which empower people to develop self-management skills may be one small part of the solution. Research of lay-led self-management programmes such as the ASMP and CDSMC has tended to demonstrate their effectiveness in improving psychosocial outcomes. Sub-group analysis of important variables such as gender, and improvers vs non-improvers, would identify characteristics of those who stand to gain most benefit, thus ensuring effective use of resources. Future research should also focus on implementation variables including how to disseminate the course widely and equitably. The full potential of self-management programmes will not be realised unless multiple referral methods and delivery methods are made widely available. Health professional approval should ensure higher attendance and lower attrition rates.

To be considered worthwhile and attractive to healthcare practitioners, healthcare purchasers and patients alike, the benefits accruing from self-management interventions should persist over extended periods of time. However, long-term evaluations are rare. Perhaps it is unreasonable to expect a brief, lay-led self-management course to maintain long-term improvements in the absence of additional, regular booster sessions. The role of booster sessions in terms of format (e.g. telephone, written or group) and regularity need to be addressed.

Finally, although we have published widely on the benefits of Lorig's Stanford lay-led self-management programmes, we recognize that it is not suitable for everyone with a LTHC and that there is a continuing role for alternative disease specific, health professional led self-management programmes.

Living with Long-Term Disabling Conditions

In: Focus on Disability: Trends in Research and Application ISBN: 978-1-60021-792-0
Editor: Thilo Kroll, pp. 165-180 © 2008 Nova Science Publishers, Inc.

Chapter X

Coping with Cancer: Family Caregivers and Psychological Burden

Maria Fotiadou

Interdisciplinary Research Centre in Health, School of Health & Social Sciences, Coventry University, CV1 5FB, UK.

Abstract

Important advances in medical care have been achieved in the last few decades, both in prevention of cancer and the development of effective cancer treatment. Nevertheless, the incidence of cancer has increased during the last decade and cancer is considered to be the leading life-threatening illness in developed countries (e.g. European countries, USA). Research has acknowledged the psychological distressing experience of cancer for patients and their caregivers. Family caregivers of cancer patients can experience psychological burden that is associated with anxiety and depression, physical health problems and poor coping skills. Cancer research has often addressed the need of caregivers for information from health professionals. However, there is little in the way of formal psychosocial support or interventions for family caregivers of cancer patients.

Keywords: Family Caregivers, Cancer, Psychological Burden, Coping

Introduction

The progress in medical treatment and survival rates in the field of life threatening illnesses, such as cancer, have been major research issues in the last 30 years. Accompanying this progress has been a large number of research studies, which have focused extensively on both the physical and psychological functioning of the patient with cancer. A life threatening illness, such as cancer, can be a distressful experience for the whole family. Diagnosis of cancer, medical treatment, remission, side effects, regular hospitalisation and fear of relapse usually change family life to a great extent. Generally, the psychological burden that families of patients with cancer experience put them at a great risk of emotional and physical distress (Pearlin, Mullan, Semple and Skaff, 1990; Wright and Kirby, 1999). Caregivers have to deal with the insecurity and uncertainty that the diagnosis of cancer comprises and cope with its consequences on both the family's and individual's stability and strength.

Medical Aspects of Cancer

Epidemiology of Cancer

Cancer is a term used to describe a number of diseases that include similar characteristics that develop at different sites of the body. Cancer represents different types of diseases (Corner & Bailey, 2001; Hancock, 1996; Nevidjon & Sowers, 2000) that can differ in their treatment, progress, and outcomes. Cancer is a type of disorder that is characterised by uncontrolled development of cells that exceeds that of the cell typology that it originates from. There are two main reasons that explain the malignant nature of the disease. As Stanford Cancer Centre in USA (2005) states:

"Cancer is malignant because it can be 'locally invasive' and 'metastatic':

- Locally invasive: the tumour can invade the tissues surrounding it by sending out 'fingers' of cancerous cells into the normal tissue.
- Metastatic: the tumour can send cells into other tissues in the body, which may be distant from the original tumour." (Stanford Cancer Centre website, http://cancer.stanfordhospital.com/healthInfo/cancerOverview/default, 2005)

Early diagnosis in some types of cancer can lead to prevention of further development and to long-term survival (Langton, 2000). Absence of early treatment leads to spread and increased growth of cells. Further exposure to external factors, the so called 'promoters' (e.g. ionising radiation) has also been found to increase the abnormal growth of carcinogenic cells (Nevidjon and Sowers, 2000).

Cancer is one of the main causes of death in European Union (Cancer Research UK, http://info.cancerresearchuk.org/cancerstats/geographic/world/commoncancers, 2005). Between 2000 and 2004 new cases of cancer increased from 1.9 to 2.9 million. Most of the people diagnosed with cancer were over 65 years of age. The rates showed that one in three people in European Union will develop cancer during their life (Cancer Research UK, website, http://info.cancerresearchuk.org/cancerstats/geographic/cancerineu, 2005). During 2004 there were approximately 1.7 million deaths from cancer. Rates of cancer have increased dramatically, with lung, colorectal, breast and stomach cancer being the leading types of cancer and causes of death throughout the European countries (Corner & Bailey, 2001). Among women, breast cancer is the most common type of cancer and, lung and prostate cancer are the most common type of cancer in men (Nevidjon and Sowers, 2000).

Leukaemia and brain tumours have found to be the most common cases of cancer in children and adolescents (Langton, 2000).

Causes of Cancer and Risk Factors

There are three primary factors that can influence the cancer development: 1. environmental exposure to carcinogens (e.g. sun), 2. genetic predisposition to cancer and, 3. immune system status. However, cancer development can take years and varies depending on both tumour and individual factors, such as age and gender (Visovsky & Workman, 2000). Environmental factors include physical and chemical agents. Physical agents can damage DNA and lead to cancer development. Ionising radiation, radiation therapy, industrial accidents and chronic irritation or tissue trauma are the most common examples of physical agents. Several chemicals and drugs that are used in every day life are considered to be carcinogenic including alcohol and tobacco. Chronic exposure to these chemicals has been proven to increase the risk of developing cancer (e.g. lung cancer, uterine cervix cancer) (Visovsky & Workman, 2000).

Individual factors can also influence someone's chances to develop cancer. Age is a very important risk factor in the development of cancer. Half of the cases of cancer happen in people older than 65 years of age (American Cancer Society, 1998). Cancer occurs less in the age group of 18-40 years of age. In addition, the predisposition to cancer is greater for people from families with previous cancer history. Gender is another important factor as well. For instance, women are more likely to develop breast cancer. Incidence also differs among races. African Americans for example, are at greater risk for developing prostate cancer or uterine cancer than Caucasians (American Cancer Association, 1998) Finally, people with weak immune functioning, such as children under the age of 2 years and people older than 60 years, organ transplant receivers, are more vulnerable to cancer (Visovsky & Workman, 2000).

There are specific causes for some types of cancer. For example lifestyle factors such as sunbathing and smoking are causes of melanomas and lung cancer respectively and changes in lifestyle will reduce or eliminate the risk of these types of cancer. However, causes are not known for all types of cancer. In such cases, early detection can prevent further development or spread of the tumour, increase treatment effectiveness and improve survival rates (Visovsky & Workman, 2000).

Treatment of Cancer and Side Effects

Chemotherapy is one of the most effective treatments in treating cancer. Chemotherapy is the use of anticancer drugs that act on the causes of the disorder. The main effect of the therapy is to stop the spreading of the carcinogenic cells to other parts of the body. (Langton, 2000). However, one of the major problems of this treatment is that the drugs act not only on the tumour but also on all rapidly dividing cells (Nevidjon & Sowers 2000). Thus, they may influence the bone marrow, and contribute to hair loss, anorexia, nausea, vomiting, diarrhea, paleness, melancholy, and lethargy. Chemotherapy constitutes the only treatment when the spread of cancer is not controllable and other treatments are not suitable (Fisch & Bruera, 2003; Nevidjon & Sowers, 2000)

Electromagnetic radiation is believed to be the most important treatment of cancer and is conducted by X-rays or gamma rays directed to tissue (Langton, 2000). *Radiotherapy* is used to treat different types of cancer and at different stages of disease. As far as the process is concerned, the radiation passes into the diseased tissue in order to destroy it or to prevent further spreading in various types of cancer, especially in metastatic tumours. Radiotherapy is also considered appropriate in cases where tumours cannot be removed by surgery (Cooper and Watson, 1991; Nevidjon and Sowers, 2000). As with chemotherapy, radiotherapy may cause unpleasant side effects, such as nausea, fatigue, vomiting and loss of hair (Barraclough, 1999; Hancock, 1996; Schou & Hewison, 1999). A late and very important effect of both chemotherapy and radiotherapy may be an increased possibility of cancer relapse (Langton, 2000).

Depending on the success of chemotherapy and radiotherapy as well as the nature of the disease, *surgery* may be necessary. Surgery is mainly appropriate for solid tumours. The primary approach of treatment in cancer is to reduce the size of the tumour and the spread of the carcinogenic cells. The progress in surgical techniques means that the cancer patient recovers quicker and experiences less side effects or disability compared to the other treatments. Surgery is not successful in cases where cancer has spread to tissues that can not be removed or the metastases are not isolated (Fisch & Bruera, 2003; Nevidjon & Sowers, 2000).

Bone marrow transplantation (BMT) is mainly used to treat leukaemia (Acute Lymphoblastic Leukaemia (ALL), Acute Myeloid Leukaemia (AML) and some cases of solid tumours (e.g. lymphomas). Patients under this treatment receive bone marrow from a donor after they have been treated with high doses of chemotherapy and in some cases radiotherapy in order to eliminate the malignant cells. Anaemia and fatigue are some of the side effects of BMT. Because of the high health risks, BMT is only recommended when other treatment can not assure cure of cancer.

FAMILY CAREGIVERS AND CANCER

The Tasks of Caregiving

The physiological side effects of the different treatments may cause patients to experience fatigue, feelings of isolation, insecurity, fear of death, low self-esteem and negative affect (Barraclough, 1999; Cooper & Watson, 1991; Langton, 2000). All these factors can make it an extremely difficult time for caregivers of patients with cancer. Caregiving is the most common and important type of assistance provided by family or friends. The obvious complexity of the meaning of caregiving has led the British Medical Association (1995) to describe the caregiver as someone, who provides unpaid regular care to another family member or friend, who has a disability or chronic illness and is incapable to support him/herself (Barer & Johnson, 1990). Caregiving research has focused on the family environment, and in particular on the role of spouses (Gray, Fitch, Phillips, Labrecque & Fergus, 2000; Gritz, Wellisch, Siau &Wang, 1990; Manne & Glassman, 2000; Morse & Fife, 1998), and children (Lewis, Hammond & Woods, 1993) as caregivers. However, caregivers can also be non-family members, such as close friends or neighbours. There is lack of research on caregivers of cancer patients.

Caregivers are confronted with many different tasks that vary depending on the problems experienced by the patient. Generally, the concerns of caregivers focus on their ability to provide physical care in order to meet patients' daily demands, (e.g. bathing, dressing, transportation and medical issues) and psychological care to meet the patient's emotional demands (e.g. help reduce anxiety and depression) (Hileman, Lackey, & Hassanein, 1992). Being the caregiver of a child patient with cancer usually

> "Requires a fundamental redefining of their self-identities and represents the beginning of a 'passage through crisis'. Although they are not themselves ill, caregivers experience many of the consequences of chronic illness, including biographical disruption, compromise in role function and deterioration in quality of life." (Young, et al., 2002, p.210).

Adaptation to a Chronic Stressor

Sometimes, cancer is compared to a crisis (Lalos, 1992). A diagnosis of cancer is an intensely strong experience for the patient but what is not well documented is how much the entire family is influenced by the diagnosis. Caregiving for a patient with cancer can be a source of severe distress, as patients usually experience chronic pain and fear of death (Kurtz, et al., 1995; Munkres, Oberst & Hughes, 1992). The word 'cancer' sometimes causes feelings of fear, dread and terror, even in cases of good prognosis (Gotay, 1984). More recently, Perrson, and his colleagues (1998) also found that spouses of cancer patients were experiencing feelings of being in a crisis situation. Zarit (1989) first established that caregiving is a stressful activity, which influences both caregiver's well being and quality of life. This distress has often been called "caregiver burden". Schultz, Newsom, and their collaborators (1997) argued that the demands and the level of stress of caregiving usually vary across individuals, because of the severity of the activities and difficulties of the illness or disability. The diagnosis of cancer has short as well as long-term effects on family's well-being. Anxiety, denial, anger, and guilt are among the initial emotional reactions family members experience after the diagnosis of cancer (Adelman, Albert, Rabkin, Del Bene, Tider, O'Sullivan, 2004; Haley, 2003). In the short-term family's social relationships, daily routine, employment and financial issues are often affected (Goldbeck, 2001). In the long-term, family functioning sometimes remains disrupted because of the fear of a future relapse (Goldbeck, 2001). A number of variables have been investigated in the context of a caregiving profile and include emotional distress, diminished social participation, physical illness, changed relationships with other family members, and financial issues and difficulties in work (Gatz, Bengtson, & Blum, 1990). Research suggests that family caregivers find emotional problems the most difficult to cope with (Northouse, 2005; Young et al., 2002).

The combination of pressure, stress and anxiety has a direct impact on a caregiver's health. General homemaking and housekeeping activities such as cleaning, shopping, laundry, and transportation require energy and can be exhausting, particularly when added to existing tasks in one's personal life (Baider, et al., 1998; Twigg, 1992). Family caregivers of cancer patients frequently state that their physical health has been influenced by caregiving including interrupted sleep, chronic weakness, muscle pain, changes in eating, and lack of time to take care of themselves (Corner & Bailey, 2001). Caregivers have a greater susceptibility to physical problems than the normal population, which can sometimes lead to impaired immune functioning and enhanced use of psychotropic drugs (King & Brassington, 1997; Stein & Nyamathi, 1998; Vitaliano, 1997). In addition, caregivers are often unable to problem solve and manage some of the daily tasks, as many of them are usually unprepared to deal with demands of caregiving for a relative with cancer.

Communication with Health Professionals

According to Oberst and his colleagues (1989), the level of caregiving demands and often the reduced help from health professionals increase caregivers' feelings of inability to cope with the stress of caregiving. Dealing with cancer includes several complex communication issues for both caregivers and health professionals. Caregivers confront several difficulties and illness related demands and so, the need for information becomes greater. A major concern of caregivers involves attempts to find meaning and information during the experience of taking care of a loved one with cancer. For families to cope, they need appropriate support from health care professionals and the health care system. Hinds (1985) reported that caregivers of cancer patients required more comprehensive information from doctors (e.g. symptom control, likely pain levels, medication). Families carry much of the responsibility of cancer care as patients' health deteriorates.

Nolan and his colleagues (1996) found that health professionals tend to use a scientific and technical language, in order to describe illness symptoms, which limits the understanding of caregivers. Northouse and Northouse (1987) found that limited communication and absence of clear information can easily lead to misunderstandings and also to feelings of helplessness and further psychological burden.

Theoretical Framework for Looking at Caregiver Burden

The theoretical perspective of Lazarus and colleagues (1987) has guided caregiving research. In essence, the theoretical framework explains adjustment to illness and appraisal of caregiving in terms of cognition and emotional reactions (Cassidy, 2000; Ferguson, Matthews & Cox, 1999). Lazarus and Folkman (1984) determined that cognitive appraisal is critical to the psychological adjustment of the chronic illness. They argued that the impact of stress cannot be predicted from the event itself. They concluded that, in order to understand the meaning of stress in people's life, it is necessary to take into account the differences that exist among individuals (David and Suls, 1999; Forbes and Eisenberg, 1997). Hence, factors that can play important role in family's perception of the illness and their coping ability are gender, age, education, socioeconomic status, type of employment, marital status, culture and religion. Additional significant factors in family's adjustment in cancer can be the prognosis and the time of diagnosis, treatment and related side effects, family's perception of the illness as well as communication with the medical staff (Cooper & Watson, 1991; Munkres, et al., 1992; Schou & Hewison, 1999; Stern & Sekeres, 2004).

According to Lazarus' and Folkman's (1984) *cognitive-phenomenological model of stress*, an individual tends to evaluate the meaning of an event as stressful and threatening to his/her well being – this process is known as primary appraisal (Cohen, Kessler & Gordon, 1997). Secondary appraisal refers to the individual's evaluation of whether he/she has the ability and the resources to cope with the stressful situation (Lazarus, 1993; Munkres, et al., 1992; Ogden, 2000; Sheridan et al, 1992). Lazarus and Folkman's theory refers to three primary appraisals: threat (psychological and physical harm), challenge (potential for growth and gain) and loss (injury already happened) (Cassidy, 1999; Ferguson, Matthews & Cox, 1999; Lazarus & Folkman, 1984). Montgomery, Gonnyea and Hooyman (1985) also proposed that the basic contribution of the theoretical framework is the concept of psychological burden. The appraisal of a situation as threatening and dreadful is most of the times burdensome. This theoretical approach has important implications on caregiving theories. What gives this relationship between caregiving and psychological burden great meaning is that caregiving can be a demanding and hard experience and that most of the times it represents a possible threat to mental and physical health (Cochrane, Goering & Rogers, 1997; Ferguson, Lawrence & Matthews, 2000).

Zarit (1989) also emphasised the association between caregiving and stress, and proposed that the factors that contribute to caregiving burden and their relations are especially complex. Lawton, Kleban et al. (1989) reported a strong relationship among caregivers' appraisals, coping strategies, reappraisal and psychological burden. As illness progresses, caregivers tend to appraise their role as burdensome and stressful rather than a source of life satisfaction. George and Gwyther (1986) thought that caregiving could be associated with psychological wellbeing as well as psychological burden. Lawton and colleagues (1991) identified that both individual dispositions and particular situation stressors, such as caring for a relative with a chronic illness, have an impact on the psychological well being.

McCorkle, et al. (1993) reported high levels of psychological burden among caregivers of cancer patients that were accompanied with significant mental health problems, such as depressive symptoms, irrespective of treatment duration and progress. Gaynor (1990) suggested this relationship is stronger over long periods of care, especially after the first two years the diagnosis of cancer. Amongst these negative outcomes, depression is believed to represent the greatest risk. Clinical studies revealed that 50 percent of caregivers of cancer patients get depressed during the first year of caregiving (Butler, 1992). Caregivers of cancer patients are more likely to receive psychiatric treatment, and have more symptoms of overall psychological distress than the general population (Iconomou, Vagenakis & Kalofonos, 2001; Neundorfer, 1991).

"a substantial number of caregivers may be experiencing depression of a severity that could warrant intervention and treatment" (Schulz et al, 1995, p. 772).

Feelings of guilt, helplessness and being out of control are common in caregivers and are often derived from feeling unable to help the patient and meet his/her expectations (Manne & Glassman, 2000). Importantly, perceived control in demanding situations, such as cancer, together with low levels of self-esteem are likely to lead to the development of severe stress symptoms (Cassidy, 1999; Newsom & Schulz, 1998). Consistent with findings reported by Gritz and his colleagues (1990), caregivers increased levels of mental health problems, such as anxiety, were predicted by feeling out of control and dealing with emotions of helplessness. Fabes and Eisenberg (1997) asserted that the greater the intensity of an event the more negative emotion people will experience. They examined people's responses to control over stressful life events and found that they may react more effectively in controllable situations.

Social Relationships

As well as caring for the patients, caregivers have to deal with other different tasks such as, maintaining family stability, financial and work issues and balance the needs of the family member with cancer with the needs of other family members. Social, leisure and relaxation activities of caregivers resulting in social isolation and exclusion (Manne, Taylor, Dougherty & Kementy, 1997; Pistrang, Barker & Rutter, 1997). The majority of caregivers report impaired social relationships (Helgeson & Cohen, 1996). Caregiving responsibilities and other social obligations, misunderstandings among family members about the time or amount of caregiving, changes in social roles, emotional impacts of caregiving, and feelings of family stigma enhance distress among family and social system (Bass, 1990; Becker, Aldridge & Dearden, 1998). Impaired social relationships and poor social support can lead to lower life satisfaction, increased feelings of psychological burden, lower adjustment to illness and in some cases impaired communication with the patient (Lewis, Hammond & Woods, 1993; Manne, et al., 1997; Manne & Glassman, 2000). Perrson, Rasmusson and Hallberg (1998) found that the spouses of cancer patients experience feelings of distress, social isolation and restricted or lack of social support.

According to Walsh (1996), there are a number of important characteristics and traits that characterize family and social relationships of caregivers. Specifically, resilience in social relationships is associated with cohesion, flexibility, open communication, and problem solving, and with information seeking and communication with the doctor. Another essential characteristic of caregiving resilience is the accessibility of support group resources (e.g. caregivers of cancer patients groups) (Walsh, 1996). Sheehan & Nuttall (1988) underlined the importance of self-help support groups, which have been created by caregivers to share experiences, and exchange support and information.

Gender seems to have a very strong influence in the adjustment of cancer and the role of caregiving. Stein and Nyamathi (1999) found that female caregivers tend to experience greater levels of severe depressive symptoms compared to male caregivers. In particular, married female caregivers report high levels of mental health problems. Miller (1990) suggests that differences in social and domestic roles and responsibilities explains the greater susceptibility of female caregivers to greater levels of mental and physical health problems compared to male caregivers. Gender differences may not always be significant, as they depend on the time spent caregiving, the patient's diagnosis and prognosis and finally, the contribution of other family members in caregiving tasks (Allen, 1994; Young & Kahana, 1989). Gaynor (1990), Allen (1994) and Gray et al. (2000) pointed out that women, and in particular spouses are more likely than men to receive support from relatives and friends as they have wider social networks. However, this effect may change over the progress of treatment (Epping-Jordan et al., 1999). Interventions that provide practical and emotional support to caregivers could help reduce caregiver burden, reduce social isolation and improve coping skills (Cawley & Gerdts, 1988; Kramer, 1997; Toseland, Rossiter, Peak & Smith, 1990).

Coping

Existing research has identified that the needs of patients with cancer and the burdens that these needs inflict on caregivers seem to influence not only the psychological reaction but the coping skills of caregivers, as well (Given & Given, 1992; Nolan, et al., 1996). Coping is considered to be a mediator between stress and adaptation (Folkman and Moskowitz, 2004). It is mainly defined as individuals' ability to change their emotional, behavioural and cognitive efforts in order to manage internal or/and external demands over different situations (Folkman, Lazarus, Dunkel-Schetter, Delongis and Gruen, 1986). Folkman and Lazarus (1988) first made a distinction between two main categories of coping: problem-focused coping or active coping (effort to change the source of stress) and emotion-focused coping (reduce and manage stress-related emotions). Specifically, problem-focused coping refers to strategies such as information seeking, decision making, and managing the situation. Emotion-focused coping refers to suppression of negative emotions, seeking social and emotional support. Folkman and Lazarus (1988) proposed that problem-focused coping tends to predominate and be more adaptive in cases where individuals feel that something practical and beneficial can be done, whereas emotion-focused coping tends to predominate in situations where individuals believe that stressors have to be tolerated. However, the research literature often identifies appraisal-focused coping (changing the meaning of the experience in order to re-appraise potential stressors) as a third category of coping strategies (Patterson, Holm & Gurney, 2004).

According to a study on coping and parental adaptation to illness, parents used emotion-focused strategies in order to better cope with their child's illness. Positive outlook, suppression of negative emotions and fears, denial, fantasy, and intellectualization were among the most common coping strategies parents reported using (Sharan, Mehta & Choudhry, 1995).

Folkman and Moskowitz (2000) argued that the different approaches to caregiving agree on the following points:

1. Coping has multiple functions including the management of stressors in a situation;
2. Coping is influenced by the individuals' appraisal of the situation, including controllability;
3. Coping is influenced by social relationships;
4. Coping is influenced by personality dispositions including neuroticism, extraversion and optimism.

However, they argued that psychologists have not made enough progress in explaining how different coping strategies help individuals to minimize and control mental and physical health reactions of stress.

Coping and Caregivers of Cancer Patients

The few interventions that have previously developed for caregivers of cancer patients have shown that caregivers had higher scores of problem-solving after taking part in an educational intervention (Bucher, et al., 2001; Houts, Nezu, Nezu & Bucher, 1996). Engagement with creative activities (e.g. art) has also been proven to be helpful for caregivers of cancer patients (Walsh & Weiss, 2003). A study of adult daughter caregivers found that dispositional optimism was associated with lower depressive symptoms and better life satisfaction (Given, et al., 1993). Caregivers sometimes use avoidant coping strategies, such as denial and suppression as emotional coping strategies (Sharan et al., 1995). Grootenhuis and Last, (1997) reported that parents of cancer patients usually use two coping strategies, withdrawal and wishful thinking. Similarly a recent study found that caregivers of cancer patients tended to use more adaptive coping strategies (active coping) than maladaptive, such as withdrawal (Trask, Amber, et al., 2003). The family caregiving literature has identified a variety of coping strategies that could influence a family's adjustment to illness. Grootenhuis and Last (1997) argue that particular coping strategies, such as information seeking, maintaining positive emotions and social support, should be examined in relation to emotional adjustment to the illness in order to better understand the efficacy of control strategies. Folkman (1984) argued that in uncontrollable situations, emotion-focused coping strategies (e.g. distraction, avoidance) may be the only possible coping responses.

CONCLUSION

Cancer is very common in European countries. Advances in detection and treatment of cancer have led to higher rates of survival in patients with cancer. However, the life-threatening nature of cancer and intensive and protracted treatment regimens constitute a stressful and difficult experience not only for the patient but for family caregivers as well.

The supportive and important role of family caregivers for cancer patients is well documented (Carter and Chang, 2000; Schrerbring, 2002; Haley, 2003). Research has shown that generally caregivers experience high levels of psychological burden, which together with caregivers' poor adjustment to the illness, daily tasks related to caregiving and the lack of effective coping strategies can lead to both mental and physical health problems. Caregivers of patients with cancer can experience, fatigue, anxiety and depression. (Gaston-Johansson, Lachica, Fall-Dickson & Kennedy, 2004 Nijboer, et al., 1998).

Most medical and support services are provided for cancer patients. There is a limited awareness of the importance of the role of caregivers, which results in inadequate resources. Recognition of the importance and need of family caregivers is necessary. Health professionals, such as doctors and nurses, clinical and health psychologists, should be aware of the health and support issues surrounding caregivers. Communication, information and financial and social support from healthcare settings are also crucial in improving the ability of caregivers in coping for a patient with cancer and its related implications. More research is necessary to provide information on caregiving burden and its impact as well as to determine appropriate interventions that aim to help caregivers to cope with psychological burden and stress.

ACKNOWLEDGEMENTS

I wish to thank Dr Andy Turner for his valuable contribution to this chapter and encouragement. I would also like to thank Christian Heathcote–Elliot for his important comments and support.

REFERENCES

Adelman, E.E., Albert, S.M., Rabkin, J.G., Del Bene, M.L., Tider, T. O'Sullivan, I. (2004). Disparities in perceptions of distress and burden in ALS patients and family caregivers. *Neurology, 62*, 1766-1770.

Allen M.S. (1994). Gender Differences in Spousal Caregiving & Unmet Need for Care. *Journal of Gerontology 49* (4), S187-S195.

American Cancer Society (1998). *Cancer Facts and Figures* – 1998 (98-300M-No.5008.98). Atlanta: American Cancer Society.

Baider l., Koch, U., Esacson R. & Kaplan De-Nour A. (1998). Prospective Study of Cancer Patients & their Spouses: The Weaknesses of Marital Strength. *Psycho-Oncology. 7*, 49-56.

Barer M.B. & Johnson C.L. (1990). A Critique of the Caregiving Literature. *The Gerontologist 30* (1), 26-29.

Barraclough J. (1999). *Cancer & Emotion. A Practical Guide to Psycho-Oncology*. 3rd ed. Chichester: John Wiley & Sons.

Bass D.S. (1990). Caring Families: Supports and intervention. Silver Spring, MD: NASW Press.

Becker S., Aldridge J. & Dearden C. (1998). *Young Carers & their Families*. London: Blackwell Science.

British Medical Association (1995). *Taking care of the carers*. London: BMA.

Bucher, J.A., Loscalzo, M., Zabora, J., Houts, P.S., Hooker, C. & BrintzehofeSzoe, K. (2001). Problem-solving cancer care education for patients and caregivers. *Cancer Practice*, *9*, 66-70.

Butler R. (1992). Aging and mental health: Prevention of caregiver overload, abuse and neglect. *Geriatrics, 47*, 53-58.

Cancer Research UK, (2005). Commonly diagnosed cancers worldwide. London, UK. [Online] Available at http://info.cancerresearchuk.org/cancerstats/geographic/world/commoncancers (accessed on 15/07/05)

Carter, P.A. & Chang, B.L. (2000). Sleep and depression in cancer caregivers. *Cancer Nursing*, *23* (6),410-415.

Cassidy T. (2000). Stress, healthiness & Health Behaviours: An Exploration of the Role of Life Events, Daily Hassles, Cognitive Appraisal & the Coping Process. *Counseling Psychology Quarterly 13* (3), 293-311.

Cassidy T. (1999). *Stress, Cognition & Health*. London: Routledge.

Cawley M.M. & Gerdts K.E. (1988). Establishing a Cancer Caregivers Program. An Interdisciplinary Approach. *Cancer Nursing 11* (5), 267-273.

Cohen S., Kessler R.C. & Gordon LU. (1997). *Measuring Stress*. London: Oxford University Press.

Cochrane J.J., Goering N.P. & Rogers M.J. (1997). The mental Health of Informal Caregivers in Onterio: An Epidemiological Survey. *American Journal of Public Health 87* (12), 2002-2007.

Cooper L.C. & Watson M. (1991). *Cancer & Stress. Psychological, Biological & Coping Studies*. Sussex: John Wiley & Sons.

Corner J. & Bailey C. (2001). *Cancer Nursing. Care in Context*. Kent: Blackwell Science.

Ell O.K., Nishimoto H.R., Mantell E.J. & Hamovitch B.M. (1988). Psychological Adaptation to Cancer: A Comparison among Patients, Spouses & Nonspouses. *Family Systems Medicine 6* (3), 335-348.

Epping-Jordan E.J., Compas E.B., Osowiecki M.D., Oppedisano G., Gerhardt C., Primo K. & Krag N.D. (1999). Psychological Adjustment in Breast Cancer: Processes of Emotional Distress. *Health Psychology 18* (4), 315-326.

Iconomou, G., Vagenakis, A.G. & Kalofonos, H.P. (2001). The informational needs, satisfaction with communication, and psychological status of primary caregivers of cancer patients receiving chemotherapy. *Supportive Care in Research*, *9* (8), 591-596.

Fabes A.R. & Eisenberg A. (1997). Regulatory Control & Adults' stress-Related Responses to Daily Life Events. *Journal of Personality & Social Psychology*, *73*:5, 1107-1117.

Ferguson E., Matthews G. & Cox T. (1999). The Appraisal of Life Events (ALE) Scale: Reliability & Validity. *British Journal of Health Psychology 4*, 97-116.

Ferguson, E., Lawrence, C. & Matthews, G. (2000). Associations between primary appraisals and life-events while controlling for depression. *British Journal of Clinical Psychology*, *39*, 143-155.

Fisch, M.J. & Bruera, E. (2003). *Handbook of Advanced Cancer Care*. Cambridge: University Press.

Folkman S. (1984) Personal Control & Stress & Coping Processes: A Theoretical Analysis. *Journal of Personality and Social Psychology 46*, 839-852.

Folkman, S., Lazarus, R.S., Dunkel-Schetter, C., DeLongis, A. & Gruen, R.J. (1986). Dynamics of a stressful encounter: Cognitive appraisal, coping and encounter outcomes. *Journal of Personality and Social Psychology, 30* (5), 992-1003.

Folkman S., Lazarus R.J., Pimley S. & Novacek J. (1987). Age Differences in Stress & Coping Processes. *Psychology & Aging, 2*, 171-184.

Folkman, S. & Lazarus, R.J. (1988). *Manual for Ways of Coping Questionnaire*. Palo Alto, CA: Consulting Psychologists Press.

Folkman, S. & Moskowitz, J.T. (2000). Positive affect and the other side of coping. *American Psychologist, 55*, 647-654.

Folkman, S. & Moskowitz, J.T. (2004). Coping: Pitfalls and Promise. *Annual Rev. Psychol., 55*, 745-774.

Forbes A. & Roger D. (1999). Stress, Social Support & Fear of Disclosure. *British Journal of Health Psychology 4*, 165-179.

Gaston-Johansson, F., Lachica, E. M., Fall-Dickson, J. M., & Kennedy, M. J. (2004). Psychological distress, fatigue, burden of care, and quality of life in primary caregivers of patients undergoing autologous bone marrow transplantation. *Oncology Nursing Forum, 31(6)*, 1161-1169

Gatz M., Bengtson V., & Blum M. (1990). *Caregiving families*. Cited in J.E. Birren and K.W. Schaie (Eds.), *Handbook of the Psychology of Ageing* (3rd ed., pp. 404-426). San Diego: Academic Press.

Gaynor S. (1990). The Long Haul: The effects of home care on caregivers. *Image: Journal of Nurse Scholarship. 22*, 208-212.

George L.K & Gwyther L.P. (1986). Caregiving Well Being: A Multi-Dimensional Examination of Family Caregivers of Demented Adults. *The Gerontologist, 26*, 253-259.

Given B. & Given W.C. (1992). Patient & Family Caregiver Reaction to New & Recurrent Breast Cancer. *JAMWA 47* (5), 201-206.

Given W.C., Stommel M., Given B., Osuch J., Kurtz E.M. & Kurtz J.C. (1993). The Influence of Cancer Patients' Symptoms & Functional States on Patients' Depression & Family Caregivers' Reaction & Depression. *Health Psychology 12* (4), 277-285.

Goldbeck, L. (2001). Parental coping with the diagnosis of childhood cancer: Gender effects, dissimilarity within couples, and quality of life. *Psycho-Oncology, 10*, 325-335.

Gotay C. (1984). The Experience of Cancer during Early & Advanced Stages: The Views of Patients & their Mates. *Social Science Medicine 18*, 605.

Gray E.R., Fitch M., Phillips C., Labrecque M. 7 Fergus K. (2000). Managing the Impact of Illness: The Experiences of Men with Prostate Cancer & their Spouses. *Journal of Health Psychology 5* (4), 531-548.

Gritz R.E., Wellisch K.D., Siau J. & Wang H.J. (1990). Long-Term Effects of Testicular Cancer on Marital Relationships. *Psychosomatics 31* (3),301-312.

Grootenhuis, M.A., & Last, B.F. (1997). Adjustment and coping by parents of children with cancer: A review of the literature. *Supportive Care in Cancer, 5*, 466-484.

Haley, W.E. (2003). Family caregivers of elderly patients with cancer: Understanding and minimizing the burden of care. *Supportive Oncology*: *1* (2), 25-29.

Haley, W.E. (2003). Family caregivers of elderly patients with cancer: Understanding and minimizing the burden of care. *Journal of Supportive Oncology, 1* (2), 25 -29.

Hancock B. (1996). *Cancer Care in the Community*. Oxford: Radiliffe Medical Press.

Hart K. (1986-87). Stress Encountered by Significant Others of Cancer Patients Receiving Chemotherapy. *Omega 17* (2), 151-167.

Helgeson S.V. & Cohen S. (1996). Social Support & Adjustment to Cancer: Reconciling Descriptive, Correlational 7 Intervention Research. *Health Psychology 15* (2), 135-148.

Hileman J.W., Lackey N.R.& Hassanein R.S. (1992). Identifying the needs of home caregivers of patients with cancer. *Oncology Nursing Forum*, *19* (5), 771-777.

Hinds C. (1985). The Needs of Families Who Care for Patients with Cancer at Home: Are We Meeting Them? *Journal of Advanced Nursing 10*, 575-581.

Houts, P., Nezu, A., Nezu, C., & Bucher, J. (1996). The prepared family caregiver: A problem-solving approach to family caregiver education. *Patient Education and Counselling, 27* (1), 63-73.

King C.A. & Brassington G. (1997). Enhancing Physical & Psychological Functioning in Older Family Caregivers: The Role of Regular Physical Activity. *Annals of Behavioural Medicine*, *19* (2), 91-100.

Kramer B. (1997). Gain in the caregiving experience: Where are we? What next? *The Gerontologist*, *37*(2), 218-232.

Kurtz E.M., Kurtz J.C., Given C.W. & Given B. (1995). Relationship of Caregiver reactions & Depression to Cancer Patients' Symptoms, Functional States & Depression – A Longitudinal Study. *Social Science Medicine 40* (6), 837-846.

Lalos A. (1997). The Impact of Diagnosis on Cervical & Endometrial Cancer Patients & their Spouses. *Journal of Gynaecological Oncology*, *18* (6), 513-519.

Langton, H. (2000). *The Child with Cancer. Family-Centred Care in Practice*. London: Bailliere Tindall.

Lawton P.M., Kleban H.M., Moss M., Rovine M. & Glicksman A. (1989). Measuring Caregiving Appraisal. *Journal of Gerontology 44* (3), P61-71.

Lazarus, R. & Folkman, S. (1984). *Stress, Appraisal and Coping*. New York: Springer.

Lazarus R.S. (1993). From Psychological Stress to the Emotions: A History of Changing Outlooks. *Annu. Rev. Psychol. 44*, 1-21.

Lewis, M.F., Hammond M.A. & Woods N.F. (1993). The Family's Functioning with Newly Diagnosed Breast Cancer in the Mother: The Development of the Explanatory Model. *Journal of Behavioural Medicine 16* (4), 351-370.

Manne S. & Glassman M. (2000). Perceived Control, Coping Efficacy, & Avoidance Coping as Mediators Between Spouses' Unsupportive Behaviours & Cancer Patients' Psychological Distress. *Health Psychology 19* (2), 155-164.

Manne L.S., Taylor L.K., Dougherty J. & Kemeny N. (1997). Supportive & Negative Responses in the Partner Relationship: Their Association with Psychological Adjustment among Individuals with Cancer. *Journal of Behavioral Medicine 20* (2), 101-125.

Miller B. (1990). Gender differences in spouse caregiver strain: Socialization & role explanations. *Journal of Marriage & the Family 52*, 311-321.

Montgomery R.J.V., Gonyea J.G. & Hooyman N.R. (1985). Caregiving & the Experience of Subjective & Objective Burden. *Family Relations 34*, 19-26.

Morse R.M. & Fife B. (1998). Coping with a partnern's Cancer: Adjustment at four stages of the Illness. *Oncology Nursing Forum 25* (4), 751-759.

Munkres, A., Oberst T.M, Hughes H.S. (1992). Appraisal of Illness, Symptom Distress, Self-Care Burden & Mood States in Patients Receiving Chemotherapy for Initial & Recurrent Cancer. *Oncology Nursery Forum 19* (8), 1201-1209.

Neundorfer M.M. (1991). *Family caregivers of the frail elderly: Impact of caregiving on their health and implications for interventions*. Community Health, *14*, 48-58.

Nevidjon M.B. & Sowers W.K. (2000). *A Nurse's guide to Cancer Care*. Philadelphia: Lippincott.

Newsom J.T., & Schulz R. (1998). Caregiving from the recipient's perspective: Negative reactions to being helped. *Health Psychology 17*, 172-181.

Nijboer C., Tempelaar R., Sanderman R., Triemstra M, Spruijt R.J., van den Bos G.A. (1998). Cancer and caregiving: the impact on the caregiver's health. Psycho Oncology. *7*(1), 3-13.

Nolan M., Grant G. & Keady J. (1996). *Understanding Family Care*. Buckingham: Open University Press.

Northouse L.L. (1995). The Impact of Cancer in Women on the Family. *Cancer Practice 3* (3), 134-142.

Northouse G.P. & Northouse L.L. (1988). Communication & Cancer: Issues Confronting Patients, Health Professionals & Family Members. *Journal of Psychosocial Oncology 5* (3), 17-46.

Oberst T.M., Thomas E.S., Gass A.K. & Ward E.S. (1989). Caregiving Demands & Appraisal of Stress among Family Caregivers. *Cancer Nursing 12* (4), 209-215.

Ogden J. (2000). *Health Psychology, A textbook*. 2nd edition. London: Open University Press.

Patterson, J.M., Holm, K.E. and Gurney, J.G. (2004). The impact of childhood cancer on the family: A qualitative analysis of strain resources and coping behaviours. *Psycho-Oncology*, *13*, 390-407.

Pearlin I.L., Mullan T.J., Semple J.S. & Skaff M.M. (1990). Caregiving & the Stress Process: An Overview of Concepts & their Measures. *The Gerontologist 30* (5), 583-594.

Perrson L., Rasmusson M. & Hallberg I.R. (1998). Spouses' view during their partners' illness and treatment. *Cancer Nursing 21* (2), 97-105.

Pistrang N., Barker C. & Rutter C. (1997). Social Support as Conversation: Analysing Breast Cancer Patients' Interactions with their Partners. *Social Science Medicine 45* (5), 773-782.

Schou K.C. & Hewison J. (1999). *Experiencing Cancer*. Buckingham, London: Open University Press.

Schrerbring, M. (2002). Effect of caregiver perception of preparedness on burden in an oncology population. *Oncology Nursing Forum*, *29* (6), 70-76.

Schulz R., Newsom J.T., Mittelmark M., Burton L., Hirsch C. & Jackson S. (1997). Health Effects of Caregiving: The cardiovascular Health Study. *Annals of Behavioural Medicine 19*, 110-116.

Sharan, P., Mehta, M. and Choudhry, V.P. (1995). Coping and adaptation in parents of children suffering from Acute Lymphoblastic Leukaemia. *Indian Journal Pediatr., 62*, 737-741.

Sheehan W.N. & Nuttall P. (1988). Conflict, emotion & Personal Strain among Family Caregivers. *Family Relations 37*, 92-98.

Stanford Cancer Centre (2005), Cancer Overview. Stanford, USA [Online] Available at http://cancer.stanfordhospital.com/healthInfo/cancerOverview/default (accessed on 13/07/05)

Stein A.J. & Nyamathi A. (1999). Gender differences in relationship among stress, coping and health risk behaviours in impoverished, minority populations. *Personality & Individual Differences 26*, 141-157.

Stern, T.A. & Sekeres, M.A. (2004). *Facing Cancer. A complete guide for people with cancer, their families and caregivers.* New York: McGraw-Hill.

Toseland R., Rossiter C., Peak T. & Smith G. (1990). The comparative effectiveness of individual and group interventions to support family caregivers. *Social Work, 35*, 209-219.

Trask, P.C., Paterson , A.G., Fardig , J. & Smith, D.C. (2003). Course of distress and quality of life in testicular cancer patients before, during, and after chemotherapy: results of a pilot study. *Psycho Oncology*, *12*(8), 814-20

Twigg J. (1992). *Carers. Research & Practice*. London: HMSO.

Visovsky, C. & Workman, M.L. (2000). Cancer Biology. In A nurse's guide to Cancer Care by Nevidjon, B.M. & Sowers, K.W. Philadelphia: Lippincott Williams & Wilkins.

Vitaliano P.P. (1997). Physiological & Physical Concomitants of Caregiving: Introduction to Special Issue. *Annals of Behavioural Medicine*, *19* (2), 75-77.

Walsh F. (1996). The concept of family resilience: Crisis and challenge. *Family Process 35*, 261-281.

Walsh, S.M. & Weiss, S. (1993). Online exclusive: art intervention with family caregivers and patients with cancer. *Oncology Nursing Forum*, *30*(6), 115-120.

Wright J.S. & Kirby A. (1999). Demonstrating Conceptualisations to Chronic Illness. *Journal of Health Psychology 4* (2), 259-272.

Young, B., Dixon-Woods, M. and Heney, D. (2002). Identity and role in parenting a child with cancer. *Pediatric Rehabilitation*, *5* (4), 209-214.

Young F.R. & Kahana E. (1989). Specifying caregiver outcomes: gender & relationship aspects of caregiving strain. *The Gerontologist 29* (5), 660-666.

Zarit S.H. (1989). Do we need another "Stress & Caregiving" study? *The Gerontologist 29*, 147-148.

In: Focus on Disability: Trends in Research and Application ISBN: 978-1-60021-792-0
Editor: Thilo Kroll, pp. 181-205 © 2008 Nova Science Publishers, Inc.

Chapter XI

EXPERIENCES WITH HEALTHCARE SERVICES AND QUALITY OF LIFE AMONG GERMAN PEOPLE WITH MYASTHENIA GRAVIS

Sabine Twork[1], Joerg Klewer[2], Dieter Poehlau[3] and Joachim Kugler[1]
[1]Public Health, Dresden Medical School, Dresden, Germany;
[2]Department of Public Health and Nursing Sciences, University of Applied Sciences Zwickau, Zwickau, Germany;
[3]Department of Neurology, Kamillus-Hospital, Asbach, Germany.

SUMMARY

Myasthenia gravis (MG) is a neuromuscular disease with a prevalence in Germany of around 10 per 100,000 residents. Progress in medical therapy has increased life expectancy in MG patients. This study focuses on identifying impairment, therapeutic course, use of complementary and alternative medicine (CAM), the impact of age-related retirement), and determinants of quality of life in German MG patients.

In collaboration with the German Myasthenia Association, 2150 German people with MG were asked to complete a mailed questionnaire. Questions addressed demographic information, impairments, therapeutic course, use of CAM, costs related to illness, and quality of life (SF-36). 1518 patients participated, for a response rate of 71%, and 1316 patients responded to all items of the questionnaire. Demographic findings were as follows: average age: 57 years; proportion of females: 60%; single households: 20%; average duration of disease: 10 years.

More than two thirds of all patients, and especially females, reported impaired mobility due to muscle weakness. One third of patients cited symptoms concerning primarily facial muscles. Additional problems reported were mainly joint disorders and cardiovascular disease. The investigated MG patients were mainly treated by neurologists and general practitioners. Only 11% of MG patients used physiotherapy. Nearly all patients had experience with acetylcholine esterase inhibitors, and nearly two thirds with azathioprine. Additional expenses due to MG amounted 50 EURO per month. This was mainly spent on pharmaceuticals, housekeeping assistance, and transportation. The overall quality of life was reduced in all dimensions of the SF-36.

Participants using CAM (n=422) were mainly female, living alone, and with a long duration of MG. They were more likely than others to have had impairments related to walking or muscle weakness of the upper limbs. Despite their increased use of physiotherapy and visits to physicians, they did not differ in therapeutic course from patients not using CAM. In general, they did spend more money per month due to MG (median 50 EURO). CAM users had a lower perceived quality of life in all dimensions of the SF-36. Factors leading to use of CAM were joint problems, difficulties with chewing, long duration of MG, younger age, increasing expenses due to MG, and the absence of dysfunctions of the urinary tract.

Patients on pensions (65 years of age and older, n=502) often lived alone and in bigger towns. They mainly cited walking problems and weakness of the upper limbs, and they spent more money than the group on average for assistance with housekeeping and physiotherapy. Perceived quality of life was mainly reduced due to physical impairments.

The results indicate that despite prolonged life expectancy, quality of life was still reduced in people with MG. Reduced quality of life resulted mainly from impaired mobility. Furthermore, MG patients spent a considerable amount of money on CAM, even in a health care system in which medical therapy, but not CAM, is covered by statutory health insurance. Therefore, improving the mobility, mental well-being, and social network of MG patients could lead to increased quality of life

1. Introduction

1.1. Myasthenia Gravis – Etiology, Epidemiology, and Clinical Presentation

Myasthenia gravis is a chronic autoimmune disorder that leads to the disturbance of neuromuscular transmissions due to the production of antibodies that act against acetylcholine-receptors (AchR). These antibodies impair neuromuscular transmission mainly by complement-mediated focal destruction of postsynaptic membrane structures, accelerated degradation of AchR, and direct blocking of AchR ligand binding [31]. Myasthenic symptoms concern striated muscles, and the course of disease is chronically progredient. The annual incidence of MG is 0.5-1/100.000 and prevalence is 8-15/100.000 [34]. The first peak of onset is around the second and third decades of age; another is around the fifth and sixth decades of age. Early onset of MG often occurs in young females, whereas older males or patients with a thymoma are mostly affected at higher ages [3,19,24,28,33]. Genetic components in the etiology of MG, probably HLA-related, are under discussion [9]. A recurrence risk of 2-4% is described for relatives of Caucasian MG patients [9,19].

A history of fluctuating weakness of extraocular, faciopharyngeal, or skeletal muscles or aggravation of weakness following physical strain leads to the presumption of the diagnosis of Myasthenia gravis. Antibodies against the AchR can be detected in 80-90% of MG patients [24]. These antibodies occur in 50-60% of cases with ocular manifestation of MG, in 80-90% of patients with generalized MG, and in nearly all patients with paraneoplastic MG and thymoma. The release of antibodies against AchR results from immunologic processes in the thymus gland [9], occurring in response to the production by myoid cells of surface structures identical to AchR [15,19,33]. Additional antibodies are often seen in thymoma patients [15,31,33]. Other myasthenic diseases such as congenital MG, neonatal MG, penicillamine-induced MG, and Lambert-Eaton syndrome must be discriminated from [15,19,24].

Table 1. MGFA Clinical Classification of Myasthenia Gravis 2002 [12]

Class	Characteristics
I	Any ocular weakness May have weakness of eye closure All other muscle strength is normal
II	Mild weakness affecting other than ocular muscles May also have ocular muscle weakness of any severity
IIa	Predominantly affecting limb or axial muscles, or both May also have lesser involvement of oropharyngeal muscles
IIb	Predominantly affecting oropharyngeal or respiratory muscles, or both May also have lesser or equal involvement of limb or axial muscles, or both
III	Moderate weakness affecting other than ocular muscles May also have ocular muscle weakness of any severity
IIIa	Predominantly affecting limb or axial muscles, or both May also have lesser involvement of oropharyngeal muscles
IIIb	Predominantly affecting oropharyngeal or respiratory muscles, or both May also have lesser or equal involvement of limb or axial muscles, or both
IV	Severe weakness affecting other than ocular muscles May also have ocular muscle weakness of any severity
IVa	Predominantly affecting limb and/or axial muscles May also have lesser involvement of oropharyngeal muscles
IVb	Predominantly affecting oropharyngeal or respiratory muscles, or both May also have lesser or equal involvement of limb or axial muscles, or both
V	Defined by intubation, with or without mechanical ventilation, except when employed in routine postoperative management. The use of a feeding tube without intubation places the patient in class IVb.

Ossermann and Genkins distinguished between ocular MG and different grades of generalized myasthenia [21]. Their classification was revised by the Myasthenia Gravis Foundation of America (MGFA) in 2000 (table 1) [12]. Patients with MG start to complain about diplopia, often combined with uni- or bilateral ptosis. Additional findings are bulbar symptoms, such as speech or chewing disorders or dysphagia. Weakness of the facial muscles (facies myopathica) and of proximal limb and trunk muscles can occur. In general, the myasthenic symptoms worsen during daytime. In the worst cases, increasing weakness of respiratory muscles can lead to respiratory insufficiency. Besides neuromuscular transmission, cognitive functions are affected by MG: mild but significant difficulties in cognitive functions such as response fluency, information processing, and verbal and visual learning were found in MG patients. Mood disturbances were not observed. The reasons for cognitive impairments are still under discussion; suggested causes include breathing abnormalities due to diaphragm exhaustion and leading to desaturation of oxygen during sleep, the effects of nonspecific immunological processes triggered by the influx of antibodies to the central nervous system, and development of fatigue over the course of testing [25].

MG is normally diagnosed by detection of antibodies against the acetylcholine receptor, electrophysiological signs of > 9% decrement by repetitive 3-Hz stimulation of a suitable nerve, a positive Tensilon® or Mestinon® test, and increased jitter at single-fiber electromyography. In the majority of cases, no abnormal radiological findings are present. Only in 10%-15% of patients is thymoma the underlying cause; these patients tend to be elderly or male. In 70-85% of patients with autoimmune myasthenia gravis a hyperplasia of the thymus gland can be found. Approximately 70% of patients present with inflammation of the thymus tissue in histological investigations [3,15,29,31,33].

Depending on the etiology of MG, several therapeutical strategies for myasthenia gravis do exist. An increased resting time of acetylcholine in the synaptic gap can be realized by means of acetylcholine esterase inhibitors such as pyridostigmin [15,19,33]. Immunosuppression or immunomodulation by means of azathioprine, corticosteroids, cyclosporin A, methotrexate, cyclophosphamide, mycophenolate mofetil, or FK506 (Tacrolimus®) is another therapeutic alternative [5,14,15,19,20,33,35]. Additionally, the thymus gland, as a source of antigens, is removed in most cases, especially in younger patients and those with thymoma [19,24], although patients with seronegative MG do not seem to profit from thymectomy [15]. A benefit of thymectomy in nonthymomatous autoimmune MG has not been established conclusively [10,37]. Plasmapheresis or immunoadsorption is applied in severe cases for elimination of circulating antibodies. The clinical effects of both methods seem to be similar [11,38]. Treatment with intravenously applied immunoglobulins is another possibility, conducted in cases of MG crisis or severe weakness poorly controlled with other agents, as a preoperative boost, or in combination with plasma exchange. The explanations of its therapeutical effects include inhibition of complement binding, prevention of membrane attack complex (MAC) formation, and other mechanisms [2,15,19,24,33]. Less is known about the effects of physiotherapy in people suffering from MG. Physical training strengthens muscle and eases weakness [17], but exacerbation of MG during therapeutic electric stimulation has been reported [27].

MG is a chronic disabling disease that brings the risk of life-threatening episodes, via respiratory failure. Some patients find their own strategy to cope with MG. Others may need professional help. Doering et al. stated that "psychotherapeutical techniques may be helpful in patients with neurotic or reactive psychiatric symptoms, but there is no general implication for psychotherapy in myasthenic patients, especially if there is adequate 'somatic' therapy" [4]. The persistent experience of muscle weakness may negatively influence patients' perceived quality of life, especially among individuals for whom demands of work, family, and other responsibilities require significant physical involvement [26].

1.2. Study Aims

To date there are no comprehensive studies focusing on experiences with health care and quality of life in large samples of MG patients. This study focuses on demographic data, identification of MG-related impairments, therapeutic course, use of complementary and alternative medicine (CAM), the impact of living on disability benefits and forced retirement ("disability pensioner"), and determinants of quality of life in German MG patients.

2. Methods and Sample

In cooperation with the German Myasthenia Association, the self-help organization for myasthenia gravis (MG) patients, all 2150 members in Germany with confirmed MG were asked to fill out a mailed, anonymous questionnaire. The standardized questions were related to demographical data, physical impairments, additional disorders, therapeutic course, satisfaction with therapists, use of complementary and alternative medicine (CAM), illness-related costs, and quality of life. A cover letter explained the purpose of the study, and a pre-paid envelope to return the questionnaire was included. In total 1518 patients participated, resulting in a response rate of 70.6%. Drop-out criteria were missing or implausible data for gender, age, age at first symptoms (< 0 years), age at diagnosis (> actual age), and duration of diagnosis (< 0 years). Thus, data of 1316 patients were included.

2.1. Demographic Data of 1316 Patients

The sample consists of 39,6% (n=521) male and 60.4% (n=795) female patients. Average age of the patients was 56.7 (± 16.6) years, ranging from 18 to 94 years (figure 1). Females (average age 52.0 (± 16.8) years) were significantly younger than males (average age 63.8 (± 13.6) years) (t-test, $p<0.001$). Around 13.1% of the patients were single, 68.5% were married, and 9.7% were widowed. The rest (8.7%) reported being separated or being divorced. 20.4% of patients lived alone in a single household. The majority of the investigated patients (64.7%) lived in towns with less than 100,000 residents, 19.4% in towns with 100,000-500,000, and 14.6% in towns with more than 500,000 residents. Most patients had 10-13 years of pre-college schooling (moderate-to-high level in the German system), and 26.4% of respondents were working more than 15 hours a week. Only 3.3% reported working less than 15 hours per week. 68.5% of patients were not employed, and 1% were on leave. The main reason for unemployment in 85.3% of the unemployed patients was being already retired; 12.7% of this subgroup were housewives/ -men and only 2% of all participants were unemployed.

Altogether 76.1% of the investigated individuals were insured by statutory health insurance. An additional 10.9% were insured by statutory health insurance combined with private supplementary insurance. A further 12.8% had private health insurance, and 0.1% of patients were insured by the social welfare office.

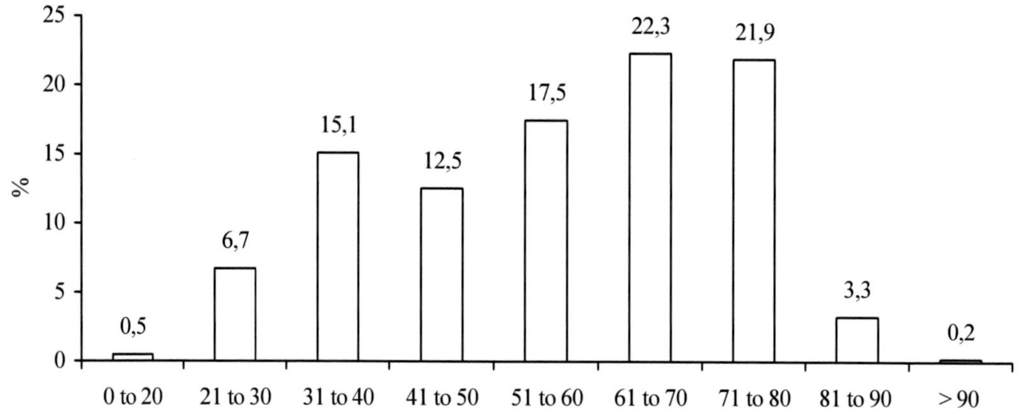

Figure 1. Age of investigated 1316 MG patients.

3. RESULTS

3.1. Disease-Related Data

The average age at occurrence of first symptoms was 43.7 years (table 2). At time of first symptoms, females were on average age 37.1 years and males 53.7 years (figure 2). Two peaks within the age distribution were found in the sample: the first one around the second and third decade and the second one from the fifth to the seventh decade.

Table 2. MG-related medical history (n = 1316)

	mean of years (range)	sd+	gender	mean of years	sd+	Statistical differences
age at first symptoms	43.7 (0-93)	19.4	male	53.7	16.5	t-test
			female	37.1	18.3	
age at diagnosis	46.4 (0-93)	18.5	male	55.6	15.6	p<0.001
			female	40.4	17.8	
duration of diagnosis	2.8 (0-67)	6.0	male	1.9	4.7	
			female	3.3	6.6	
years with symptoms	13.0 (0-70)	11.4	male	10.1	9.2	
			female	14.9	12.3	
duration of disease	10.3 (0-53)	9.3	male	8.2	7.6	
			female	11.6	10.1	

+ sd = standard deviation.

The proportion of female patients decreases with increasing years of age (figure 3). The proportion of males trends in the opposite direction (Chi², $p<0.001$). The average age at time of diagnosis was 46.4 years (± 18.5), and males were significantly older at this time (55.6 years) than females (40.4 years; t-test, $p<0.001$). The diagnostic period was ranged from the first onset of MG up to the moment when the diagnosis of MG was confirmed. On average, the diagnostic period lasted 2.8 years (± 6.0); in males it was significantly shorter than in females (table 2). The length of the diagnostic period was shorter in patients diagnosed during the previous five years (average of 0.6 [± 2.5] years) than in those diagnosed in past decades. Almost no changes in diagnostic period duration were found for the periods of last 6 to 10 and 11 to 15 years (1.6 [± 2.1] years and 1.8 years, respectively). However, more than 15 years ago, the diagnostic period was about 6.4 years (± 9.7 years). The investigated MG patients had experienced MG symptoms on average for about 13.0 years, females significantly longer than males (table 2). The duration of disease was defined as the period from confirmed diagnosis of MG up to the moment of survey. In this sample, the average duration of disease was 10.3 years.

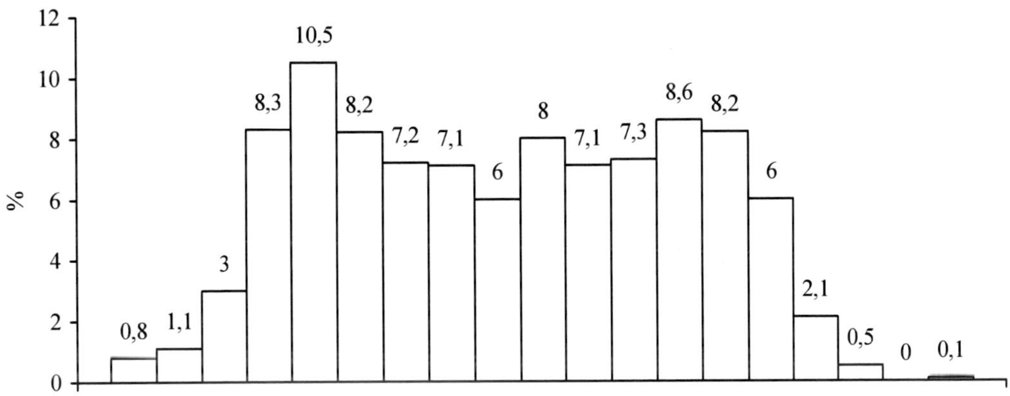

Figure 2. Age at occurrence of first MG symptoms [n=1316].

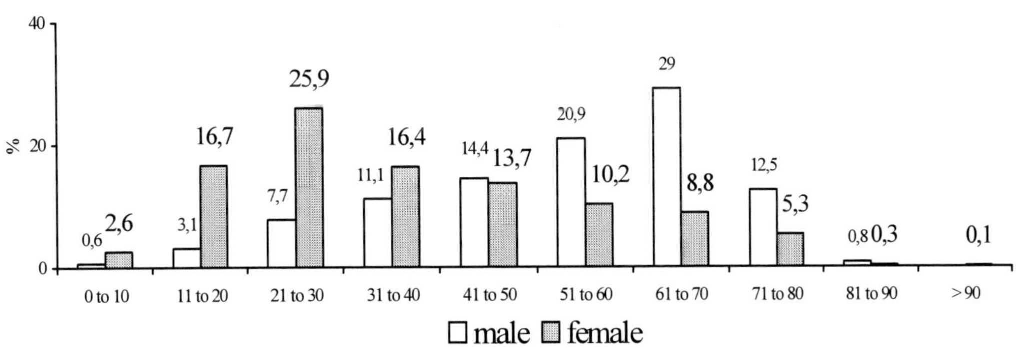

Figure 3. Age at occurrence of first MG symptoms – female versus male MG patients (Chi², p<0,001).

Altogether 67.8% of the investigated MG patients were AchR-antibody positive, 8.7% of the patients were antibody negative, 3.8% stated that they had never been tested, and 17.9% were unsure of their antibody condition. No gender differences in antibody condition could be found.

79.3% of patients stated a stable course of MG. Only 16.3% complained of instability. No gender difference with regard to stability of MG could be found. 2.8% of patients had an affected family member. In 8 cases the mother, in 6 the father, in 7 the brother, in 4 the sister, in 1 the son, in 2 the daughter, and in 13 cases other family members also had MG.

Table 3. Gender differences in MG related impairments*

Impairments	Proportion of patients in %	Gender		Statistical differences
Muscle weakness after physical strain	75.5	females	81.3%	Chi² ***
		males	72.3%	
Weakness of upper limbs	71.6	females	77.6%	Chi² ***
		males	65.7%	
Walking problems	69.8	females	73.8%	Chi² *
		males	68.5%	
Dysphagia	43.6	females	46.9%	Chi² n.s.
		males	43.1%	
Chewing problems	39.4	females	41.3%	Chi² n.s.
		males	39.6%	
Ptosis	38.4	females	41.5%	Chi² n.s.
		males	40.0%	
Defecation problems	38.1	females	42.0%	Chi² n.s.
		males	37.2%	
Diplopia	37.9	females	38.9%	Chi² n.s.
		males	40.1%	
Neck weakness	31.7	females	37.2%	Chi² ***
		males	26.1%	
Speech disorders	28.6	females	29.9%	Chi² n.s.
		males	32.1%	
Facial expression disorders	25.8	females	32.7%	Chi² **
		males	23.4%	
Miction disorders	24.9	females	23.5%	Chi² **
		males	32.4%	
Sexual disorders	18.7	females	13.1%	Chi² ***
		males	33.8%	
Muscle weakness at rest	16.6	females	19.4%	Chi² n.s.
		males	18.8%	

* = Multiple answers possible.

*** = $p<0.001$, ** = $p<0.01$, * = $p<0.05$, n.s. = not significant.

Due to the design of the study, it was impossible to assess patients' exact grade of MG according to the MGFA Classification. Patients were asked about MG-related symptoms as well as urinary tract disorders, problems with defecation, and impaired sexuality (table 3). More than two thirds of patients, especially females, complained about limited mobility due to muscle weakness. About one third, mainly females, experienced symptoms concerning the oculofaciopharyngeal and neck musculature or defecation. Symptoms such as speech, facial expression, or urinary tract disorders or sexual dysfunction were less often reported (table 3).

Altogether 92.6% of the investigated MG patients did not need assistance from mobile nursing care services.

3.2. Additional Health Problems

More than one third of the patients reported additional joint problems and cardiovascular diseases, mood disorders, or hormone disorders (table 4). Less frequent were osteoporosis, metabolic disorders, and malignancies. About 10% of patients experienced other conditions involving the immune system. Atopic diseases (allergies, neurodermatitis, asthma, or hayfever) were reported in 5.9% of cases. Immunodeficiency, multiple repeating infections, or herpes zoster were reported by 3.0% of the investigated patients. Health problems reported by less than 1% of patients in the sample included lupus erythematosus, Morbus Crohn or colitis ulcerosa, Morbus Bechterew, Hashimoto's thyreoiditis, multiple sclerosis, celiac disease, rheumatoid arthritis, Morbus Basedow or sarcoidosis, autoimmune vasculitis, hepatitis, and gastritis.

Table 4. Additional disorders in MG patients§

Additional disorders	Proportion of patients in %	Gender prevalence (Chi^2-test)		Statistical differences
Joint problems	40.2	females	46.1%	Chi^2 n.s.
		males	42.8%	
Cardiovascular diseases	38.9	females	38.8%	Chi^2 **
		males	47.9%	
Mood disorders	38.1	females	43.4%	Chi^2 n.s.
		males	42.4%	
Hormone disorders	24.4	females	37.1%	Chi^2 ***
		males	17.1%	
Osteoporosis	16.3	females	24.8%	Chi^2 ***
		males	14.1%	
Metabolic disorders	12.0	females	10.1%	Chi^2 ***
		males	19.9%	
Other immunological disorders	11.0	females	19.7%	Chi^2 ***
		males	9.4%	
Malignancies	7.8	females	9.4%	Chi^2 n.s.
		males	9.4%	

§ Multiple answers possible.
*** $p<0.001$, ** $p<0.01$, * $p<0.05$, n.s.=non significant.

Gender differences were found regarding osteoporosis, other immunological diseases, and hormone disorders, with increased occurrence in females (table 4). More males were affected by cardiovascular problems and metabolic disorders. There were no gender differences in the occurrence of cancer, joint problems, or mood disorders.

3.3. Health Practitioners and Patients' Satisfaction with them

Nearly all participants (98.2%) reported visits at health professionals during the 12 month before the study. The health professionals most often consulted by patients for the treatment of MG were neurologists in private practice and general practitioners. Patients less often visited hospital outpatient departments, specialists in internal medicine, physiotherapists, and nonmedical health practitioners (table 5).

Table 5. Therapists consulted for myasthenia gravis§

Therapist	Proportion of patients in %
Neurologist in private practice	62.2
Family doctor/general practitioner	50.3
Hospital doctor	38.9
Specialist in internal medicine in private practice	16.4
Physiotherapist	11.3
Non-medical practitioner	4.0

§ Multiple answers possible.

For the most part significant gender differences in the choice of health professionals were not found, the exception being in the choice of physiotherapists and nonmedical practitioners. These were both more often attended by females than by males (physiotherapists: 23.8% females, 16.3% males, Chi²-test: $p<0.05$; nonmedical practitioners: 10.1% females, 4.9% males, Chi²-test: $p<0.05$). The majority of the participants reported more than six visits to their health professional within the previous 12 months, and most of these reported more than 12 visits (table 6). Patients reporting an unstable course of disease visited their therapists more often than patients experiencing a stable disease course (54.7% versus 30.8%, Chi²-test: $p<0.001$). Furthermore, more females than males were seeking for therapy (37.4% versus 31.0%, Chi²-test: $p<0.01$).

Table 6. Number of visitations at the therapist in the previous 12 months

number of visits	none	1-3	4-6	7-9	10-12	> 12
N	24	144	240	221	220	454
%	1.8	10.9	18.2	16.8	16.7	34.5

Respondents were also asked to express their satisfaction with the professional and communication skills of their doctors, using a rating scale of 1 (very satisfied) to 6 (absolutely not satisfied). Male patients assessed the professional skills of their practitioners higher than did female patients (t-test, $p<0.01$). Similar results were found for communication skills (t-test, $p<0.05$). 35.3% of all patients claimed they would change their doctor if someone were to recommend a "good expert for MG in town". 43.9% of patients said such a recommendation would not lead them to change their doctor, and 19.5% were unsure about that option.

3.4. Experiences with Different Therapies

The majority of the investigated MG patients had been treated with acetylcholine esterase inhibitors, azathioprine, or corticosteroids or had undergone thymectomy (table 8). The MG patients in the sample had less experiences with cyclosporine A, intravenous immunoglobulin therapy, plasmapheresis or immunoadsorption, re-thymectomy, or radiation.

11.3% of patients had been treated by physiotherapists in the previous three months. More females than males used physiotherapy (23.8% females, 16.3% males, Chi²-test: $p<0.05$). 7.5% of patients had sought physiotherapeutic support more than 10 times during the previous three months, but the majority (79.9%) never used it (table 7). No significant gender differences were found.

Table 7. Frequency of physiotherapy in the previous 12 months

number of visitations	none	1-3	4-6	7-9	10-12	> 12
n	1051	66	50	25	40	59
%	79.9	5.0	3.8	1.9	3.0	4.5

Table 8. Immunosuppressive therapies used§

Therapy	Proportion of patients using (%)
Acetylcholine esterase inhibitors	92.4
Azathioprine	73.1
Corticosteroids	56.2
Thymectomy	50.2
Intravenous immunoglobulin therapy	14.3
Plasmapheresis/Immunoadsorption	11.2
Cyclosporine A	4.3
Radiation	4.1
Rethymectomy	1.5

§ = Multiple answers possible.

Psychotherapy had never been provided to 57.1% of the respondents. When psychotherapy was offered, it was offered significantly more often to females than to males (59.9% versus 56.3%, Chi²-test: $p<0.01$). 16.5% of the MG patients were not interested in having psychotherapy, especially males (18.8% males versus 15.2% females, Chi²-test: $p<0.01$). 13.6% of the patients had no experience with psychotherapy but were interested in getting it. 11.8% of the patients had received psychotherapy, and 63.9% of that group had experienced it as helpful, while 36.1% mentioned no positive effects.

3.5. Financial Situation and Expenses due to MG

Patients were asked about the number of people who contributed financially to their household's net income. 52.9% of respondents mentioned support by only one additional person and 45.3% were supported by several persons. The median monthly net income of patients amounted to 1750.00 EURO (approximately 2100 USD) (± 2324.53 EURO).

Patients faced considerable expenses due to MG, with median monthly expenditures of about 50 EURO (60 USD): In 29.6% of the patients, expenditures were up to 25 EURO (30 USD); in 21.2%, up to 50 EURO; in 22.0%, up to 250 EURO (300 USD); in 4.9%, up to 500 EURO (600 USD); and in 1.1%, more than 500 EURO per month. Only 18.5% of all patients stated they did not spend any additional money due to MG. The monthly financial burdens consisted mainly of paying for pharmaceuticals, housekeeping assistance, and transportation (table 9).

Table 9. Monthly expenses due to MG*

Expenses	Median of monthly expenses in EURO (sd[§])
Housekeeping assistance	50.00 (± 222.45)
Transportation (taxi, public transport)	25.00 (± 270.28)
Prescribed medications	15.00 (± 174.52)
OTC medications	10.00 (± 69.18)
Analgesics	5.00 (± 48.09)
Physiotherapy	5.00 (± 34.30)
Voluntary treatment courses (sports, diet cooking, relaxation)	2.50 (± 39.19)

* = multiple answers possible.
[§] = standard deviation.

3.6. Quality of Life in MG Patients

Only few of the investigated MG patients stated that the onset of MG had influenced their educational choice (1.8%) or job training (8.0%). 8.9% of patients had changed jobs due to MG, 21.4% experienced disadvantages in their job due to the disease, and 28.9% of patients were had retired prematurely.

Subjective quality of life was measured using a rating scale ranging from 0 to 100 and by the German version of the SF-36 [1]. The SF-36 was developed to examine the impact of disease on perceived well-being and has been used extensively to assess quality of life in patients with various diseases [26]. The questionnaire consists of 36 questions that inquire about the general health status of patients. They can be categorized as follows: physical functioning (interference with physical activities), social functioning (interference in social activities), physical role (degree to which physical health necessitated change in activities in the last 4 weeks), emotional role (degree to which emotional health necessitated change in activities in the last 4 weeks), mental health (overall mood in the last 4 weeks), vitality (perceived energy in the last 4 weeks), bodily pain (amount of pain experienced in the last 4 weeks), and general health (overall perceived health). In this study, MG patients were compared to a German normative population [6] according their quality of life (table 10).

The rating scale to assess global quality of life ranged from 0 (extremely low) to 100 (extremely high). On average, the score of the MG patients was 60.6 (± 22.9).

The results of a comparison between German MG patients and a German normative population show decreased quality of life in all eight categories of the SF-36 for the MG patients (table 10, figures 4 and 5).

Table 10. Scores for each SF-36 dimension for MG patients and the general German population*

	females		males	
SF-36 dimension	MG patients mean (sd)[+]	German population[§] mean (sd)[+]	MG patients mean (sd)[+]	German population[§] mean (sd)[+]
Physical functioning	56.8 (30.2)	82.8 (22.2)	61.0 (29.4)	88.2 (18.5)
Physical role	50.4 (42.7)	79.2 (34.8)	46.2 (43.4)	85.5 (30.0)
Bodily pain	45.4 (15.3)	63.9 (25.9)	46.8 (16.1)	71.0 (25.3)
General health	45.0 (22.4)	66.0 (18.7)	44.9 (22.8)	66.8 (17.6)
Vitality	42.8 (19.6)	57.6 (18.3)	45.3 (22.0)	62.6 (17.0)
Social functioning	68.4 (27.6)	84.2 (21.2)	68.9 (28.8)	88.6 (18.3)
Emotional role	64.7 (42.5)	86.7 (29.1)	65.7 (43.2)	91.6 (23.8)
Mental health	62.8 (19.4)	69.8 (17.6)	64.7 (21.2)	75.2 (15.3)

* = Possible scale range 0-100.
§ = data by Ellert and Bellach [6].
+ = standard deviation.

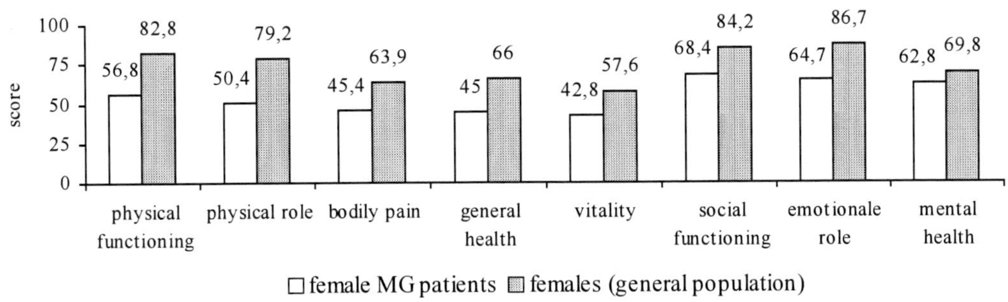

Figure 4. Quality of life (SF-36) in female MG patients compared to females from the general German population [6].

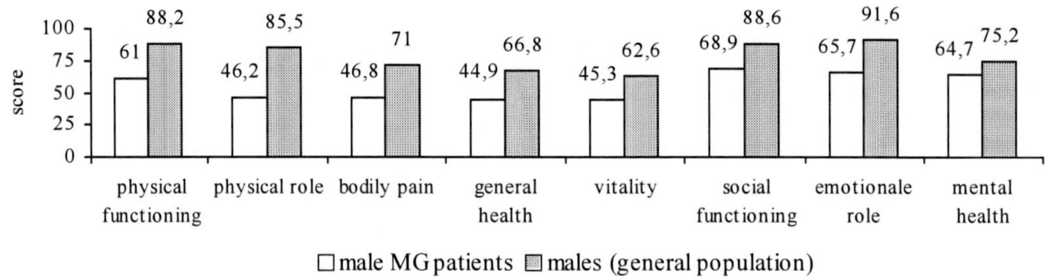

Figure 5. Quality of life (SF-36) in male MG patients compared to males from the general German population [6].

Regression analysis revealed the factors influencing quality of life, taken by the two aggregated scales of the SF-36: physical health (summary of physical functioning, physical role, bodily pain, and general health), and mental health (summary of emotional role, mental health, vitality, and social functioning) (tables 11 and 12). It became obvious that walking problems, mood disorders, muscle weakness, and dysphagia had a negative influence on the physical dimension of perceived quality of life in MG patients. Stability of MG, employment, and female gender exacted positive effects on the physical dimension of perceived quality of life . The mental dimension of the SF-36 was negatively influenced by mood and metabolic disorders, walking problems, and defecation problems. A positive effect on the mental dimension of the SF-36 was found in the stability of MG.

Table 11. Factors influencing physical health – stepwise linear regression analysis§

Independent variables	B	ß	p
Walking problems (no/yes)	-10.365	-0.229	0.000
Mood disorders (no/yes)	-7.298	-0.165	0.000
Muscle weakness after physical strain (no/yes)	-7.285	-0.141	0.000
Dysphagia (no/yes)	-5.091	-0.120	0.000
Muscle weakness at rest (no/yes)	-4.470	-0.079	0.012
Neck weakness (no/yes)	-3.567	-0.079	0.019
Visitation frequency at a doctor	-3.131	-0.224	0.000
Own monthly expenses	-2.044	-0.115	0.000
Age	-0.162	-0.123	0.001
Stability of MG (no/yes)	8.627	0.148	0.000
Employment (no/yes)	4.374	0.100	0.005
Gender (male/female)	4.093	0.097	0.004

§ = Adjusted r^2=0.623, ANOVA F=64.553, p<0.001.

3.7. Use of Complementary and Alternative Medicine (CAM)

All study participants were asked about their use of complementary and alternative medicine (CAM) since the onset of MG. Participants were classified as CAM-users when they classified themselves as CAM-users, or if they reported visits to nonmedical practitioners, or if they stated that they spent money on homeopathic remedies or one of the different CAM therapies mentioned in the questionnaire. This classification scheme was used because no exact definition of CAM or CAM-users currently exists [13].

Table 12. Factors influencing mental health – stepwise linear regression analysis§

Independent variables *	B	ß	p
Mood disorders (no/yes)	-19.227	-0.411	0.000
Metabolic disorders (no/yes)	-5.527	-0.072	0.022
Walking problems (no/yes)	-4.633	-0.099	0.003
Defecation disorders (no/yes)	-4.336	-0.092	0.004
Facial expression disorders (no/yes)	-3.676	-0.075	0.027
Dysphagia (no/yes)	-3.445	-0.076	0.033
Own monthly expenses	-2.470	-0.132	0.000
Frequency of visits to doctor	-1.797	-0.121	0.000
Stability of MG (no/yes)	10.696	0.174	0.000

§ = Adjusted r^2=0.474, ANOVA F=57.240, p=0.000.

Table 13. Complementary and alternative therapies (CAM) used by 422 MG patients

CAM	Proportion of patients in %
Vitamins	39.6
Homeopathic agents	33.2
Antioxidants	29.4
Acupuncture	29.4
Bach flower therapy	13.3
Special diets	11.8
Heavy metal removal	11.1
Other alternative therapies	9.7
Bioresonance therapy	6.4
Healing stones	4.5

In total 422 patients were classified as CAM-users (table 13). These were especially women and tended to be unmarried and to live in a single-person household (table 14). There was no difference in age, educational level, or size of place of residence compared to non-CAM-users. CAM-users had had MG significantly longer than non-CAM users (12.1 years (± 10.6 years) versus 9.4 years (± 8.5 years), t-test: p<0.001) and had more often experienced an unstable course of disease. They reported more physical impairments than non-CAM-users (table 14). In more than 75% of these patients, the most severe symptoms were general muscle weakness after physical strain, weakness of upper limbs, and walking problems. About half of patients reported dysphagia, chewing problems, diplopia, and ptosis.

Table 14. Differences between CAM-users and patients not using CAM

	CAM-users	Non-CAM-users	Statistical differences
Female sex	70.9%	55.5%	Chi^2 ***
Married	62.3%	71.4%	Chi^2 **
Single-person household	24.5%	18.6%	Chi^2 *
Duration of MG in years (sd) §	12.1 (± 10.6)	9.4 (± 8.5)	t-test ***
Unstable disease course	20.7%	15.2%	Chi^2 *
Muscle weakness after physical strain	82.2%	75.7%	Chi^2 *
Weakness of upper limbs	77.0%	71.0%	Chi^2 *
Walking problems	75.6%	69.8%	Chi^2 *
Dysphagia	50.4%	43.1%	Chi^2 *
Chewing problems	49.9%	36.4%	Chi^2 ***
Diplopia	48.1%	35.3%	Chi^2 ***
Ptosis	45.1%	39.0%	Chi^2 *
Defecation disorders	43.0%	38.8%	Chi^2 n.s.
Neck weakness	42.2%	28.4%	Chi^2 ***
Facial expression disorders	37.0%	25.3%	Chi^2 ***
Speech disorders	34.5%	29.0%	Chi^2 n.s.
Miction disorders	28.2%	26.5%	Chi^2 n.s.
Sexual problems	24.2%	20.3%	Chi^2 n.s.
Muscle weakness at rest	20.8%	18.4%	Chi^2 n.s.
Joint problems	52.2%	39.2%	Chi^2 ***
Mood disorders	49.5%	37.7%	Chi^2 ***
Cardiovascular diseases	44.6%	40.3%	Chi^2 n.s.
Hormone disorders	32.8%	24.7%	Chi^2 *
Osteoporosis	23.2%	16.6%	Chi^2 *
Other immunological diseases	20.9%	10.2%	Chi^2 ***
Metabolic disorders	13.2%	13.8%	Chi^2 n.s.
Malignancies	9.2%	8.9%	Chi^2 n.s.
Handicapped person's pass	64.8%	56.7%	Chi^2 **
% of handicap (sd)§	71.3 (± 20.4)	66.4 (± 19.8)	t-test ***
Consulting a physical therapist	32.6%	15.2%	Chi^2 ***
> 12 visits at a doctor past year	41.1%	31.9%	Chi^2 *
Psychotherapy not offered	51.9%	60.5%	Chi^2 ***
but interested	16.0%	12.7%	

*** = $p<0.001$, ** = $p<0.01$, * = $p<0.05$.

§ = standard deviation, CAM = Complementary and alternative therapy.

Compared to non-CAM-users, no differences were found in muscle weakness at rest, urinary tract disorders, nor with regard to problems with defecation or sexual dysfunction. About half of the patients using CAM reported joint problems, mood disorders, and cardiovascular problems. Compared to non-CAM-users, no significant differences in occurrence of cardiovascular or metabolic disorders were found. Further, no differences were found in experience with immunosuppressive therapies or in type of main health care practitioner, despite the more frequent visits to physical therapists made by CAM-users. In general, CAM-users reported more visits to their therapists. They were more interested in psychotherapy, which was less often withheld from them. CAM-users spent proportionately more money related to MG, with a median expenditure of up to 50 EURO (60 USD) per month (versus non-CAM-users with up to 25 EURO (30 USD), Chi²-test: $p<0.001$). On average, they additionally spent 25 EURO (median) for alternative therapies and 12.5 EURO (15 USD) (median) for homeopathic remedies. No differences between CAM-users and non-CAM-users were found in employment, number of persons contributing to household net income, or in monthly net income.

Subjective quality of life, assessed by the rating-scale, was reduced in both groups. By using the SF-36, significant differences between CAM and non-CAM users were found in the health-related quality of life for all eight scales (figure 6).

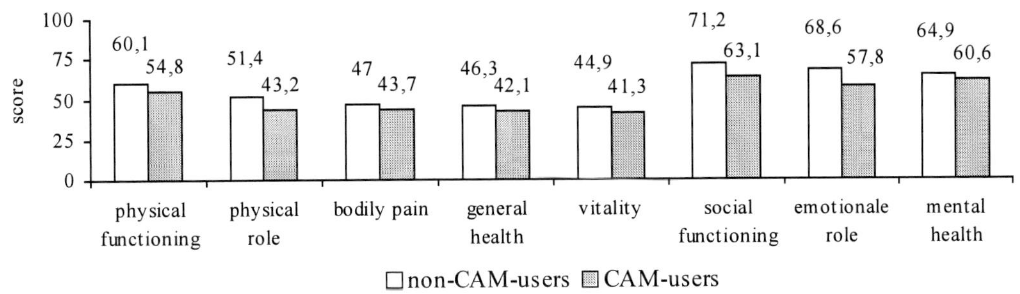

Figure 6. Differences in quality of life (SF-36) between users of complementary and alternative medicine (CAM) and non-CAM-users. (t-test, *** = $p<0.001$, ** = $p<0.01$).

By means of stepwise linear regression analysis, joint and chewing problems, additional monthly expenses due to MG, longer duration of disease, younger age, and not suffering from urinary tract disorders were extracted as the factors most strongly associated with the use of CAM in people with MG (table 15).

Table 15. Factors influencing use of CAM - stepwise linear regression analysis§

	B	ß	p
Joint problems (no/yes)	0.122	0.122	0.001
Additional monthly expenses	0.09543	0.246	0.000
Chewing problems (no/yes)	0.0847	0.088	0.018
Duration of MG	0.00488	0.091	0.012
Miction disorders (no/yes)	-0.0867	-0.073	0.049
Age	-0.00231	-0.081	0.033

§ = adjusted $r^2=0.098$, ANOVA $F=13.848$, $p=0.000$.

CAM = Complementary and alternative therapy.

Table 16. Characteristics of pensioners versus non-pensioners

		Pensioners	Non-pensioners	Statistical differences
Age in years (sd)§		73.4 (± 5,8)	46.3 (± 12,1)	t-test ***
Female proportion		42.2%	71.6%	Chi^2 ***
Married		67.3%	69.2%	Chi^2 ***
Single household		27.8%	16.0%	Chi^2 ***
Place of residence	< 100'000	58.5%	69.9%	Chi^2 ***
with number of	100-500'000	24.0%	17.0%	
residents	> 500'000	17.5%	13.1%	
AchR antibodies		61.2%	73.8%	Chi^2 ***
Walking problems		80.5%	66.4%	Chi^2 ***
Muscle weakness after physical strain		76.3%	78.6%	Chi^2 n.s.
Weakness of upper limbs		70.5%	74.4%	Chi^2 n.s.
Ptosis		52.7%	32.1%	Chi^2 ***
Dysphagia		48.5%	43.5%	Chi^2 n.s.
Defecation problems		45.3%	37.1%	Chi^2 **
Chewing problems		39.7%	41.2%	Chi^2 n.s.
Miction disorders		38.3%	20.5%	Chi^2 ***
Diplopia		35.9%	41.5%	Chi^2 n.s.
Speech disorder		31.3%	30.4%	Chi^2 n.s.
Neck weakness		30.1%	34.4%	Chi^2 n.s.
Sexual disorders		29.6%	17.6%	Chi^2 ***
Muscle weakness at rest		21.0%	18.1%	Chi^2 n.s.
Facial expression disorders		20.5%	33.7%	Chi^2 **
Joint problems		61.2%	32.5%	Chi^2 ***
Cardiovascular diseases		59.6%	30.9%	Chi^2 ***
Mood disorders		40.5%	42.0%	Chi^2 n.s.
Osteoporosis		29.2%	12.7%	Chi^2 ***
Hormone disorders		23.6%	29.3%	Chi^2 n.s.
Metabolic disorders		22.0%	8.7%	Chi^2 ***
Malignancies		11.2%	7.7%	Chi^2 n.s.
Other immunological diseases		9.0%	16.0%	Chi^2 ***
Services by nursing care insurance		8.8%	4.8%	Chi^2 *
% of handicap (sd)§		74.2 (± 18.6)	64.3 (± 20.1)	t-test ***
Neurologist		81.0%	75.1%	Chi^2 **
Family doctor/general practitioner		74.1%	65.0%	Chi^2 **
Internist		35.0%	25.6%	Chi^2 **
Thymectomy		30.8%	73.4%	Chi^2 ***
Immunoglobulin therapy		17.6%	21.6%	Chi^2 **
Plasmapheresis or Immunoadsorption		14.4%	16.6%	Chi^2 *
Cyclosporine A		7.4%	5.8%	Chi^2 **
Psychotherapy	not offered	63.0%	54.4%	Chi^2 *
	not interested in	12.6%	14.5%	
> 1 person with financial contribution to net income		40.0%	49.9%	Chi^2 ***
Median of monthly net income in EURO		1600 (± 990.38)	2000 (± 2827.66)	t-test ***
Expenses for assistance in housekeeping in EURO (sd)§		137.68 (± 332.95)	67.88 (± 89.81)	t-test **
Expenses for physiotherapy in EURO (sd)§		23.97 (± 32.83)	13.81 (± 34.55)	t-test *

*** = p<0.001, ** = p<0.01, * = p<0.05, n.s. = not significant.

§ = standard deviation.

3.8. Comparison of Retirees and Working Age Adults

To test for potential differences between age-related retirees (patients age 65 years and older, n=502) and working-age adults (< 65 years of age, n=814), the overall cohort was divided into the subgroups. (Note: In Germany, healthy workers retire not later as at age of 65 years. In people with disabilities, the German system „forces" people out of the work force if a rehabilitative evaluation has determined that they would functionally not benefit from additional rehabilitation efforts that would allow a return to work.).

Average age in the group of pensioners was 73 years, and this group consisted of 212 females and 290 males. The group of non-pensioners included 231 male and 583 female MG patients, with an average age of about 46 years (table 16). Pensioners more often lived in single-person households and in bigger towns. The proportion of married persons among pensioners was lower. Concerning the duration of disease and stability of MG, no differences were found. The proportion of AchR antibody-positive patients among pensioners was lower than among non-pensioners.

In general, the surveyed pensioners with MG stated mostly walking problems and weakness of the upper limbs (table 16). Compared to non-pensioners, they experienced significantly more from walking problems, ptosis, and defecation and urinary tract disorders as well as sexual problems. Non-pensioners reported loss of facial expression. No significant differences were found in diplopia, dysphagia, chewing or speech problems, weakness of muscles at rest or after physical strain, or weakness of the upper limbs or neck. In pensioners with MG, additional disorders of the joints and the cardiovascular system were frequently reported (table 16). Mood disorders were mentioned by nearly half of the pensioners with MG. Compared to non-pensioners, the proportion of pensioners experiencing joint problems, cardiovascular diseases, osteoporosis, and metabolic disorders was significantly higher. Non-pensioners reported more frequently additional immunologic diseases.

The investigated pensioners with MG required assistance by nursing services more often than did non-pensioners. No difference in the total number of visits to the doctor was found. The pensioned MG patients visited their neurologists, general practitioners, and specialists in internal medicine more often (table 16). Supporting psychotherapy was offered less often to pensioners than to non-pensioners. Fewer pensioners were interested in receiving psychotherapy.

In contrast to non-pensioners, pensioners with MG had less frequently undergone thymectomy and were less often treated with immunoglobulins, plasmapheresis, or immunoadsorption. Treatment with steroids, acetylcholine esterase inhibitors, azathioprine and radiation did not differ between the two groups.

The monthly net income of pensioners was significantly lower than that of non-pensioners. Despite increased additional payment for assistance in housekeeping and physiotherapy, pensioners and non-pensioners did not differ in overall additional expenses due to MG.

Pensioners with MG presented with significantly lower quality of life in the SF-36-scales measuring physical functioning, physical role, and bodily pain than did the non-pensioners (figure 7). Similar findings were found for general health, vitality, and social functioning. No statistical differences between pensioners and non-pensioners were found for the scales 'emotional role' [??] and 'mental health'.

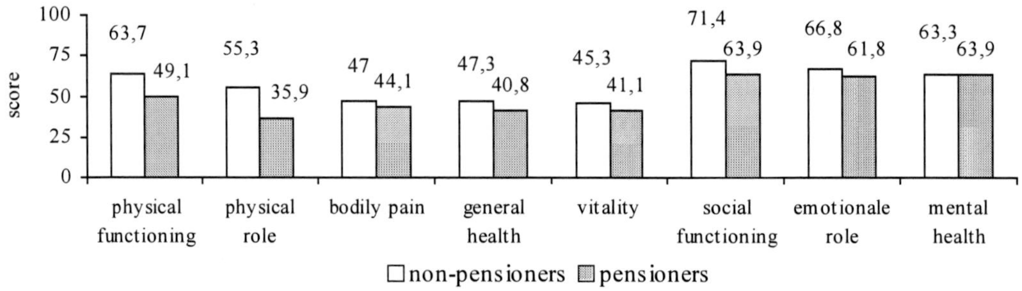

Figure 7. Differences in quality of life (SF-36) between pensioners and non-pensioners (t-test: *** = p<0,001, ** = p<0,01, n.s. = not significant).

4. Discussion and Conclusion

Progress in medical therapy and intensive care technology have increased life expectancy in MG patients [24]. Until now, not much has been known about the health care experiences and quality of life of MG patients. To fill this gap, this study focused on impairments, therapeutic course, use of complementary and alternative medicine, the impact of living as a pensioner, and the determinants of quality of life in German MG patients. Given the limited sample sizes in previous studies evaluating quality of life in MG patients, this study represents one of the largest samples of people with MG in the world. The German study sample is representative for people with MG in Germany and reflects the demographic makeup of the MG population in Western countries [34].

Unfortunately, it was not possible to assess patients' exact clinical status according to the MGFA Classification [11]. Clinical assessment of each study participant MG would have required extensive use of trained neurologists, which, given the large sample size, was impossible in the end. Perhaps future studies should include examinations of a portion of MG patients so that these assessments can be compared by experts with the self-completed answers by the patients, in order to get more information on the validity of the results.

Poulas et al. described differences in the average age of disease onset in males and females - 55.1 years versus 40.1 years, respectively - in Greek patients [28]. Mantegazza also showed two peaks of onset (females: third decade; males: sixth decade) in an Italian MG cohort [18]. The results presented in this study (53.7 versus 37.1 years) are similar to the findings presented by Poulas and Mantegazza. It remains unclear why these two different peaks of onset in male and female MG patients occur. Due to the study design, it is impossible to explain an underlying reason. Perhaps future studies should address existing theories under discussion: initiation of antibody production seems to take place in the thymus by exposing AchR-like epitopes [9,33], thymoma with a higher incidence in elderly male patients and thymus hyperplasia in younger females [18,3,9].

The rate of confirmed AchR antibodies (67.8%) was lower than in previous studies (80-90%) [24].It must be taken into account that about 20% of the MG patients in this sample did not know whether they had antibodies or not; thus, the true AchR antibody rate was probably higher. Mantegazza et al. reported similar results in their cohort of 756 MG patients (73.2%) [18]. Taking blood to analyze the presence of antibodies would have been interesting but was impossible to consider as part of the chosen study design.

The diagnostic period amounted on average to 2.8 years. In male patients the diagnosis was made significantly earlier than female MG patients. It has to be taken into account that, in some cases, the process of diagnosing MG took place in the middle of the last century. The duration of diagnostic period within the previous five years was 0.6 years. Weizer et al. revealed in their study a duration of 12.8 months for the diagnostic period, with an advantage for male patients. In addition, they referred to other studies that reported the diagnostic period length as from one year in 57% of patients to two years in 74% of the patients (males 99% and females 66% within 2 years), and 39.8 months in ocular MG patients [36]. Concerning the gender difference,I it can be asked whether male and female patients present with different symptoms. Perhaps symptoms are more obvious, reported more assertively, or experienced as more threatening in males than in females. These gender differences point up the problem that female MG patients are more likely than males to experience MG symptoms until the diagnosis is made and adequate treatment is started. Therefore, female patients presenting with unclear symptoms that do not exclude MG require more intensive attendance by physicians and neurologists to avoid improper care due to a prolonged diagnostic process.

The study participants had lived with MG on average for ten years. Nearly 80% of them stated a stable course of the disease. In contrast, 20% were confronted with an unstable course, combined with altering muscle weakness leading to respiratory insufficiency. It is likely that MG patients with severe symptoms are underrepresented because they were not able to complete the questionnaire. Paul et al. stated similar results in a smaller cohort with generalized MG [26]. Muscle weakness involving nearly all areas of the body was the main proble mreported, especially in female patients. The most common impairing symptom among elderly MG patients (≥ 65 years of age) were walking problems, reported by about 80% of the patients. One-third of participants complained about ptosis and problems with defecation.

Other factors influencing patients' daily activity are existing additional disorders. About one-third of the sample reported joint and cardiovascular problems (especially elderly patients) as well as mood disorders. In addition, osteoporosis and metabolic disorders were frequently present in participants on pension.

Despite living with a health care system that covers neurological therapies, German MG patients had increased additional expenses due to MG (on average about 50 EURO (60 USD) per month; in some cases up to 500 EURO (600 USD)). They mainly spent their money for pharmaceuticals, housekeeping assistance, and transportation. Pensioners with a low monthly net income were especially likely to spend an increased amount of money on MG-related therapies. Therefore, specific changes in the health care system are needed to make coping with MG easier and to alleviate extra out-of-pocket expenses, especially for pensioners, for example by providing free transportation to their health care providers.

One main purpose of this study was to assess quality of life in MG patients. Up to now only two published studies have investigated quality of life in MG patients. These studies included only small numbers of MG patients, and thus cannot be considered representative of the West-European or US MG population as a whole [22,26]. Paul et al. [26] investigated 27 patients with generalized MG. With regard to average age (56.7 years), duration of disease (7.3 years), and main complaints (arm weakness 70%, leg weakness 59%, ptosis 37%) their patient sample was comparable to the MG patients investigated. Compared to findings from the general population, they found in MG patients lower scores in seven of the eight dimensions of the SF-36. Padua et al. investigated 46 MG patients, with an average age of 50.7 years [22,23]. Their quality of life was lower on all scales of the SF-36. That study is limited because most of the patients participated during worsening of symptoms [22]. In our study, reduced quality of life was found in all dimensions of the SF-36, compared to the general German population. On the other hand, due to the lack of original data, no statistical comparison between the investigated sample of people with MG and the general population could be completed. By means of linear regression analysis, we found that female sex and stability of MG seem to correlate with higher quality of life. For that reason, adequate therapy to stabilize MG is an important mainstays for keeping MG patients in the working process, leading to positive consequences such as improved health and increased net income .

Pascuzzi and Weizer et al. reported progression of MG mainly within the initial two to three years after disease onset, with a tendency toward stabilization or improvement in the following years [24,36]. Progression of ocular MG to generalized MG was reported in 49-69% of the patients [7,36]. Farrugia described a reduction of the risk of generalized MG in nearly three-quarters of MG patients when the treatment was corticosteroids or azathioprine [7]. Thus, forced immunosuppressive therapy has to be conducted, especially in the initial phase of MG. Long-term immunosuppression and thymectomy have been suspected of causing increased illness in elderly patients [36]. Thus, elderly patients require special attention from health professionals. General muscle weakness can be treated by adjusting the dose of acetylcholine esterase inhibitors. However, adverse effects as severe as cholinergic crisis often limit their application [15]. Another approach could be a forced physiotherapy to strengthen musculature as described by Lohi et al. [17], which could also improve walking abilities and mobility. Less is known about the effects of physiotherapy in myasthenic patients. In one case an exacerbation of MG during therapeutic electric stimulation was reported [27]. Logopedic methods could ease faciopharyngeal symptoms and speech difficulties. They can also reduce already-existing health problems related to higher age as well as improve cardiovascular fitness.

Paul et al. also proposed that emotional health should remain an important clinical focus [26]. Therefore, MG patients should receive psychotherapy, especially if they are interested in getting it or if they expect positive results from it, as this may help them to cope with the disease-related burden. Due to the fact that conventional therapy of MG does not offer sufficient cure in all patients, and that immunosuppressive therapy is connected with severe side effects, additional therapeutic use of CAM should be considered. This study shows a high acceptance of CAM among MG patients. On the other hand, it remains unclear whether CAM is helpful in easing MG-related problems. The MG patients using CAM were predominantly females in single households, with unstable MG, a longer duration of disease, and reduced quality of life. This patient subgroup patients requires increased efforts by health care providers to ease MG-related problems and to prevent these patients spending considerable amounts of money for CAM which may be useless or dangerous.

The study indicates that while life expectancy has been prolonged, quality of life is still reduced in MG patients. Impaired quality of life resulted mainly from symptoms that impair mobility and mental health. MG may not be a major public health problem in terms of the number of patients affected, but as a chronic illness, it has major financial impacts on patients and the health care system. MG patients spent a considerable amount of money for pharmaceuticals, housekeeping assistance, transportation, physiotherapy, and CAM, even in a health care system in which neurological therapy is covered by statutory health insurance. It follows that successful managed care in MG patients depends not only on evidence-based therapies but also on other measures that improve quality of life. By improving mobility, mental well-being, integration into social surroundings, and the possibility of employment according to physical abilities, and by improving stability of disease, increased quality of life in MG patients could be achieved. Standardized guidelines for the therapy of MG patients are recommended to avoid inadequate treatment of this rare disease. Tight networks between general practitioners and neurologist are required to ensure proper health care for the MG patients. Consequently, implementation of disease-management programs for MG patients in Germany should be discussed in the near future.

5. References

[1] Bullinger M, Kirchberger I. *Questionnaire to investigate health related quality of life (SF-36)*. Göttingen: Hogrefe Verlag, 1998. (Original in German)

[2] Dalakas MC: Intravenous immunoglobulin in autoimmune neuromuscular diseases. *The Journal of the American Medical Association 291* (2004): 2367-2375.

[3] De Perrot M, Liu J, Bril V, McRae K, Bezjak A, Keshavjee SH: Prognostic significance of thymomas in patients with myasthenia gravis. *The Annals of Thoracic Surgery 74* (2002): 1658-1662.

[4] Doering S, Henze T, Schussler G: Coping with myasthenia gravis and implications for psychotherapy. *Archives of Neurology 50* (1993): 617-620.

[5] Drachman DB, Jones Rj, Brodsky RA: Treatment of refractory myasthenia: “Rebooting” with high dose cyclophosphamide. *Annals of Neurology (53)* 2003: 29-34.

[6] Ellert U, Bellach BM: German National Health Survey 1998 – Description of an Update Random Sampling Test. *Gesundheitswesen 61* (1999) Sonderheft 2: S184-S190. (Original in German)

[7] Farrugia ME: A limited epidemiological study of seropositive myasthenia gravis in Tayside. *Scottish Medical Journal* 2002 (6): 132-135.

[8] Finkel AG, Howard JF, Mann JD: Successful treatment of headache related to intravenous immunoglobulin with antimigraine medications. *Headache 38* (1998): 317-321.

[9] Garchon HJ: Genetics of autoimmune myasthenia gravis, a model for antibody-mediated autoimmunity in man. *Journal of Autoimmunity 21* (2003): 105-110.

[10] Gronseth GS, Barohn RJ: Practice parameter: thymectomy for autoimmune myasthenia gravis (an evidence-based review). *Neurology 55* (2000): 7-15.

[11] Haupt WF, Rosenow F, van der Ven C, Birkmann C: Immunoadsorption in Guillain-Barré syndrome and myasthenia gravis. *Therapeutic Apheresis 4* (2000): 195-197.

[12] Jaretzki A, Barohn RJ, Ernstoff RM, Kaminski HJ, Keesey JC, Penn AS, Sanders DB: Myasthenia gravis: recommendations for clinical research standards. *Neurology* (2000) 55: 16-23.

[13] Kaptchuk TJ, Eisenberg DM: Varieties of healing. 2: A taxonomy of unconventional healing practices. *Annals of Internal Medicine 135* (2001): 196-204.

[14] Komiyama A, Arai H, Kijima M, Hirayama K: Extraocular muscle reponses to high dose intravenous methylprednisolone in myasthenia gravis. *Journal of Neurology, Neurosurgery and Psychiatry 68* (2000): 214-217.

[15] Leitlinienkommission. Guidelines in neurology, 2nd edition, 2003. (Original in German)

[16] Lloyd JM, Mitchell RG: Myasthenia gravis as a cause of facial pain. *Oral Surgery Oral Medicine and Oral Pathology 66* (1988): 45-46

[17] Lohi EL, Lindberg C, Andersen O: Physical training effects in myasthenia gravis. *Archives of Physical Medicine and Rehabilitation 74* (1993): 1178-1180.

[18] Mantegazza R, Baggi F, Antozzi C, Confalonieri P, Morandi L, Bernasconi P, Andreetta F, Simoncini O, Campanella A, Beghi E, Cornelio F: Myasthenia gravis (MG): Epidemiological Data and prognostic factors. *Annals of the New York Academy of Sciences 998* (2003): 413-423.

[19] Masuhr KF, Neumann M: *Neurology*. 4th edition. Stuttgart: Hippokrates, 1998: S 442-445. (Original in German)

[20] Meriggioli MN, Ciafaloni E, Al-Hayk KA, Rowin J, Tucker-Lipscomb B, Massey JM, Sanders D: Mycophenolate mofetil for myasthenia gravis. An analysis of efficacy, safety, and tolerability. *Neurology 61* (2003): 1438-1440.

[21] Ossermann KE, Genkins G: Studies in myasthenia gravis: review of a twenty-years experience in over 1200 patients. *Mount Sinai Journal of Medicine 38* (1971): 497-537.

[22] Padua L, Evoli A, Aprile I, Caliandro P, Mazza S, Padua R, Tonali P: Health-related quality of life in patients with myasthenia gravis and the relationship between patient-oriented assessment and conventional measurements. *Neurological Sciences 22* (2001): 363-369.

[23] Padua L, Evoli A, Aprile I, Caliandro P, D'Amico P, Rabini A, Tonali P: Quality of life in patients with myasthenia gravis. *Muscle and Nerve 25* (2002): 466-467.

[24] Pascuzzi RM: Myasthenia gravis and Lambert-Eaton syndrome. *Therapeutic Apheresis 6* (2002): 57-68.

[25] Paul RH, Cohen RA, Gilchrist JM, Aloia MS, Goldstein JM: Cognitive dysfunction in individuals with myasthenia gravis. *Journal of the Neurological Sciences 179* (2000): 59-64

[26] Paul RH, Nash JM, Cohen RA, Gilchrist JM, Goldstein JM: Quality of life and well-being of patients with myasthenia gravis. *Muscle and Nerve 24* (2001): 512-516.

[27] Pease WS, Lagattuta FP: Exacerbation of a case of myasthenia gravis during therapeutic electric stimulation. *Archieves of Physical Medicine and Rehabilitation 68* (1987): 568-570.

[28] Poulas K, Tzartos SJ: The gender gap in autoimmune disease. *The Lancet 357* (2001): 234.

[29] Rilling G, Tettenborn B: Therapy of Myasthenia gravis. *Schweizer Rundschau für Medizin Praxis 90* (2001): 1350-1354. (Original in German)

[30] Rostedt A, Stalberg E: Joint pain and hyperalgesia due to pyridostigmine bromide in a patient with myasthenia gravis. *Neurology 62* (2004): 835-836.

[31] Romi F, Skeie GO, Gilhus NE: Muscle antibodies in subgroups of myasthenia gravis patients. *Journal of Neurology 247* (2000): 369-375.

[32] Scheschonka A, Beuche W: Treatment of post-herpetic pain in myasthenia gravis: exacerbation of weakness due to gabapentin. *Pain 104*(2003): 423-424.

[33] Schneider-Gold C, Hartung HP: Myasthenia gravis: Pathogenesis, diagnosis and therapy. *Fortschritte der Neurologie-Psychiatrie 72* (2004): 45-57 (Original in German).

[34] Vincent A, Palace J, Hilton-Jones D. Myasthenia gravis. Lancet. 2001; 357: 2122-2128.

[35] Wakata N, Saito T, Tanaka S, Hirano T, Oka K: Tacrolimus hydrate (FK 506): therapeutic effects and selection of resonders in the treatment of myasthenia gravis. *Clinical Neurology and Neurosurgery* (2003) 106: 5-8.

[36] Weizer JS, Lee AG, Coats DK: Myasthenia gravis with ocular involvement in older patients. *Canadian Journal of Ophthalmology 36* (2001): 26-33.

[37] Werneck LC, Cunha FMB, Scola RH: Myasthenia gravis: a retrospective study comparing thymectomy to conservative treatment. *Acta Neurologica Scandinavica 101* (2000): 41-46.

[38] Yeh JH, Chiu HC: Comparison between double-filtration plasmapheresis and immunoadsorption plasmapheresis in the treatment of patients with myasthenia gravis. *Journal of Neurology 247* (2000): 510-513.

In: Focus on Disability: Trends in Research and Application ISBN: 978-1-60021-792-0
Editor: Thilo Kroll, pp. 207-226 © 2008 Nova Science Publishers, Inc.

Chapter XII

OBESITY IN CHILDREN AND ADOLESCENTS: PSYCHOLOGICAL AND SOCIAL ASPECTS

Petra Warschburger*
Department of Psychology, University of Potsdam, 14415 Potsdam, Germany.

Childhood obesity has been identified as a major health threat to children and adolescents. The rate of obesity in children and adolescents continually increases, with almost every fifth child affected (Troiano & Flegal, 1998). This trend takes place in all industrial nations all over the world and it already affects the group of preschool children (Livingstone, 2000). In the meantime, obesity has already been noticed as a serious problem in some developing countries as well (De Onis & Blössner, 2000). Childhood obesity has become one of the most prominent public health concerns worldwide. Some researchers speak about a global obesity epidemic (e.g. Dietz, 2001; James, Leach, Kalamara & Shayeghi, 2001; Robinson, 2000). The health-political relevance of obesity is based on two aspects: firstly, the associated health problems and secondly, the enormous stability of obesity from childhood to adolescence. Obesity is not only a widespread phenomenon, but it also involves a range of secondary diseases. The following contribution deals with the psychological, social and functional consequences of obesity in childhood and adolescence above all. Empirical studies are to be illustrated in more detail and the role of psychosocial aspects of obesity, related to its maintenance and treatment is to be discussed. However, first it has to be explained what is understood by obesity and how the pathogenesis of this disease is explained.

* Correspondence concerning this article should be addressed to: Petra Warschburger, University of Potsdam, Department of Psychology, Postfach 60 15 53, 14415 Potsdam, Germany. Phone: 0049 / 331 9772988; Fax: 0049 / 331 9772794; E-mail: warschb@rz.uni-potsdam.de.

1. Defining Obesity

Obesity describes the health impairing excess adiposity. Since the direct measurement of the body composition is large-scale and cost-intensive, its extent is estimated indirectly. Obesity is usually defined in terms of the body mass index (BMI). The BMI is the ratio of weight in kilograms to the square of height in meters. It is widely used to define overweight and obesity because of its relative good correlation with extent of body fat. The BMI not only changes during lifetime but it also differs concerning age and sex. Therefore BMI percentile curves are employed in childhood and adolescence. The critical point for differentiating between overweight and obesity partly varies a little in different countries. However, meanwhile it has been more and more accepted, that the 97. percentile related to national standard values is enlisted to define adiposity, the 90. percentile is enlisted to mark overweight. Especially in America the 85. respectively the 95. percentile is sometimes enlisted for the classification of overweight and adiposity as well (see Lobstein, Bauer & Uauy, 2004). Cole, Belizzi, Flegal und Dietz (2000) recently presented a classification of obesity for children and adolescents suggesting age- and sex-specific BMI cut-off points, which is based on the BMI age curves passing into the BMI-values of 25 and 30 (cut-off points used in adults to define overweight and obesity) at the adult age. This classification is supposed to form the basis for international and national surveys in the future.

2. Increasing Prevalence

As already mentioned, the prevalence of obesity is national and international of a very high level and it has obtained „pandemic“ (Kimm & Obarzanek, 2002). In general it is possible to speak of a secular increase. Ogden, Troiano, Briefel, Kuczmarski, Flegal and Johnson (1997) for instance detected nearly a quadrupling of the prevalence of obesity in the group of six- to eleven-year-olds (from 4 to 15%) and a trebling for adolescents (from 5 to 16%) since the beginning of the sixties. In Germany, between 1975 and 1995 a doubling of the frequency of obesity as well as overweight was noticeable for children from East Germany (Kromeyer-Hausschild, Zellner, Jaeger & Hoyer, 1999). The increasing global dissemination of adiposity even with children at preschool age is alarming (Kalies, Lenz & von Kries, 2002; Mei, Scanlon, Grummer-Strawn, Freedman, Yip, & Trowbridge, 1998; Ogden et al., 1997). For example, the prevalence for 2-year-old children was already 6% in a British study (Reilly, Dorosty & Emmett, 1999). With the increasing age of children the dissemination of adiposity increases (see Troiano & Flegal, 1998). Several studies reveal that in the last decades not only more children are becoming obese but also these children have been getting heavier (e.g. Barth et al., 1997; Jolliffe, 2004). Environmental variables such as altered nutrition- and exercise behavior are mainly held responsible for this trend (Hill & Peters, 1998; Lobstein et al., 2004).

Obesity is not distributed equally over all groups: there is a significant overrepresentation of the lower social classes (vgl. Alaimo, Olson & Frongillo, 2001; Goodman et al., 2003; Haas, Lee, Kaplan, Sonneborn, Philips & Liang, 2003; Sorensen, 1995). Moreover, clear ethnic differences were not only observable in the prevalence (e.g. Kimm et al., 2001, 2002;

Haas et al., 2003), but also in the increasing incidence: Between 1986 and 1998 the spread of overweight in children (4-12 years) of Hispanic and Afro-American descent rose twice as fast as in children of Caucasian origin (Strauss & Pollack, 2001). Children of parents with a low income and an offer of poor cognitive stimulation clearly show a higher risk of excessive adiposity (Strauss & Knight, 1999). We may speak of an accumulation of risk factors in these groups: the socioeconomic status of a child is linked in a multifaceted way with risk factors such as nutrition, physical exercise or inactivity. These risk factors and the models of explanation for the development and maintenance of obesity are to be dealt with in the following part.

3. Medicial Comorbidities and Economic Burden

For many years it has been widely accepted that health problems associated with obesity only emerge in adulthood and that they are of minor importance for childhood and adolescence. However, current research indicates that childhood obesity is a risk factor for several major diseases – among them type 2 diabetes, hypertension, coronary heart disease and orthopaedic problems – already in childhood and adolescence (e.g. Dietz, 2002; Reilly et al., 2003). In addition, the numerous health problems in adulthood have to be taken into account (see Field, Barnoya & Colditz, 2002 for a review): Obesity in adulthood increases not only the risk for cardiovascular disease or diabetes, but also for certain cancers and mortality. Must, Jacques, Dallal, Bajema and Dietz (1992) presented results of a 55-year follow-up study examining the effects of overweight in adolescence on morbidity and mortality in adulthood. 508 lean and overweight adolescents (aged 13 to 18 years) participated in the study. Among overweight men, the relative risk for mortality of all causes increased to 1.8, for mortality from coronary heart disease to 2.3 and from atherosclerotic cerebrovascular disease to 13.2 compared with lean men. No increase in relative risk from death was found among overweight women. In the course of 40 years, Mossberg (1989) demonstrated that overweight in childhood and adolescence (age: 0 16 years) involves increased morbidity and mortality.

In addition, obese children and adolescents are at increased risk of becoming obese adults. Across all ages, the risk of adult obesity was at least twice as high for obese children as for non-obese children. The risk grows with increasing levels of obesity and increasing age (Serdula, Ivery, Coates, Freedman, Williamson & Byers, 1993). Children being obese at the age of four to ten years become obese adults in about 30%, whereas obese adolescents between 11 and 17 years become the same in about 50% (Danielzik, Langnäse, Mast, Spethmann & Müller, 2002; Lake, Power & Cole, 1997; Whitaker et al., 1997). Furthermore, an early increase of the „adiposity rebound" during the time of school enrolment is prognostic (Whitaker et al., 1998). The BMI of the parents is an independent risk factor as well as it is linked with further risk fators like early rebound (Dorosty, Emmett, Cowin & Reilly, 2000).

The health political relevance of obesity has gained interest in times of limited resources. The precise measurement of expenses is difficult and the economic burden upon the health services can often only be estimated. There are no facts about the expenses caused specifically by overweight and obese children. The costs in the age of adulthood are considered above all. Thompson and Wolf (2001) compiled 18 global studies in a current survey that deal with the expenses of the medical care of obesity. The studies focus on very different secondary diseases and their costs and they partly apply different BMI cut-off points. The percentage of the national health expenses which can be attributed to obesity is around 5.5 to 7% in the USA, and this amounts up to US $ 70 billion. In France and Portugal the total share was visibly lower with a percentage of 2 resp. 3.5%. Moreover, an increase of the costs by 25 to 44% seems to exist in comparison to normal weight. The different methodical standards are problematic with all analyses. Many estimations are rated in a conservative way since some relevant factors such as the psychic and social consequences were not considered in the analyses.

4. Obesity as a Multifactoral Disease

Obesity is a very heterogeneous disease with many different factors contributing to its etiology and maintenance. Plainly speaking, we gain weight if we consume more energy (food) than we expend. But which factors contribute to this positive energy relation? Contrary to the popular belief, childhood obesity is only rarely caused by an underlying disease (e.g. Prader Willi or tumour of the hypothalamus). The most prominent risk factor seems to be genetic influence. Many studies have demonstrated that obesity runs in families and that children from obese or overweight parents take a heightened risk of becoming obese themselves (e.g. Stunkard, Harris, Pederson & McClearn, 1990). Studies of mono- and dizygotic twins and of those brought up in separate environments have shown that a genetic predisposition to gain weight accounts for 60-85% of the variation in obesity (Bouchard et al., 1989, 1990; Stunkard, Harris, Pederson & McClearn, 1990). Besides this high level of genetic predetermination, physical and social environments as well as certain behaviors may particularly encourage or trigger excessive weight gain, e.g. dietary patterns characterized by a strong preference for high-fat diets, decline in physical activity or increase in sedentary behavior.

Besides resting metabolic rate, physical activity is an essential additional source of energy expenditure. It was assumed that overweight children exercise less often and less intensively and therefore show decreased need for energy. Waxman and Stunkard (1980) for example observed that overweight children were less active at home than their normalweight brothers and sisters; such differences were not yet observable at the playground. Further cross-sectional studies also reasoned that obese children and adoloscents exercise less than normalweight peers (e.g. Davies, Gregory & White, 1995; Sallis et al., 1993). Epstein, Smith, Vara and Rodefer (1991) were able to reveal in an experimental study that overweight children particularly avoid physical exercise when it is linked with high costs. Researchers agree in terms of the contribution of lacking physical activity on the maintenance of obesity. However, these studies do not allow to conclude whether physical inactivity substantially supports the its pathogenesis. Prospective studies on this are contradictory. Thus, in the course of one year Berkey and collagues (2000) detected a higher increase of the BMI with adolescents exercising less. All in all the effect was referred to as rather minor, but on the other side it also appeared that a cumulation of risks like caloric intake and time spent with TV or games ought to be considered.

Several studies have specially examined the links between the amount of watching television and children's risk of overweight and obesity. Two prospective studies by Gortmaker (Dietz & Gortmaker, 1985; Gortmaker et al., 1996) have demonstrated that children who watched television five or more hours a day were five times more likely to be overweight after four years than those watching fewer than two hours a day. This relationship remained even stable after adjusting several confounding factors (like child's weight status, maternal weight, socio-economic status). The contribution of television viewing seems to be partially mediated by a higher food intake and a lower general activity level (Klesges, Shelton & Klesges, 1993). It also applies for this that the interrelations are rather minor and that they could not be replicated in each study (Robinson et al., 1993). The reduction of TV consumption proved to be an efficient preventive strategy in school samples (Robinson, 1999).

Food intake and physical activity themselves as potential risk patterns for becoming obese are influenced by many factors: Facilities for sporting activities, parental knowledge, attitudes or beliefs concerning consumption of certain foods (like high-caloric density foods) play an important role. In contrary to adults, children are only partly responsible for their nutrition and activity habits as well as for their spending of leisure time. Parents and other attachment figures influence the behavior of their children in a manifold way, inter alia by their own model behavior and the providing of alternatives and their support (e.g. Birch & Fisher, 1998; Borah-Giddens & Falciglia, 1993;; Cutting, Fisher, Grimm-Thomas & Birch, 1999; Davison & Birch, 2001; Nadar, 1993). For instance Epstein (2000) found out that children of active parents are up to six times more active than children of inactive parents. Burke, Beilin und Dunbar (2001) observed correlations between the unhealthy life-style of parents and their children in a prospective study. The socioeconomic background has to be taken into consideration too. Thus, Dennison, Erb and Jenkins (2002) report on a high rate of own TV sets for preschool children (!) at socially discriminated families. An own TV set was also linked with a higher obesity rate. Furthermore, children of a lower social layer eat fruits and vegetables less regularly (Neumark-Sztainer, Story, Resnik & Blum, 1996).

To summarize, it can be retained that current explanations centralize the genetic predisposition (mediated e.g. by a reduced metabolic rate or a particular preference for high-fat foods). Nutrition behavior (in the sense of quantity and quality of nourishment; distribution through the day etc.) and activity and inactivity profile are regarded as important interventional factors. At the same time it should be taken into account that the direct and indirect social environment may affect the concrete behavior and thus the obesity risk.

5. Psychosocial Consequences of Obesity

There is a long tradition of a psychosocial consideration of obesity. Accordingly, there is a wide range of psychosocial impairments and problems that have been investigated in association with obesity. In the following, the multitude of studies at childhood and adolescence according to the following categories is to be analysed: (1) social discrimination and teasing experiences (2) emotional problems (such as anxieties, depression or self-worth) (3) school and functional restrictions as well as (4) effects on the quality of life.

5.1. Social Discrimination and Teasing Experiences

Obesity is a highly visible disorder. Everybody can assess your weight status and comment on it. Besides visibility, obese persons are thought to be strongly responsible for their condition. There is a clear and consistent scientific literature showing bias against and consequent discrimination of overweight people. In an excellent review Puhl and Brownell (2001) describe detailed stigmatization and discrimination in three important areas of life: education, employment and health care. They report on studies which underline that even the attitudes of health professionals towards obese people were very negative. They often associated obesity with poor compliance, hostility and absent self-control (e.g. Jelalian, Boergers, Alday & Frank, 2003). Such attitudes and the reluctance perceived by the concerned persons may lead to their hesitation to seek for medical or for psychotherapeutic help too.

Negative stereotypes of obese people emerge early in life. In the study from Goldfield and Chrisler (1995) first graders were shown a set of body silhouettes. The children significantly wanted to be less often friends with an endomorphic child. Hill and Silver (1995) asked 9-year-old children to rate four different body figures. The obese figures were rated as having fewer friends, doing less well at school and being less liked by their parents. The children's own weight only marginally influenced these stereotypical judgements. These studies and others (e.g. Hill & Silver, 1995; Kraig & Keel, 2001; Wardle, Volz & Golding, 1995) are suggestive of the prevalent aversion to "chubbiness", even in young children. The negative attitudes neither changed even if the children were given a medical explanation pattern in the run-up to it (Bell & Morgan, 2000).

Given the high prevalence of obesity in our society, Latner and Stunkard (2003) hypothesized that the degree of disapproval of obesity could have been declined during the last decades. They replicated a study from the sixties in which children were asked to rank six different drawings ("healthy", "wheelchair", "crutches", "facial disfigurement", "left hand missing" and "obese") according to which degree they liked the child. The most important finding of their study was that the bias against obese children was even stronger in 2001 than it had been 40 years ago. Nearly half of the children rated the obese child last, whereas only 5.1% rated this body figure first compared to 57.1% for the healthy figure.

In addition to results from hypothetical paradigms, numerous studies have also documented repeated negative social experiences of obese children and adolescents. Physical attributes, including weight, are common targets for teasing among children and adolescents. Recent research by several authors has indicated that overweight and obese children and adolescents experience a range of negative experiences. Neumark-Sztainer, Story and Faibisch (1998) interviewed overweight girls to explore their weight-related negative experiences. Nearly all girls reported hurtful indirect and direct comments, being treated differentially or even rejected because of their overweight. Peers were most frequently involved in hurtful experiences, but also other children, family members or strangers.

These observations correspond with our own results exploring the role of teasing and coping behavior in a group of heavily overweight children and adolescents. 158 children and adolescents were asked to fill in the "Physical Appearance-Related Teasing Scale" developed by Thompson, Fabian, Moulton, Dunn and Altabe (1991). As expected, the obese children and adolescents reported a significantly higher level of weight-related teasing compared with performance-related teasing. Yet, girls and boys did not differ from each other in the perceived frequency of teasing behavior; but girls still perceived it to be more stressful. In addition, children were asked to rate their experienced frequency of teasing by different people or groups. As shown in figure 1 unfamiliar children and classmates were reported to tease most commonly. Dealing with teasing experience the children and adolescents reported that they fell back on internal and avoidant coping behaviors more likely.

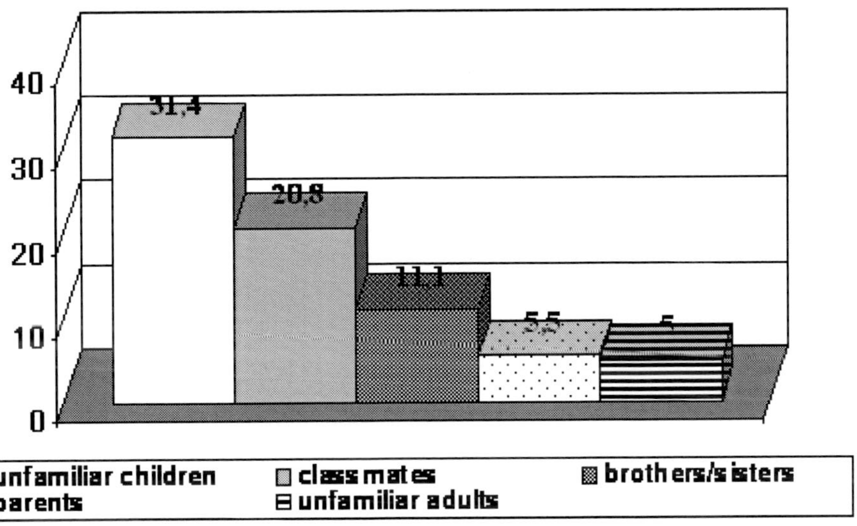

Figure 1. Frequency of weight-teasing by different persons or groups.

Within the scope of samples referred to population-based studies, statistically significant associations between perceived weight-teasing and weight status were detectable as well. Among average weight children, 18.7% of the girls and 13% of boys reported frequent weight teasing. Among obese children, this percentage rose to 45.3% for the girls and to 50.2% for the boys (Neumark-Sztainer, Falkner, Story, Perry, Hannan & Mulert, 2002). Beyond it, Pearce, Boergers and Prinstein (2002) were able to demonstrate that especially obese girls dispose of dating experiences considerably less seldom. Teasing related to weight was not only associated with a disturbedbody image and current eating disorder (e.g. Jackson, Grilo & Masheb, 2000; Neumark-Sztainer et al., 2002) but also with reduced physical activity levels (Faith, Leone, Ayers, Heo, & Pietrobelli, 2002).

These studies might suggest that obese children and adolescents are merely the victims of bullying. A recent report from Jansen et al. (2004) challenges that view. The authors examined more than 5000 children and adolescents, who were not only asked if they experienced bullying in school in the last two months but also if they took part in bullying themselves. Furthermore, they differentiated between verbal, relational, physical and sexual bullying behaviors. 11.6% of the children reported being bullied. Across all age groups the prevalence of victims rose with increasing BMI category (normal weight, overweight and obese) from 10.7% to 18.5%. In addition to being more frequently a victim of bullying, overweight and obese children were also more often the perpetrators of bullying themselves. These behaviors might establish a vicious circle of hurting others (verbally or physically) and being harmed by others. This thesis could also be supported by Baum and Forehand (1984), who observed a negative social interactive behavior with moderately and highly overweight children.

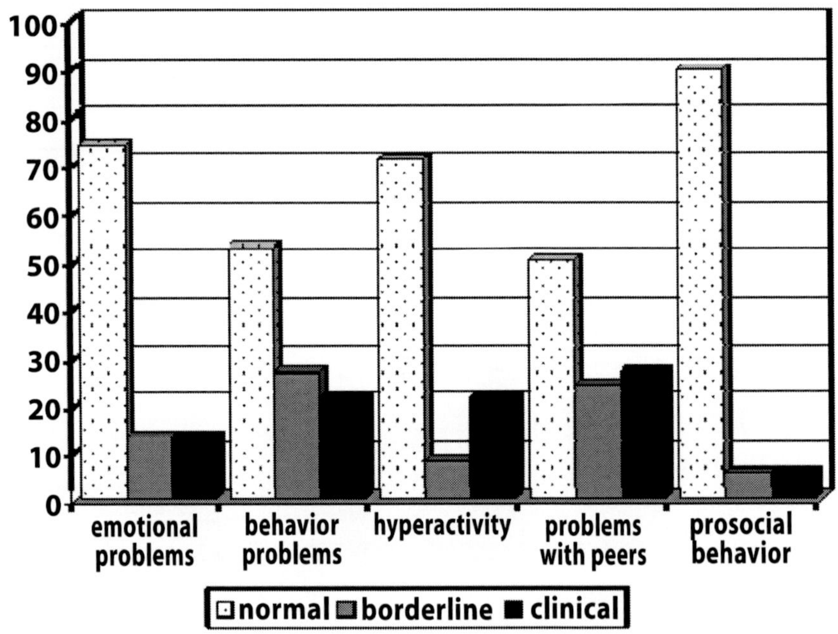

Figure 2. Frequency of parent-reported problems in obese boys (SDQ; Warschburger, 2004).

Keeping the negative social experiences in mind, these children may have limited chances to develop social competences and supporting social relationships. The thesis does not seem to be true in this general sense. It is true that indications of a lower popularity of obese children and adolescents were found in several studies (e.g. Kimm et al., 1991; Manus & Killeen, 1995), but others did not find such an effect (e.g. Israel & Ivanova, 2002; Philipps & Hill, 1998). If you use the parent assessment as a basis, social problems will be among the most frequent strains for obese children and adolescents. In an examination of 88 adolescents (aged 10 to 17 years) seeking inpatient treatment due to their obesity, the parents were given the SDQ (Strengths and Difficulties Questionnaire), which asks for problems with peers among other things:: 50% of the boys and even 58.3% of the girls had at least borderline problems in this field (see figure 2 and 3). The parents of all girls and of 89,4% of the boys regarded prosocial behavior (e.g. helping others) as unproblematic. As figures 2 and 3 reveal, above all emotional problems (like being anxious, feeling blue) were reported for girls and behavior problems (like aggressiveness) for boys.

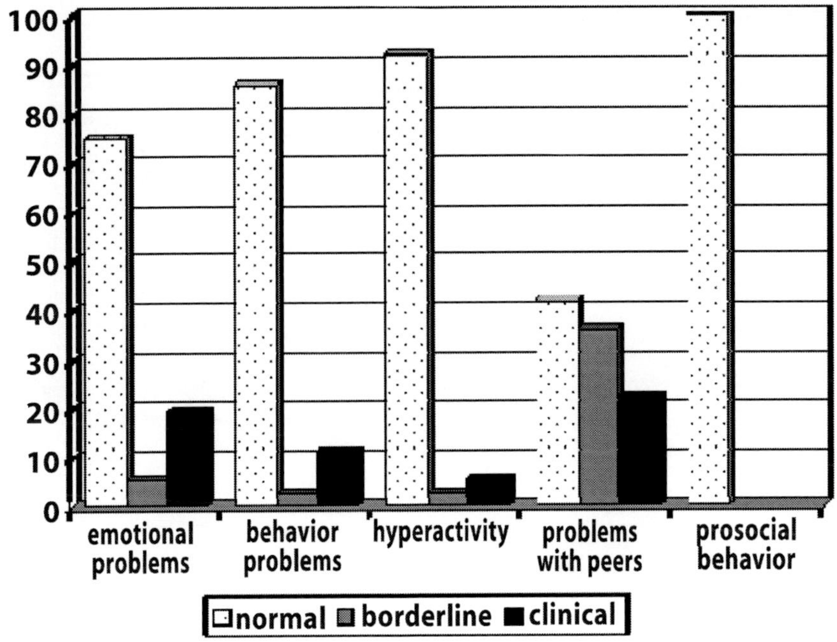

Figure 3. Frequency of parent-reported problems in obese girls (SDQ; Warschburger, 2004).

5.2. Emotional Problems

The strong aversion against overweight as well as the clinical impression indicated that obese children and adolescents might experience significant restrictions. Psychological problems suggested to be associated with obesity included negative self-esteem, elevated anxiety and depression levels. However, this clinical observation did not always coincide with the results of studies. The magnitude of association between weight status and psychological problems varies and suggests that obesity does not inevitable lead to psychosocial strain (see French, Story & Perry, 1995; Friedman & Brownell, 1995; Warschburger, 2000). This conclusion is to be reinforced by means of the empirical data situation.

A first access to this subject was made by psychopathological approach: The frequency of psychiatric disorders was meant to be heightened with obese children and adolescents. Therefore, the Child Behavior Checklist (CBCL) was particularly applied in the Anglo-American region to test this thesis. The results of these studies are summarized in table 1. Altogether, we may note (down) that between 29% and 49% of the obese children had clinically relevant scores in the papers of Epstein and colleagues (Epstein, Klein & Wisniewski, 1994; Epstein, Myers & Anderson, 1996). Social problems and internalizing behaviors were reported most frequently with the children. The missing control group and the fact that only children being in treatment because of their weight were criticized above all.

Table 1. Studies that applied the CBCL with obese children and adolescents

Publication	Sample characteristics	Major Results
Braet et al. (1997)	n = 92 obese children (from clinics) n = 47 obese children (from school) n= 150 normal-weight children age: 9 – 12 years	• total problem score: 20% of the clincal group had elevated scores in the clinical range compared with 4% in the non-clinical obese group and 3% of the controls • in all subscales the clinical group scored higher than the controls • in all subscales with the exception of the activity and social competence scales the clinical group reached higher means than the non-clinical comparison group.
Epstein et al. (1994)	N = 59 obese children age: 8 – 11 years	• 71% of the children were in the normal range • in the subscale „social problems“ 20% of obese boys and 12,8% of girls had elevated scores • 10% of boys and 2.6% of girls showed internalizing behavior disorder • 15% of the boys and 5.2% of the girls showed elevated anxiety/depression scores
Epstein et al. (1996)	N = 152 obese children age (mean): 10 ± 1.3 years	• 20% of the boys and 10.9% of the girls showed elevated internalizing problem scores • 5% of the boys and 12% of the girls showed elevated externalizing problem scores • social problems were reported for 45% of the boys and 28.3% of the girls in the sample
Eremis et al. (2004)	n = 30 obese children (from clinics) n = 30 obese children (from school) n= 30 normal-weight children age: 12 – 16 years	• no significant differences for activity competence, social and total competence and thought problem scores • in nearly all other scales the clinical group scored higher than the normal-weight controls and non-clinical obese controls • the non-clinical obese controls only scored in four scales higher than the normal-weight controls: social problems, somatic problems, internalizing behavior and total problem score
Tershakovec et al. (1994)	n = 25 obese schoolchildren n = 35 normal-weight children age: 8 – 12 years	• all study children showed significantly higher CBCL scores than the population means • obese children scored higher in the total problem score and internalizing problems
Vila et al. (2004)	n = 155 obese children n = 171 diabetic children age: 5 – 17 years	
Wallander et al. (1988)	n = 80 diabetic children n = 77 children with spina bifida n = 40 hemophilic children n = 30 obese children n = 24 rheumatic children n = 19 children with cerebral palsy age: 4 – 16 years	• as a group the chronically ill and handicapped children reported to display significantly more behavior problems and a lower level of social competence than normative samples • obese children were not different from all other chronic physical disorders
Young-Hyman et al. (2003)	N= 117 overweight children age: 5 – 10 years	• 3% fell into the clinical range for total social competence • 8% fell into the clinical range for total problems score • a BMI above the 99th percentile was associated with more somatic complaints, more social problems, more aggression and more total problems

Braet, Mervielde and Vandereyken (1997) were able to demonstrate in an impressive way that such an approach causes skewed results. They compared three groups: obese children being medically treated, a normalweight and an obese school group. The affiliation to the clinical status proved to be a significant predictor for the extent of psychological problems. Concerning their means, the obese children of the nonclinical sample were comparable with the normal weight controls relating to the dimension of behavior problems (assessed with the CBCL). Significant differences were found for the self-competence, namely the physical and general self-worth subscales, indicating that both obese groups scored lower than the normal-weight controls. This setting effect could recently be confirmed in a further study as well (vgl. Eremis, Cetin, Tamar, Bukusoglu, Akdeniz & Goksen, 2004). In a non-clinical group of obese children Young-Hyman, Schlundt, Herman-Wenderoth and Bozylinski (2003) too detected only 8% whose total score fell into the clinical range.

Compared to other clinically relevant clinical pictures, the results are not clear: whereas Wallander et al. (1988) did not find any differences between children with varying syndromes (diabetes among others as well), Vila et al. (2004) lately reported a multiplied occurence externalizing and internalizining behaviors among obese children compared with diabetic children. Since Wallander et al. (1988) concentrated above all on children of the lower social class and only considered 30 children with obesity, this might explain the absent effects.

Some papers recorded psychiatric diagnoses and detected high prevalences especially in clinical groups. Britz et al. (2000) for instance reported on a clinical group of 47 extremely obese adolescents, that 70% met the criteria for at least one DSM-IV diagnosis: 42.6% for mood disorder, 40.4% for anxiety disorder (especially social phobia: 29.8%). The rates were both clearly increased compared with a control group and with an obese population-based control group. In the study of Buddeberg-Fischer, Klaghofer and Reed (1999) with a non-clinical sample of 136 female adolescents even 87% of the overweight persons received at least one psychiatric diagnosis. Mustillo, Worthman, Erkanli, Keeler, Angold and Costello (2003), who also observed the progress of obesity between 9 and 16 years in a representative study, detected visibly smaller numbers: They especially found an increased rate of psychiatric disorders when a chronic obesity existed (14.6% of the population). This applied to oppositional disorder and depression (only for boys) above all.

On the other hand, the high rate of anxieties with obese children and adolescents in in-patient settings could be confirmed with other chronic diseases as well. Thus we interviewed 55 obese and 44 asthmatic children and adolescents about the occurence of anxieties, inter alia by the STAI-C and the German version of the Social Anxiety Scale for children. 43.9% of the obese children and adolescents showed clinically demonstrative anxiety scores in the STAI compared to 27.8% of asthmatic children and adolescents. Almost four times as many children and adolescents with obesity reported clinically significant levels of fear of negative evaluation as the children with asthma (Stöckel & Warschburger, 2004; Warschburger & Stöckel, in preparation). These results underline the observations of a large-scale clinical study which detected significantly higher STAI-scores with obese children and adolescents in comparison to children with asthma and atopic dermatitis (Warschburger, 1998). Therefore anxiety seems to play a crucial role with obesity.

Significant differences with a control group only showed in 4 of 19 studies in an own survey (Warschburger, 2000). These observations have lead to many discussions about the inquiry about psychosocial consequences for obese children and adolescents. Several features of the research might have contributed to the inconsistency of its outcome. As already pointed out, the definition of obesity or overweight used by researchers varies from study to study. The considered age-group shows big differences between the studies as well, but still it also partly demonstrates large scopes within one study. Kimm et al. (1991) investigated 130 obese children and adolescents aged 8 to 17 years: With increasing age the self-concept became worse. Strauss (2000) point to clear age and gender differences as well: negative effects are expected only in adolescence and mainly with girls.The inquiry about the methodical approach is another factor that can help to explain the contradiction in the findings. The sample size is often very small: Therefore differences between groups can hardly be detected. Another point is, that the clinical impression is usually based on a highly selective group of patients which undergoes medical treatment because of their obesity. As already demonstrated, a high dissemination of demonstrative features can be expected in such a group. An access through schools was chosen in many examinations that did not discover differences between normal weight and overweight/obese children and adolescents (e.g. Wadden et al., 1989). According to these authors, we should not speak about psychiatric problems of obese children and adolescents but about a strong dissatisfaction with their own body. Complementary it has to be added that this dissatisfaction can still lead to psychological problems. Another important aspect within the scope of self-worth research is the fact that global but not dimensional measures were often applied. Differences between obese and non-obese children and adolescents are expected the earliest withing the field of physical competence and body esteem. Here the findings are comparatively consistent as well (e.g. Renmann et al., 1999; Stradmeijer et al., 2000).

In this connection it is to be mentioned, that besides the fact that clinical groups are more demonstrative, it can be differentiated within the clinical groups again. Thus more and more studies indicate that the existence of a Binge Eating Disorder or of binging-behavior is linked with higher psychosocial strain (e.g. Decaluwé, Braet & Fairburn, 2002; Isnard et al., 2003).

The majority of reported studies so far are cross-sectional surveys with already manifest obese people. The emotional problems in this connection are rather understood as a consequence of obesity than as their cause. However, such studies cannot tell something about the temporal or causal relationship. Yet, several third-generation papers, that deal with the relationship between depression and obesity in the first place, already exist by now. The findings are also contradictory in this case: Conduct disorder, but not depression in early adolescence predicted BMI and obesity in adulthood (Pine, Cohen, Brook & Coplan, 1997), whereas such connections were also found with the control of potential confounders (like social class; parental BMI or health style) in three further studies (Goodman & Whitaker, 2002; Pine, Goldstein, Wolk & Weissman, 2001; Richardson et al., 2003: only among girls). Many explanations for this connection, such as reduced physical activity or changed eating behavior, seem to be possible due to the multifactorial genesis of obesity. The coherences are often low and they also plead for a closer inspection of subgroups in this case again.

5.3. School Difficulties and Functional Impairments

Surprisingly little research has been carried out on the social consequences of obesity for children and adolescents. Two significant studies addressed the issue of social consequences of obesity in young adulthood. In a longitudinal study, Gortmaker, Must, Perrin, Sobol and Dietz (1993) investigated among other things the association between overweight and subsequent educational attainment, marital status and household income in 10,039 young people. Seven years later, overweight women had completed fewer years of school, earned less money and were less likely to be married. Men were eleven percent less likely to be married but did not differ in other ways from non-overweight men. These results are noteworthy since the authors were able to show that other chronic conditions like asthma did not affect the reported socio-economic characteristics in a comparable way. Sargent and Blanchflower (1994) also found a correlative connection between a higher weight state and a lower income with young women, whereas no differences existed with men.

More significant in childhood and adolescence are certainly the studies about the school situation. At the same time the papers still concentrated less on the question of absent school days or the absence at sports classes, but rather on the intelligence and achievement problems of the students. In the majority, the present results indicate intensified problems of children and adolescents in this field. Thus,Tershakovec, Weller and Gallagher (1994) detected a twice as high rate of children who needed specific learning aids among obese children. Mo-suwan, Lebel, Puetpaiboon and Jujana (1999) only detected a negative coherence between the BMI and progress at school with adolescents, but not with primary schoolchildren . In a prospective analysis of Lissau and Sorensen (1993) these difficulties at school proved to be a predictor for an increased risk of obesity ten years later. Mo-suwan et al. (1999) detected a similar connection as well: poor progress at school with adolescents proved to be a predictor for the development of obesity. At the moment it can only be speculated on the interpretation of such associations. Besides higher emotional stress with the use of food as a coping strategy, a link between lower progress at school and the inability to control the own eating behavior is also possible. According to this, the poor achievements at school would be an indicator for lacking self-organization. In accordance with that view, in the performance IQ but not in the verbal IQ with severely obese children Li (1995)detected significant lower test scores compared with the normal weight controls.

Functional restrictions owing to obesity have to be looked for mainly in the field of physical activity and agility. For instance, problems with breathing or joint difficulties play an important role (Redline et al., 1999). In a semi-structured interview 54 obese children and adolescents were asked about the activities while they felt bothered from their obesity the most. The interviewed felt most bothered with sports activities such as running, athletics or sports lessons, daily activities like bying clothes or general walking as well as social activities like going to disco or eating out with friends, too (Warschburger, Buchholz & Petermann, 2001). Such functional restrictions in evervday life were given specific attention in quality of life studies.

5.4. Quality of Life

Many studies have tended to examine psychosocial impairments from a psychopathological point of view. These measures often focus on specific issues (like anxiety or depression) but they do not account two important aspects: firstly, the potential consequences of obesity on general health and well-being and secondly, the limitations of well-being that do not fulfil diagnostic criteria (subclinical range). As a multidimensional construct health related quality of life aggregates the emotional and social well-being, physical health and the functional ability associated with a chronic disease.

The quality of life of obese children and adolescents has hardly been examined yet. Whereas on the one hand results with generic instruments like the SF-36 existed for adults, (e.g. Brown, Mishra, Kenardy & Dobson, 2000; Fontaine et al., 1999; Kaukua, Pekkarinen, Sane & Mustajoki, 2002) and on the other hand weight related measuring instruments were developed (e.g. Butler, Vallis, Perey, Veldhuyzen van Zanten, MacDonald & Konok, 1999; Kolotkin, Crosby, Koslsoki & Williams, 2001), this field was rather neglected in childhood and adolescence. However, first studies in this area have been submitted lately. Wake, Salmon, Waters, Wright und Hesketh (2002) presented the CHQ to the parents of 2863 schoolchildren in Australia. Numerous restrictions in the quality of life, presenting themselves in the areas physical functioning, bodily pain, general health, mental health and self-esteem, showed especially for boys. The parents additionally stated that they felt emotionally distressed and limited in time due to the state of health of their child. In the group of girls demonstrative scores only displayed according to general health and self-esteem.

Significant setting effects appeared in the studies on quality of life as well. An own study referring to the weight-related quality of life was able to confirm this observation. More than 500 children being in treatment due to their obesity and 800 school-children were interviewed. As expected, within the group of school-children scores differentiated between the different weight levels: Overweight children reported a lower quality of life compared to normalweight or underweight children and adolescents (Warschburger, Fromme & Petermann, in press). Furthermore, compared to the clinical group of overweight and obese children, their quality of life was higher. Beyond it, higher impairments in the quality of life of children with obesity compared with children suffering from asthma or atopic dermatitis were also found (Ravens-Sieberer, Redegeld & Bullinger, 2001).

6. Conclusion

Obesity is a widespread problem in our society and current epidemiological data underscore the urgency of dealing with this topic. Only the medical aspects of obesity have been given special emphasis for a long time. However, in childhood and adolescence the negative social and psychological consequences of obesity are more important and more prevalent than the medical problems. From the existing research results to date, it can be delineated that obesity affects the psychosocial well-being in many different ways: Firstly, sociocultural pressures center around the idealization of a slimness and the disparagement of overweight. Secondly, social restrictions, for instance referred to the interaction with age-mates and teachers but also to the professional career, were reported. Social expectations cannot only cause the discrimination and stigmatization of the concerned persons, but also self-worth and behavioral problems for them. Here, the enormous heterogeneity of findings and therefore of obese children and adolescents especially displays with the analysis of cross-sectional studies.

Taking this into account, Friedman and Brownell (1995) proposed a generational research approach. First generation studies compared obese/overweight and non-obese persons regarding psychological variables. The problem is that group comparisons often hide existing differences within the group and assume that groups are very homogeneous within themselves. Still, the investigations have partially displayed very big differences within the group of obese persons. Yet, it can be demonstrated, that at least a subsample of obese children and adolescents substantially suffers from their weight and some have pronounced psychological problems. The majority of children, particularly when they are asked in schools, reports on negative experiences, but not so much on psychiatric problems. They are dissatisfied above all and feel restricted in their quality of life. According to Friedman and Brownell it is time to identify which groups are particularly restricted in their well-being (second generation): The strains seem to increase with age, just as gender differences are expected to appear, but they have to be analysed more carefully for the examined fields (e.g. self-esteem, anxiety or conduct disorder) once more. Children who undergo treatment represent a high risk-population. However, this group is also very heterogeneous and within this group the existence of binging is an important discriminative variable. After it, the identified clusters of risk factors should be examined in third-generation studies for interactions, succession of time and so on.

Considering the psychological literature, these data suggest that obesity is accompanied by more strongly developed psychosocial problems and lower weight-related quality of life in clinical groups. Therefore, the findings highlight the importance of developing effective treatments for obese children and adolescents that take account of the social and psychological consequences of obesity. Obesity cannot to considered as a medical problem but a chronic disease which affects all aspects of everyday life. In many cases we cannot assume that we can cure obesity, but the concerned people have to learn strategies to get their weight under control and to reduce the potential secondary risks. The consequences of obesity are very widespread and they primarily affect the emotional, social and functional well-being in childhood and adolescence.

In our society obesity is often regarded as an individual problem, for solving the concerned people are exclusively responsible. Such a one-sided ascription of responsibility does no justice to our knowledge of the emergence and maintenance of obesity. We live in an „obese world“ that arranges all environmental factors in a way that we are confronted with resisting unhealthy behavior again and again. Besides the personal responsibility for our own actions, there is also a social responsibility for the general conditions. Not only the availability of less density-rich foods or the integration of physical exercise into everyday life, but also the personal dealing with the own image of „obese persons“ belong to these general conditions. More and more people become bigger, moreover even increasingly bigger, but on the other side slimness up to a rather anorectic appearance is propagated as the ideal of our society. Children and adolescents who wish to correspond to this ideal often suffer from their own physical appearance and are at risk to reach for drastic weight regulating measures.

7. REFERENCES

[1] Alaimo, K., Olson, Ch. M. & Frongillo, E. A. (2001). Low family income and food insuffiency in relation to overweight in US children. Is there a paradox? *Archives of Pediatric and Adolescent Medicine, 155*, 1161-1167.

[2] Barth, N., Ziegler, A., Himmelmann, G. W., Coners, H., Wabitsch, M., Henninghausen, K., Mayer, H., Remschmidt, H., Schäfer, H. & Hebebrand, J. (1997). Significant weight gains in a clinical sample of obese children and adolescents between 1985 and 1995. *International Journal of Obesity, 21*, 122-126.

[3] Becker, E. S., Margraf, J., Türke, V., Soeder, U. & Neumer, S. (2001). Obesity and mental illness in a representative sample of young women. *International Journal of Obesity, 25*, S5-S9.

[4] Berkey, C. S., Rockett, H. R. H., Field, A. E., Gillman, M. W., Frazier, A. L., Camargo, C. A. & Colditz, G. A. (2000). Activity, dietary intake, and weight changes in a longitudinal study of preadolescent and adolescent boys and girls. *Pediatrics, 105*, www.pediatrics.org.

[5] Birch, L. L. & Fischer, J. O. (1998). Development of eating behaviors among children and adolescents. *Pediatrics, 101Supp*, 539-549.

[6] Bouchard, C. (1997). Genetics of human obesity: recent results from linkage studies. *The Journal of Nutrition, 127(Suppl.)*, 1887S-1890S.

[7] Britz, B., Siegfried, W., Ziegler, A., Lamertz, C., Herpetz-Dahlmann, B. M., Remschmidt, H., Wittchen, H.-U. & Hebebrand, J. (2000). Rates of psychiatric disorders in a clinical study group of adolescents with extreme obesity and in obese adolescents ascertained via a population based study. *International Journal of Obesity, 24*, 1707-1714.

[8] Brown, W. J., Mishra, G., Kenardy, J. & Dobson, A. (2000). Relationships between body mass index and well-being in young Australian women. *International Journal of Obesity, 24*, 1360-1368.

[9] Burke, V., Beilin, L. J. & Dunbar, D. (2001). Family lifestyle and parental body mass index as predictors of body mass index in Australian children: a longitudinal study. *International Journal of Obesity, 25*, 147-157.

[10] Butler, G. S., Vallis, T. M., Perey, B., Veldhuyzen van Zanten, S. J. O., MacDonald, A. S. & Konok, G. (1999). The obesity adjustment survey: development of a scale to assess psychological adjustment to morbid obesity. *International Journal of Obesity, 23*, 505-511.

[11] Cole, T. J. , Bellizzi, M. C. , Flegal, K. M. & Dietz, W. H. (2000). Establishing a standard definition for child overweight and obesity worldwide: international survey. *British Medical Journal, 320*, 1240-1243.

[12] Davison, K. K. & Birch, L. L. (2001). Child and parent characteristics as predictors of change in girls`body mass index. *International Journal of Obesity*, *25*, 1834-1842.

[13] De Onis, M. & Blössner, M. (2000). Prevalence and trends of overweight among preschoolchildren in developing countries. *American Journal of Clinical Nutrition*, *72*, 1032-1039.

[14] Dennison, B. A., Erb, T. A. & Jenkins, P. L. (2002). Television viewing and television in bedroom associated with overweight risk among low-income preschool children. *Pediatrics*, *109*, 1028-1035.

[15] Dietz, W. H. (2001). The obesity epidemic in young children. *British Medical Journal*, *322*, 313-314.

[16] Dietz, W. H. (2002). Overweight and precursors of type 2 diabetes mellitus in children and adolescents. *The Journal of Pediatrics*, *138*, 453-454.

[17] Dietz, W. H. & Gortmaker, S. L. (1985). Do we fatten our children at the television set? Obesity and television viewing in children and adolescents. *Pediatrics*, *75*, 807-812.

[18] Dorosty, A. R. , Emmett, P. M. , Cowin, I. S. & Reilly, J. J. (2000). Factors associated with early adiposity rebound. *Journal of Pediatrics*, *105*, 1115-1118.

[19] Epstein, L. H., Klein, K. R. & Wisniewski, L. (1994). Child and parent factors that influence psychological problems in obese children. *International Journal of Eating Disorders*, *15*, 151-157.

[20] Epstein, L. H., Myers, M. D. & Anderson, K. (1996). The association of maternal psychopathology and family socioeconomic status with psychological problems in obese children. *Obesity Research*, *4*, 65-74.

[21] Epstein, L. H., Smith, J. A., Vara, L. S. & Rodefer, J. S. (1991). Behavioral economic analysis of activity choice in obese children. *Health Psychology*, *10*, 311-316.

[22] Eremis, S., Cetin, N., Tamar, M., Bukusoglu, N., Akdeniz, F. & Goksen, D. (2004). Is obesity a risk factor for psychopathology among adolescents? *Pediatrics International*, *46*, 296-301.

[23] Faith, M. S., Leone, M. A., Ayers, T. S., Heo, M. & Pietrobelli, A. (2002). Weight criticism during physical activity, coping skills, and reported physical activity in children. *Pediatrics*, *110*, e23.

[24] Gortmaker, S. L., Must, A., Perrin, J. M., Sobol, A. M. & Dietz, W. H. (1993). Social and economic consequences of overweight in adolescence and young adulthood. *New England Journal of Medicine*, *329*, 1008-1012.

[25] Gortmaker, S. L., Must, A., Sobol, A. M., Peterson, K., Colditz, G. A. & Dietz, W. H. (1996). Television viewing as a cause of increasing obesity among children in the United States, 1986-1990. *Archives of Pediatrics and Adolescent Medicine*, *150*, 356-362.

[26] Haas, J. S., Lee, L. B., Kaplan, C. P., Sonneborn, D., Philips, K. A. & Liang, S. (2003). The association of race, socioecomic status, and health insurance status with the prevalence of overweight among children and adolescents. *American Journal of Public Health*, *93*, 2105-2110.

[27] Hill, A. J. & Silver, E. K. (1995). Fat, friendless and unhealthy: 9-year old children's perception of body shape stereotypes. *International Journal of Obesity*, *19*, 423-430.

[28] Hill, J. O. & Peters J. C. (1998). Environmental contributions to the obesity epidemic. *Science, 280*, 1371-1374.

[29] Jackson, T. D., Grilo, C. M. & Masheb, R. M. (2000). Teasing history, onset of obesity, current eating disorder psychopathology, body dissatisfaction, and psychological functioning in binge eating disorder. *Obesity Research, 8*, 451-458.

[30] James, Ph., T., Leach, R., Kalamara, E. & Shayeghi, M. (2001). The worldwide obesity epidemic. *Obesity Research, 9 (Suppl. 4)*, 228S-233S.

[31] Janssen, I., Craig, W. M., Boyce, W. F. & Pickett, W. (2004). Associations between overweight and obesity with bullying behaviors in school-aged children. *Pediatrics, 113*, 1187-1194.

[32] Jelalian, E., Boergers, J., Alday, C. S. & Frank, R. (2003). Survey of physician attitudes and practices related to pediatric obesity. *Clinical Pediatrics, April 2003*, ????.

[33] Jolliffe, D. (2004). Extent of overweight among US children and adolescents from 1971 to 2000. *International Journal of Obesity, 28*, 4-9.

[34] Kaukua, J., Pekkarinen, T., Sane, T. & Mustajoki, P. (2002). Health-related quality of life in WHO Class II-III obesemen losing weight with very-low-energy diet andbehaviour modification: a randomised clinical trial. *International Journal of Obesity, 26*, 487-495.

[35] Kimm, S. Y. S., Barton, B. A., Obarzanek, E., McMahon, R. P., Kronsberg, S. S., Waclawiw, M. A., Morrison, J. A., Schreiber, G. B., Sabry, Z. I. & Daniels, S. R. (2002). Obesity development during adolescence in a biracial cohort: the NHLBI growth and health study. *Pediatrics, 110*, www.pediatrics.org.

[36] Kimm, S. Y. S., Barton, B. A., Obarzanek, E., McMahon, R. P., Sabry, Z. I., Waclawiw, M. A., Schreiber, G. B., Morrison, J. A., Similo, S. & Daniels, S. R. (2001). Racial divergence in adiposity during adolescence: the NHLBI Growth and Health Study. *Pediatrics, 107*, www.pediatrics.org/cgi/content/full/107/3/e34.

[37] Klesges, R. C., Shelton, M. L. & Klesges, L. M. (1993). Effects of television on metabolic rate: Potential implications for childhood obesity. *Pediatrics, 91*, 281-286.

[38] Kolotkin R. L., Crosby, R. D., Kosloski, K. D. & Williams, G. R. (2001). Development of a brief measure to assess quality of life in obesity. *Obesity Research, 9*, 102-111.

[39] Kraig, K. A. & Keel, P. K. (2001). Weight-based stigmatization in children. *International Journal of Obesity, 25*, 1661-1666.

[40] Kromeyer-Hausschild, K., Zellner, K., Jaeger, U. & Hoyer, H. (1999). Prevalence of overweight and obesity among schoool children in Jena (Germany). *International Journal of Obesity, 23*, 1143-1150.

[41] Lake, J. K., Power, C. & Cole, T. J. (1997). Child to adult body mass index in the 1958 British birth cohort: associations with parental obesity. *Archives of Disease in Childhood, 77*, 376-381.

[42] Latner, J. D. & Stunkard, A. J. (2003). Getting worse: The stigmatization of obese children. *Obesity Research, 11*, 452-456.

[43] Livingstone, B. (2000). Epidemiology of childhood obesity in Europe. *European Journal of Pediatrics, 159*, 14-34.Lobstein, T., Baur, L. & Uauy, R. for the IASO International Obesity Task Force. (2004). Obesity in children and young peopel: a crisis in public health. *Obesity Reviews, 5 (Suppl. 1)*, 4-85.

[44] Mei, Z., Scanlon, K. S., Grummer-Strawn, L. M., Freedman, D. S., Yip, R. & Trowbridge, F. L. (1998). Increasing prevalence of overweight among US low-income preschool children: The centers for disease control and prevention pediatric nutrition surveillance,1983 to 1995. *Pediatrics*, http://www.pediatrics.org/cgi/content/full/ 101/1/e12 .

[45] Mossberg, H.-O. (1989). 40-year follow-up of overweight children. *The Lancet, 2(8661)*, 491-493.

[46] Must, A., Jacques, P. F., Dallal, G. E., Bajema, C. J. & Dietz, W. H. (1992). Long-term morbidity and mortality of overweight adolescents. A follow-up of the Harvard Growth Study of 1922 to 1935. *New England Journal of Medicine, 327*, 1350-1355.

[47] Myers, A. & Rosen, J. C. (1999). Obesity stigmatization and coping: relation to mental health symptoms, body image, and self-esteem. *International Journal of Obesity, 23*, 221-230.

[48] Nader, P. R. (1993). The role of the family in obesity prevention and treatment. In C. L. Williams & S. Y. S. Kimm (Eds.), *Prevention and treatment of childhood obesity: Annals of the New York Academy of Sciences* (Vol. 699, pp. 147-153). New York: The New York Academy of Sciences.

[49] Neumark-Sztainer, D., Falkner, N., Story, M., Perry, C., Hannan, P. J. & Mulert, S. (2002). Weight-teasing among adolescents: correlations with weight status and disordered eating behaviors. *International Journal of Obesity, 26*, 123-131.

[50] Neumark-Sztainer, D., Story, M. & Faibisch, L. (1998). Perceived stigmatization among overweight African-American and Caucasian adolescent girls. *Journal of Adolescent Health, 23*, 264-270.

[51] Neumark-Sztainer, D., Story, M., Resnik, M. D. & Blum, R. W. (1996). Correlates of inadequate fruit and vegetable consumption among adolescents. *Preventive Medicine, 25*, 497-505.

[52] Ogden, C. L., Troiano, R. P., Briefel, R. R., Kuczmarski, R. J., Flegal, K. M. & Johnson, C. L. (1997). Prevalence of overweight among preschool children in the United States, 1971 through 1994. *Pediatrics, 99(4)*, http://www.pediatrics.org/cgi/content/full/99/4/e1.

[53] Pearce, M. J., Boergers, J. Prinstein, M. J. (2002). Adolescent obesity, overt and relational peer victimization, and romantic relationships. *Obesity Research, 10*, 386-393.

[54] Puhl, R. & Brownell, K. D. (2001). Bias, discrimination, and obesity. *Obesity Research, 9*, 788-805.

[55] Reilly, J. J., Dorosty, A. R. & Emmett, P. M. (1999). Prevalence of overweight and obesity in British children: cohort study. *British Medical Journal, 319*, 1039.

[56] Reilly, J. J., Methven, E., McDowell, Z. C., Hacking, B., Alexander, D., Stewart, L. & Kelnar, C. J. H. (2003). Health consequences of obesity. *Archives of Diseases in Childhood, 88*, 748-752.

[57] Robinson, T. N. (1999). Reducing children's television viewing to prevent obesity. *Journal of the American Medical Association, 282*, 1561-1567.

[58] Robinson, T. N. (2000). The epidemic of pediatric obesity. *Western Journal of Medicine, 173*, 220-221.

[59] Robinson, T. N., Hammer, L. D., Killen, J. D., Kraemer, H. C., Wilson, D. M., Hayward, C. & Taylo??? (1993). Does television viewing increase obesity and reduce physical activity? Cross-sectional and longitudinal analyses among adolescent girls. *Pediatrics*, *91*, 273-280.

[60] Sallis, J. F., McKenzie, T. L., Alcaraz, J. E., Kolody, B., Hovell, M. F. & Nader, P. R. (1993). Project SPARK: Effects of physical education on adiposity in children. In C. L. Williams & S. Y. S. Kimm (Eds.), *Prevention and treatment of childhood obesity: Annals of the New York Academy of Sciences* (Vol. 699, pp. 127-136). New York: The New York Academy of Sciences.

[61] Sargent, J. D. & Blanchflower, D. G. (1994). Obesity and stature in adolescence and earning in young adulthood. Analysis of a British birth cohort. *Archives of Pediatrics and Adolescent Medicine*, *148*, 681-687.

[62] Serdula, M. K., Ivery, D., Coates, R. J., Freedman, D. S., Williamson, D. F. & Byers, T. (1993). Do obese children become obese adults? A review of the literature. *Preventive Medicine*, *22*, 167-177.

[63] Strauss, R. S. & Knight, J. (1999). Influence of the home environment on the development of obesity in children. *Pediatrics, http://www.pediatrics.org/ cgi/content /full/103/6/e85*, *103*.

[64] Strauss, R. S. & Pollack, H. A. (2001). Epidemic increase in childhood overweight 1986-1998. *Journal of the American Medical Association*, *286*, 2845-2848.

[65] Tershakovec, A. M., Weller, S. C. & Gallagher, P. R. (1994). Obesity, school performance and behavior of black, urban elementary school children. *International Journal of Obesity*, *18*, 323-327.

[66] Thompson, D. & Wolf, A. M. (2001). The medical-care cost burden of obesity. *Obesity Reviews*, *2*, 189-197.

[67] Thompson, J. K., Fabian, L. J., Moulton, D. O., Dunn, M. E. & Altabe, M. N. (1991). Development and validation of the Physical Appearance Related Teasing Scale. *Journal of Personality Asssessment*, *56*, 513-521.

[68] Troiano, R. P. & Flegal, K. M. (1998). Overweight children and adolescents: Description, epidemiology, and demographics. *Pediatrics*, *101 (Suppl.)*, 497-504.

[69] Wake, M., Salmon, L., Waters, E., Wright, M. & Hesketh, K. (2002). Parent-reported health status of overweight and obeseAustralian primary school children: a cross-sectionalpopulation survey. *International Journal of Obesity*, *26*, 717-724.

[70] Waxman, M. & Stunkard, A. J. (1980). Caloric intake and expenditure of obese boys. *Journal of Pediatrics*, *96*, 187-193.

[71] Whitaker, R. C., Pepe, M. S., Wright, J. A., Seidel, K. D. & Dietz, W. H. (1998). Early adiposity rebound and the risk of adult obesity. *Pediatrics*, *101*, http://www.pediatrics.org/cgi/content/ full/101/1/e5.

[72] Whitaker, R. C., Wright, J. A., Pepe, M. S., Seidel, K. D. & Dietz, W. H. (1997). Predicting obesity in young adulthood from childhood and parental obesity. *New England Journal of Medicine*, *337*, 869-873.

INDEX

A

B

C

D

E

F

G

J

L

M

Q

R

S

T

U

V

W

Y